RAGS AND BONES

ADVISORY BOARD

David Evans, General Editor
Barry Jean Ancelet
Edward A. Berlin
Joyce J. Bolden
Rob Bowman
Susan C. Cook
Curtis Ellison
William Ferris
John Edward Hasse
Kip Lornell
Bill Malone
Eddie S. Meadows
Manuel H. Peña
Wayne D. Shirley
Robert Walser

RAGS AND BONES

An Exploration of The Band

Edited by Jeff Sellars and Kevin C. Neece

University Press of Mississippi / Jackson

The University Press of Mississippi is the scholarly publishing agency of the Mississippi Institutions of Higher Learning: Alcorn State University, Delta State University, Jackson State University, Mississippi State University, Mississippi University for Women, Mississippi Valley State University, University of Mississippi, and University of Southern Mississippi.

www.upress.state.ms.us

The University Press of Mississippi is a member of the Association of University Presses.

Copyright © 2022 by University Press of Mississippi
All rights reserved

First printing 2022

∞

Library of Congress Cataloging-in-Publication Data

Names: Sellars, Jeff, editor. | Neece, Kevin C., editor.
Title: Rags and bones : an exploration of The Band / edited by Jeff Sellars and Kevin C. Neece.
Description: Jackson : University Press of Mississippi, 2022. | Series: American Made Music series | Includes bibliographical references and index.
Identifiers: LCCN 2022033507 (print) | LCCN 2022033508 (ebook) | ISBN 9781496842978 (hardback) | ISBN 9781496842985 (trade paperback) | ISBN 9781496842992 (epub) | ISBN 9781496843029 (epub) | ISBN 9781496843005 (pdf) | ISBN 9781496843012 (pdf)
Subjects: LCSH: Band (Musical group) | Rock music—History and criticism.
Classification: LCC ML421.B32 R35 2022 (print) | LCC ML421.B32 (ebook) | DDC 782.42166092/2—dc23/eng/20220816
LC record available at https://lccn.loc.gov/2022033507
LC ebook record available at https://lccn.loc.gov/2022033508

British Library Cataloging-in-Publication Data available

CONTENTS

Acknowledgments vii
Introduction 3
    JEFF SELLARS

Chapter 1: Honky-Tonk Hawkin' 11
    TOBY THOMPSON

Chapter 2: The Day the Music Lived: How Bob Dylan
and The Band Paved the Way for Southern Rock 26
    CHRISTINE HAND JONES

Chapter 3: Reading Baldwin's "Sonny Blues"
while Listening to The Band 48
    CHARLOTTE PENCE

Chapter 4: Big Sound from Big Pink 61
    JEFF SELLARS

Chapter 5: "Caught in the Spotlight": The Band's Performance
Anxiety in *Stage Fright* 78
    JUDE WARNE

Chapter 6: Chasing the Music: The Sacred and Profane in
The Band's Early Years 92
    JEFFREY SCHOLES

Chapter 7: Half Past Dead: Remnant Identity in
The Band's America 104
    JOSHUA COLEMAN

Chapter 8: Entanglement and Sainthood:
Carrying "The Weight" across the Endless Highway. 118
GEORGE PLASKETES

Chapter 9: Loud Prayers: Communion, Transcendence,
and the Blues in Scorsese's *The Last Waltz* 146
KEVIN C. NEECE

Bibliography 161
Discography/Filmography 167
Contributors 169
Index 172

ACKNOWLEDGEMENTS

Jeff Sellars: Thank you to my family, friends, and colleagues for their continued help and support, especially Hollie, Eliana, Emilia, Tom, Linda, Jennifer, Dave, Jordan, Alyssa, Vickie, Skip, Samantha, Matt, Todd, Kevin, and Ed. Thanks to all the contributors in this volume for their work and patience, and a special thanks to Kevin C. Neece for his help bringing this project to fruition.

Kevin C. Neece: My thanks to all our contributors for being part of this book, especially my friend Christine Hand-Jones for bringing her particular expertise as a Dylan scholar to bear on this discussion. I also want to thank Jeff Sellars for helping me start my career as a published author, and for his long patience, persistent kindness, and friendship for several years. I'm grateful to him for letting me tag along on this project, of which he is the true architect. I also want to thank my former professor, mentor, and friend, Dr. David K. Naugle, without whose influence I would not be the person or the writer I am today. My contribution to this book was the last piece of my writing I read to him, and his enthusiasm for it was deeply honoring. I dedicate my work herein to his memory and legacy.

RAGS AND BONES

INTRODUCTION

JEFF SELLARS

My first sustained and in-depth introduction to The Band was through my own band's drummer. I, of course, knew The Band from their hits, but I was quickly converted to a true fan, thanks to his introduction (and to the film *The Last Waltz*). I vividly remember being deeply affected by Rick Danko's vulnerability in "It Makes No Difference," which hit me at a perfect time in a troubled teenage relationship. My drummer had also suggested that we play "The Weight" live. I'd heard the song, and liked it, but never considered it a song specifically for us to play live. After studying the song, I realized the depth that undergirded it: the layered harmonies, the syncopated rhythm, the high country harmony on the last verse, and, of course, the lyrics. I was very familiar with country music and its tropes, but here was something different: here was a new combination of country, blues, folk, and rock. I heard the twang and swing of the old country albums my grandfather would listen to at night lurking in the background, but there was a fresh, exciting amalgamation of sounds and influences. It was a union of forces, marshaled for the potential of artistic creativity—and I wanted to be a part of it. There was a twist on the twang. The music had a curious effect on me. I could sense a broad and sometimes dark history behind the music and meaningful philosophical quandaries about what it meant to be human. Here was a rock-country-folk-pop-blues fusion that tickled my intellect and my ears. I know I am not alone, except possibly in the particulars of my personal situation and experience, in finding a lasting personal connection to The Band and their music. It is no secret that they are one of the enduring bands of rock history, and their place in that history is a secure one. Their influence and relevance are far-reaching and enjoy a broad audience.

With this project, we hope to give The Band a broad examination, through multiple disciplines, allowing for a sophisticated reading of The Band and their work. With beginnings as a backup band, known as the Hawks, with Ronnie Hawkins, The Band eventually rose to fame as the backing band to Bob Dylan (in his controversial move to "electric" music). Through this collaboration with Dylan came the chance to expand musically:

> Over time, the music made by The Band became very different. They no longer sounded even remotely as they had behind Hawkins and Dylan, or on their own as Levon and the Hawks. Robertson remembers clearly the transformation: "[With The Band] the song is becoming the thing, the mood is becoming the thing . . . I don't mean electronic trick sounds. All of that plays a part, but there's a vibe to certain records, a quality, whether it's a Motown thing or a Sun Records thing or a Phil Spector thing . . . I wanted to discover the sound of The Band . . . I'm only going to play riffs, Curtis Mayfield kind of riffs. I wanted the drums to have their own character, I wanted the piano not to sound like a big Yamaha grand. I wanted it to sound like an upright piano. I wanted these pictures in your mind . . . I didn't want screaming vocals. I wanted sensitive vocals where you can hear the breathing and the voices coming in. This whole thing of discovering the voices—don't everybody come in together. Everybody in records is working on getting the voices together until it neutralizes itself. I like voices coming in one at a time, in a chain reaction kind of thing like the Staple Singers did. But because we are all men it will have another effect . . . This is emotional and this is storytelling. You can see this mythology. This is the record that I wanted to make."[1]

The Band's fusion of rock, country, soul, and blues music—all tinged with a southern flavor and musical adventurousness—created a daring sound. Their mostly Canadian makeup also adds an exciting element to The Band's music, invention, and foundation. The use of multiple instruments, complex song structures, and poetic lyrics—where one can feel the influence of Dylan—require an attentive listening and interpretive framework. The Band creates a paradoxically mythic and hauntingly realistic landscape for their songs—and the musicianship of The Band enlarges this intricate landscape.

The recordings of these classic rock songs also add to this landscape. The stripped-down recording techniques create a "back to basics," homespun, do-it-yourself feel. These recording techniques have changed rock history.[2] Modern-day artists still borrow from this approach.[3] These artists have heard what I've heard in the music: the deep tones of Rick Danko's bass, the thick bass drum and tubby snare of Levon Helm, the magical flourishes of

Garth Hudson, the crisp and biting guitar of Robbie Robertson, the steady keyboards of Richard Manuel—the beautiful nasal whines of the voices all creating a sense of back-home community. The expression of history, myth, politics, and culture in their music is so readily apparent. The reworking of history, from a decidedly personal perspective, in "The Night They Drove Old Dixie Down" is just one example of The Band's profoundly deep and controversial subject matter: it resonates with mythic imagery, with historical and cultural significance. With the song "King Harvest (Has Surely Come)," we get a broader message within the upbeat pop structure: its visible political messages of laborers, unions, and poverty, which creates an evocative picture of the working person's life. One may also find the deep spiritual longing, complete with quasibiblical imagery, in "The Weight" as a clear expression of and response to the cultural pangs of the song's times (circa 1968): there is a prophetic gaze in the song, seen, for example, in the lines about Miss Moses talking about the Judgment Day, that projects a cultural critique of its time and a glimpse of an uncertain future. It is clear that The Band's unique musical stylings place them amongst the most original bands to spring from the 1960s, with their southern musical influences and their penchant for melody, intricate arrangements, and poetics.

As mentioned above, The Band started their career as a backup band called "the Hawks" (of Ronnie Hawkins and the Hawks). Around 1958, Ronnie Hawkins, a friend of Levon Helm and his fellow Arkansas native, convinced Helm to join his band and have Levon play the drums. There were earlier bands for the members of the group, but The Band as we know them now formed around the central figure of Hawkins.

> Ronnie Hawkins and the Hawks worked their way up to Canada a few times before Hawkins realized that in the South they were one of several good band playing a rockabilly style that was rapidly becoming dated, whereas up in Toronto the sound was unique. As far as hipper Torontonians felt, they played the fastest, most violent rock'n'roll ever heard. Logic and money being what they are, the Hawks made Toronto their adopted home in 1958. One by one, the other members of what would be The Band entered the fold as various original Hawks succumbed to homesickness and headed back south. Jaime Robbie Robertson (born July 5, 1943) was one of the first recruits. A refugee from Robbie and the Robots, Thumper and the Trambones and Little Caesar and the Consuls, Robertson, a few months shy of his sixteenth birthday, joined early in 1960, initially on bass . . . Rick Danko (born Dec. 28, 1943) came into the Hawks the other way around. He had

been playing guitar in various bands, several featuring accordion, in the Simcoe area from the age of 12. He first saw Hawkins backed by Robertson and Helm in 1960. Quite smitten by the crazed excitement of Hawkins's camel walk and The Band's frenetic and ferocious accompaniment, Danko got himself an opening slot on Hawkins's next performance in the Simcoe area the following spring. The next night he was a Hawk, initially playing rhythm guitar before learning to play bass after Rebel Payne departed. Richard Manuel (born April 3, 1943) entered the picture later in the summer of 1961, after graduating from the Rockin' Revols, a band of hardcore rockers from Stratford who had toured the South through the Harold Kudlets connection. Originally a vocalist, Manuel played what he described as "rhythm piano," nothing too complicated but good enough when combined with his unearthly, ethereal voice that landed him a job as a Hawk. The last to sign up was the much sought after Garth Hudson. Hudson (born August 2, 1937) was older than the rest. Classically trained as a pianist, he was also infatuated with rock and roll, especially that of hard, driving tenor sax players such as Big Jay McNeely and Lee Allen. He himself had started playing sax in his teenage years (his father, a drummer in the Birr Brass Band, had a C melody sax laying around the house).[4]

The members of the Hawks that eventually became The Band (along with Jerry Penfound and Bruce Bruno) left Hawkins's group in 1964. They quickly changed their name to Levon and the Hawks and started playing gigs around the South and in Ontario. They recorded two singles, "Leave Me Alone" and "Uh-Uh-Uh" in 1964 (it was sometime during this period that Bruno and Penfound left the group).[5] Also, during this period, the group's music had grown "more black-influenced," with harder rhythm-and-blues numbers and rhythm-and-blues-inspired writing by the group (in particular by Robbie Robertson).[6]

During the summer of 1965, Bob Dylan heard about the Hawks and considered them as a possible backup band for him for his move to "electric" music. Dylan came to listen to them on their four-month stand in Somers Point, New Jersey. Eventually, Robertson convinced Dylan to hire the entire band to accompany him to New York, where they played to hostile audiences: they would "play two or three three-nights to an audience of 'folkie purists' who were engrossed in a ritual booing, viewing an electric Dylan as a sell-out to the values of folk music rather than listening to music that was years ahead of its time in power and majesty."[7] However, the experience did create a dynamic within the group's playing—something that they all recognized as exceptional.[8] Rick Danko and Richard Manuel found a big pink house in Woodstock, and soon after Danko, Hudson, and Manuel moved in, with Robertson living nearby. Helm, having left briefly due to the horrible reception they received playing with Dylan, would come soon after to complete the group's lineup. It was here at Big Pink that The Band solidified their sound and aesthetic—and found the name and inspiration for their debut album *Music from Big Pink* (1968). The song list is impressive, especially for a debut: for example, "Tears of Rage," "Chest Fever," and, of course, "The Weight."

They followed this album up quickly with the self-titled *The Band*, made in the spring following *Music from Big Pink*. The record further cemented The Band's standing in rock music and peaked at number nine on the Billboard charts. The group was flying high on accolades and success, and as is often the case with such tremendous success, there was a shadowy depth that accompanied the sunny highs. Reflecting this darkness, The Band created *Stage Fright* (1970), largely a rumination of the strangeness and dangers of fame and performance. After *Stage Fright*, The Band worked for the next year on what would become *Cahoots* (1971). The Band continued to feel the pressures of fame and success, both internally and externally, and those pressures started to create cracks in the group's cohesiveness: "The sessions were difficult.... The Band was undergoing internal problems. Hudson felt that Robertson's songs were also much more difficult. The structures, chord changes and arrangements were that much more complex.... Robertson felt a lot of the ideas were only half-finished."[9] They followed up *Cahoots* with a live double album—*Rock of Ages* (1972): "The Band planned to close out the difficult year of 1971 in a very special way.... [They] asked Toussaint to write arrangements ... to be performed at three special concerts ... culminating New Year's eve 1971 with what was then an extremely rare appearance by Bob Dylan.... All three nights were recorded for ... the live double LP *Rock of Ages*."[10]

Moondog Matinee, a collection of oldies, and *Northern Lights—Southern Cross* would come later (1973 and 1975, respectively). *Northern Lights—Southern Cross* was a return to form in many ways. The short album (only eight songs) certainly has gems, most notably "It Makes No Difference" and "Ophelia," which also have clear echoes of their earlier work.

After halting touring in 1976, The Band decided to play one last gig at Winterland in San Francisco—paying tribute to their beginnings as a group. The idea was to invite their musical friends and film the event. Of course, we know this as *The Last Waltz*, directed by Martin Scorsese. The album of the event (of the same name) appeared in April of 1978. But before they could release *The Last Waltz*, they had to fulfill their contract with Capitol Records and deliver an album. That album became *Islands*: "'We were just trying to get out of a contract. It wasn't an album,' stated Robertson emphatically.... Rather, it was bits and pieces from here and there as well as a number of new recordings. Released in March 1977, the album commercially fared worse than any Band record, reaching only #64 on Billboard's album charts."[11] The Band did continue in other forms, of course, but the original lineup officially disbanded. However, the legacy of that original lineup has endured and inspired generations of music lovers and music makers, and it is this original lineup that has inspired us to write about that legacy.

Our collection starts with "Honky-Tonk Hawkin'" by Toby Thompson. Thompson explores The Band's roots on the bar circuit and the bar scene's influence on the group's music. We continue with Christine Hand Jones's analysis of the text and music of both The Band's and Bob Dylan's work, before and after their time together, giving a glimpse into the influence each artist had on the other. Next is Charlotte Pence's "Reading Baldwin's 'Sonny Blues' while Listening to The Band," which assesses The Band in light of James Baldwin's famous story—with focus on "different strategies for the 'I' in poetry, nonfiction, and fiction." My contribution is next, which explores the cultural influence of *Music from Big Pink* and The Band's recording techniques on that album. Following this is Jude Warne's contribution, which looks at performance anxiety in *Stage Fright*. Warne emphasizes the dangers and emptiness of success and manifestations of this in the group's music and lyrics. Jeffrey Scholes's "Chasing the Music: The Sacred and Profane in The Band's Early Years" looks at The Band's relationship with religion and religious themes, the sacred and the profane. In "Half Past Dead: Remnant Identity in The Band's America," Joshua Coleman investigates American identity within The Band's work. With "Entanglement and Sainthood: Carrying 'The Weight' across the Endless Highway," George Plasketes considers The Band's music through the contextual history of the group and the content of the music: the unique characters and enduring mythology. We end with Kevin C. Neece's "Loud Prayers: Communion, Transcendence, and the Blues in Scorsese's *The Last Waltz*." Neece analyses the "religious urge" found in the film *The Last Waltz*.

Obviously, there is much to mine here, and in this collection we will attempt just that—by taking a straightforward approach to the very complex workings of The Band and their music. We will take a broad line of attack, allowing examination through sociological, historical, political, literary, religious, technological, cultural, and philosophical means. Our study will present a broad range of investigation on The Band's music and their influence. Each contributor will approach the music from her/his/their particular field of interest. In so doing, we hope to offer a more rounded examination, from several perspectives, allowing the multifaceted music and work of The Band to shine forth. We fully acknowledge our limitations: we cannot include every important aspect of The Band's music, nor can we deal with every critical angle of their work—and, as with any serious examination of artists, there will be blind spots and omissions.

If there is a thread pulled through this collection, it is the "Rags and Bones" thread (hence the name of the compilation). Historically, the "ragman" bought and sold the "junk" of various neighborhood peoples and was a searcher for anything of worth, including old rags and cloth. And we are here pulling together a collection of writers to explore elements of The Band's work, sewing together a quilt of criticism that is fundamentally ad hoc. Additionally, of course, there is a long history in the variously named "rag and bone man." Robbie Robertson found his way to the term through his own family when he discovered his Jewish roots.

> Robertson had been raised in suburban Toronto as Jaime Royal Robertson without knowing that the man he called dad, James Patrick Robertson, was not his biological father. When his mother, Dolly Robertson—who was a Mohawk raised on the Six Nations Reserve southwest of Toronto—finally had had enough of James Robertson's physical and emotional abuse, she sat her son down, explained that she was divorcing James, and revealed to him that his natural father, Alexander Klegerman, had died in a roadside accident before Robbie was born. She also told her bar-mitzvah age son that Klegerman was Jewish.... For The Band's penultimate studio album, 1975's "Northern Light, Southern Cross," Robertson wrote a song called "Rags and Bones," which seems to pay tribute to one of the professions typically filled by Eastern European Jewish immigrants to North America—the ragman—and the sounds and music one would hear in those ghetto streets."[12]

I am excited to have my minimal contribution alongside these writers' work. I have found that their ideas have given me new insights into the music of The Band, and I am eager to share their work with you.

Notes

1. Rob Bowman, *The History of The Band*, "Playing with Bob Dylan," from the article, "Life Is a Carnival," *Goldmine* magazine, July 26, 1991, vol.17, no.15, issue 287.

2. For example, the Beatles' *Let It Be* can be seen as a response to this recording style. George Harrison hung out with The Band prior to the recording of *Let It Be*: "George: I had spent the last few months of 1968 producing an album by Jackie Lomax and hanging out with Bob Dylan and The Band in Woodstock, having a great time." (*The Beatles Anthology*, the Beatles, Chronicle Books, 2000, 316). It's clear Paul was listening to The Band during 1968, as evidenced by his improvisational vocal ad lib of lyrics from "The Weight" during the Beatles' semi-live performance of "Hey Jude" on the Frost on Sunday show (airing October 2nd, 1968). Paul's improvisation can be heard in this video around the 6:19 mark: https://youtu.be/A_MjCqQoLLA.

3. One could look to Wilco's album *Being There* as a representative case of the influence of The Band's song recording grammar, for example, in some of the instrumentation, sparse recording atmosphere, and the ethos of the record (where songs were rehearsed and recorded in the same day). One can also see this influence expressed through the tribute album *Endless Highway: The Music of The Band*, which includes such diverse artists as My Morning Jacket, Death Cab for Cutie, Gomez, Guster, Bruce Hornsby, Jack Johnson and ALO, Lee Ann Womack, the Allman Brothers Band, Blues Traveler, Jakob Dylan, and more.

4. Rob Bowman, *The History of The Band*.

5. Ibid.

6. Ibid. For example, Robert noted that "The Stones I Throw" was influenced by Pop Staples: "This was a song that I wrote for the Staple Singers in my mind," recalled Robertson. "One of my favourite vocalists is Pop [Staples]. He sounds like a train when he sings. He has a quality in his voice, this whispering, haunting thing that always killed me. I didn't like us doing it. I didn't like the way it came off. I had to think of something to write (for the recording session) and because I was listening to the Staple Singers all the time this is what came to mind. It was out of context for us to do this song. But if you imagine the Staple Singers doing it, it's right in context."

7. Ibid.

8. Ibid. "By the time we did the Australia and Europe tours we had discovered whatever this thing was. It was not light, it was not folky. It was very dynamic, very explosive and very violent.' The whole experience culminated in late May 1966 at the Albert Hall in London, England. Columbia Records recorded the event for a possible live LP. The recordings show that, indeed, Dylan and The Band had discovered 'this thing,' an entity that continually ebbed and flowed as quiet sections alternated with moments of awesome volume and apocalyptic power."

9. Ibid.

10. Rob Bowman, *The History of The Band*.

11. Ibid.

12. Seth Rogovoy, "How Robbie Robertson Learned He Was Jewish and the Son of a Gangster." https://forward.com/culture/444583/how-robbie-robertson-learned-he-was-jewish-and-the-son-of-a-gangster/.

Chapter 1

HONKY-TONK HAWKIN'

TOBY THOMPSON

Before the seventeen-year-old Levon Helm entered the Rebel Club in Osceola, Florida, for his first gig as one of Ronnie Hawkins's Hawks, the band leader took Helm aside and said, "It's a rough place, son. You have to puke twice and show your razor just to get in." He added that if the owner asked, Levon was twenty-one. "Better grow some whiskers if you wanna go to Canada," Hawkins added. "I don't know how the hell I'm gonna get you into clubs up there if you keep looking like a damn choirboy."[1]

Thus commenced Helm's career as a bar musician, one that he, as a founding member of The Band, with the Canadians Robbie Robertson, Rick Danko, and Garth Hudson, would pursue for eight years before Bob Dylan made them his touring outfit. It was a run that would continue a decade after The Band's star had dimmed—culminating in 1986's spate of Holiday Inn and roadhouse bookings that Helm called "the Death Tour"—during which Manuel hanged himself from a shower rod in a motel bathroom. Robertson, after filming 1978's *The Last Waltz*, had quit the road, describing it as "a goddamn impossible way of life."[2] Yet it and its bars had been The Band's proving ground, the boot camp where they'd learned fundamentals, not just of musicianship and of pleasing a crowd, but of mesmerizing them with carnival-like theatricality.

The road and its taverns were immensely seductive. Helm remembered that as a boy, "In the dark of night I'd lie in my bed and listen to the train whistles in the distance. I wanted—I needed—to go. To me the prettiest sight in the world was a '57 Cadillac rolling down the road with a doghouse bass tied to the top. That looked like the car I wanted to be in."[3]

A few years later, Helm stated, "Ronnie Hawkins had molded us into the wildest, fiercest, speed-driven bar band in America."[4] Hawkins was the quintessential bar musician, a rockabilly James Brown who offered comparable splits, dance steps and gospel-shout vocals to his audience, anything to keep them dancing. To survive as a bar band one had to make the crowd dance; the rhythms had to pound, the arrangements had to cohere, and The Band's vocals—as in a gospel choir—had to pierce. Like Brown, Hawkins knew that rock was an angel hair's breadth removed from gospel *extasis*. Yet it championed a cruder ecstasy. Booze, pills, groupies, and prostitutes were its sacraments. Robertson said in *The Last Waltz*, that upon his hiring, Hawkins told him, "Son, you won't make much money, but you'll get more pussy than Frank Sinatra."[5] The after-hours shenanigans would be compensation for any financial shortfall. Hawkins later said of those happenings, "Let's not call them orgies. Let's just say it was seven or eight people in love."[6]

The Band—as Levon and the Hawks, once they split from Hawkins—played clubs from Texas to Ontario, honing their act behind Helm's, Manuel's, and Danko's vocals, into one of the sharpest bands working. Unlike concert groups such as Jefferson Airplane or Big Brother and the Holding Company, The Band had emerged from the bar scene. "It was a helluva circuit back then," Levon remembered. "We played places on Oklahoma Indian reservations where we felt we wouldn't get out alive."[7] Such experiences steeled them. The Band-as-Hawks could headline a bar like Tony Mart's, in Somers Point, New Jersey, "the biggest teenage nightclub in the East,"[8] where the week before, then-rocker Conway Twitty had headlined, and pulverize its crowd.

But a hit album eluded them. The Beatles, themselves bar vets, had proved that with a single hit everything could change. It wasn't until the Hawks' association with Dylan as his backup band, and the group's subsequent solo collections—*Music from Big Pink* and *The Band*—that an international reputation was secured.

Those albums' selections, and many from subsequent discs, reflected much that the group had learned about spirituality from Dylan—but also the chops it cultivated from its roadhouse days: the ability to create tight vocals and arrangements, with a precision of mood that, uptempo, made a couple want to boogie, but on slower tunes made it want to dance close and weep. Suffusing all was the carnival-like theatricality—old time instruments such as wooden drum kits and button accordions suggesting tent revivals, hootchie-cootchie shows, or juke-joint blowouts, and the promise of *extasis*, no matter how mournful a tune might prove.

That ecstasy was rooted in the pasts of both Levon Helm, the quintessential southerner, and of Bob Dylan, the north country's bard.

It is wonderful to read Levon's account of those lost, youthful years, which as Dylan wrote in a blurb, "explodes in the pure Dixie Delta dialect of rockabilly, the back beat of America."[9] Hawkins had recruited Helms from his home in Chicken Scratch, Arkansas, and broke him in at the Rebel Club in Osceola. Levon had sneaked into bars to hear music since he was fifteen. Places like the Delta Supper Club in West Helena, which he described as "one tough place," had "a big seam running down the middle of the bar where it had been glued back together after an ejected customer stormed back in with a chain saw and cut the bar in half."[10]

In that first gig at the Rebel, Hawkins showed Levon his stuff: "He was big, good looking, funny . . . he'd do his kick, that camel walk." Hawkins had been a professional diver, "so he could execute a front flip into a split that would astonish you." He shuffled onstage to a Bo Diddley beat and worked through standards like "Forty Days," "Mary Lou," "Need Your Lovin'," and "Who Do You Love." He was more of an entertainer than a musician and had an uncanny way of working a crowd. He'd run whiskey as a teenager and was part owner of various bars in Fayetteville, Arkansas. In his late twenties, he knew saloon life front and back.[11]

Canadians were hungry for border music, and "Toronto had become a major music town," Robertson recalled in *Testimony*, "with hot jazz clubs like the Colonial and the Town Tavern. . . . There weren't many places up north where a rockabilly band like ours could play for three weeks at a time, but Toronto had Le Coq d'Or." It became the group's headquarters, situated near clubs along Yonge Street that featured Bo Diddley, Jerry Lee Lewis, Carl Perkins, and others. Up the block one could hear jazz greats such as Louis Prima, Frank Sinatra, or Ray Charles.[12] Helm remembered Toronto as being "the best place for music I'd ever seen, outside Memphis." For lodging, "We joined the shady clientele at the very down-market Warwick Hotel, not far from Le Coq D'or."[13]

Robertson remembered the Warwick as "a haven for street walkers, hustlers, and tin men" near the corner of "Dundas and Jarvis, the city's vibrant crossroads of vice."[14] Ronnie bought them hipster attire—tight black suits, pointy black shoes, and black ties over white-on-white shirts—and they were ready for Yonge Street. They played each night until twelve, rehearsed for one or two hours, then partied with groupies. "Ronnie liked to tell people we had parties that Nero would have been ashamed to attend," Levon wrote. "The Hawk assiduously cultivated the worst reputation he could for us. He felt it was part of the promotion of the show."[15]

For Robertson, a teenager, this was heaven. He would write,

[Ronnie] and Levon charming the ladies was a sight to behold—the humor, the timing, an art form unto itself. . . . Night after night, an array of teachers, nurses, waitresses, students, hairdressers, salesgirls, elevator operators and telephone operators passed before my eyes.

The recommendations came with careful consideration as to who could teach me the most the quickest.... I saw in the mirror a boy turning into a man before his time.[16]

Musically, "All I could do was play like a demon." And culturally, "I had crossed the border. I had gone to the Mississippi Delta. I'd gotten hired by an official southern rockabilly band, one of the hottest around.... I stepped forward into the spotlight to take my solo."[17]

An uncle on Robertson's father's side had ties to organized crime, and the bar life Robbie was being initiated into had long been influenced by gangsters. Since Prohibition, they'd had their claws in the music business, especially that performed in saloons. Bands, when they recorded an original song, were expected to share its royalties with execs—characters such as Morris Levy, president of Roulette Records, who reportedly hung a songwriter by his ankles out a Manhattan window to acquire a signature.[18] Hawkins wanted to sign with Levy because, as he told Levon, "He's Mafia up to his eyeballs. We can't miss with these cats behind us."[19] They signed with Roulette, recorded and released *Ronnie Hawkins*. Levy (who later was convicted for the extortion of a record wholesaler and cited by the FBI as an associate of the Genovese crime family) booked them on the *The Steve Allen Show* and *American Bandstand*.

They returned to the road.

Robertson had joined the group by then, and his memories of touring are perhaps the most acute. Dive bars, with easy access to drugs, groupies, prostitutes, and danger, epitomized the hipster lifestyle during the 1950s. Its ethos was diametrically opposed to the lassitude of the Beat generation. Violence and sex was the hipster mantra, and an attraction to African American culture and its music was mandatory. Norman Mailer, in his 1957 essay "The White Negro," characterized the hipster as an American existentialist who encouraged "the psychopath in [himself]," accepting that "security is boredom and therefore sickness, and one exists in the present . . . where a man must go until he is beat . . . where he must be with it or doomed not to swing . . . one is a frontiersman of the Wild West of American nightlife." Mailer also praised "the curious community of feeling in the world of the hipster, a muted cool religious revival" and its "dynamic view of existence [which] sees every man and woman as moving individually through each moment of life forward into growth or backward into death."[20]

Dylan would paraphrase that line, in 1965's "It's Alright Ma (I'm Only Bleeding)," with "He not busy being born is busy dying."[21]

The Hawks, under Ronnie's leadership and later Helms's, would cross most lines of propriety and some of legality. Their whoring and drug use were legendary. part of their image. The drugs they used were primarily marijuana and amphetamines, but later included cocaine and heroin. "The Hawk also liked to carry 'the difference' in the glove compartment," Levon wrote of Hawkins's fondness for guns.[22] And Robertson in *Testimony* recalled The Band purchasing "small derringer pistols, switchblades, an assortment of blackjacks, brass knuckles, even tear-gas pens." They stole gasoline to reach gigs, took food from supermarkets to eat, torched a nightclub that stiffed them on a fee, and were prepared to rob at gunpoint a high-stakes poker game until that evening's festivity was called off.[23]

The low point of the Hawks' bar scuffling perhaps was a 1963 gig at the Skyline Lounge in Fort Worth, Texas. As Robertson wrote in *Testimony*, "When we arrived, our jaws dropped open. The club was burned out, blown up. It was hard to imagine it was habitable. . . . 'Looks like we finally hit the big time,' Ronnie told Levon." That first night a one-armed go-go dancer warmed the crowd of two or three couples, and a fight broke out. "There weren't enough people there to cause a fight," Robertson said. There was no roof to the club, the doors wouldn't lock, and The Band had to guard their instruments all night with their newly purchased handguns. The owner, a stocky pill popper named Jack, darted in and out. A few months later, after President Kennedy's assassination and Lee Harvey Oswald's murder, they learned his full name: Jack Ruby.[24]

Throughout this period the Hawks made extraordinary music. Levon wrote, "Despite our unsavory rep throughout the Midwest and Canada as pill-poppin', whore-visitin', gas-siphonin', girlfriend-stealin' reprobate musicians, we'd hear our competition—good bands, too—and they'd be playing our arrangements, our turnarounds, stuff we invented."[25]

Sets during this period included mostly covers—songs like "Kansas City," "Memphis," "Please, Please, Please," "No Particular Place to Go," "Turn on Your Love Light," "Georgia on My Mind," and "Short Fat Fannie."[26] Levon recalled, "We basically worked every night of the year. This made us sharp. I mean, we were *honed*."[27] The Hawks and Hawkins had parted ways, and as Levon wrote, The Band were restless to make it big. "The Hawk had taught us to sweat up a roadhouse with hard-core rock and roll, and we knew the satisfaction of wringing a crowd of Saturday night dancers dry until they were begging for more."[28] But a big break eluded them. "We were like a state secret among hip musical people because nobody else was as tight as we were."[29]

Then Bob Dylan called. The rest is history.

During the fall of 1968, and again in May 1969, I traveled to Hibbing, Minnesota, in search of Dylan's roots and to report material that would make up the bulk of *Positively Main Street*, my book about his boyhood in Minnesota. I also was scouting Hibbing's bars in anticipation of a second book, *Saloon*, about America's bar culture. I was startled by the taverns' polka music, country tunes, and traditional rock, which cut smiles into the red iron-ore dust coating the faces of the city's miners and set their feet tapping.

Like Robertston as a teen in Toronto, Dylan in Hibbing had been too young to frequent its saloons. But in *Chronicles: Volume One*, he recalled listening from the street to their accordion-driven bands: "On Saturday nights the taverns were filled with polka bands.... Polka dances always got my blood pumping. That was the first type of loud, live music I'd ever heard."[30] Hibbing's music centered around its bars and churches; there was a frontier religiosity to the north country's saloons. Hibbing, founded in 1893, enjoyed a frontier ambience. It had the world's largest open-pit iron-ore mine and was surrounded by deep forests and lakes. The first building in a frontier community often doubled as a saloon and church. That duplicity was reflected in nineteenth-century bar design, where artisans fashioned ornate front counters, reminiscent of altars, and back bars with carved entablatures and caryatids framing huge mirrors, like the reredos or altar screens of Renaissance cathedrals. The saloon's upright played both honky-tonk and hymns.

Garth Hudson, an Anglican, would speak in *The Last Waltz* of bar music's religiosity: "There is a view that jazz is evil, because it comes from evil people. But actually the greatest priests on 52nd Street [and in its nightclubs] were the musicians. They were doing the greatest healing work."[31]

In 1969, Dylan's mother, Beattie Zimmerman, told me that as a boy not only had Bob played in bands, but he had also attended every church in Hibbing. In his house at Woodstock there was "a huge Bible open on a stand in the middle of his study. Of all the books that crowd his house, *overflow* from his house, that Bible gets the most attention. He's constantly getting up and going over to refer to something."[32]

Dylan's brother, David Zimmerman, told me that musically Bob wasn't listening to much of anything "except country-western."[33]

After Dylan sustained injuries in a 1966 motorcycle accident, The Band, on retainer, moved to Woodstock. "For the first time we didn't have to play joints to stay alive anymore," Helm recalled.[34] Robertson added, "We were having a really good time writing music, hanging out. It was really the most joyous period for The Band."[35]

At Woodstock its members helped Dylan, in recovery, to create and record demos for other artists. These collaborative efforts were released first as bootlegs and later as *The Basement Tapes*. They were composed at Dylan's house and at Big Pink—Helm's, Rick Danko's, and Richard Manuel's West Saugerties residence. The Band also were composing songs—thus, *Music from Big Pink*. "This was our music," Helm wrote, "honed in isolation from the radio and contemporary trends, liberated from the world of the bars and the climate of the Dylan tours."[36]

That album, with its three songs written by or cowritten with Dylan, reflected the metaphysical path both had taken after leaving the road. Touring, with its late nights and drugs "just to keep going," Dylan told *Rolling Stone* in November of 1969, had nearly killed him. A scene in Robertson's memoir, *Testimony*, has him reviving the singer after what, presumably, was an overdose. Like many imbibers, Dylan turned to God as a proxy for drugs—be they amphetamines or the rush of screaming fans. His turn skidded him toward Old Testament lyricism and religiosity. These traits, married to a rekindled interest in traditional music, were the bedrock of his 1967 album *John Wesley Harding*. Its marriage of folk, parable, and spiritual was a perfect breeding ground for The Band's new music.

There is debate about whether the Hawks' grounding in rhythm and blues, classic rock, country, and soul pushed Dylan back from the surrealistic experimentation of *Blonde on Blonde*, or whether Dylan's encyclopedic knowledge of traditional music influenced them. In his biography *Across the Great Divide*, Barney Hoskyns wrote, "A big part of Robbie's beef with Dylan's songs [had been] their verbal complexity, their dense subjectivity; now he was leading his mentor back to simplicity, to the concise Americana that as a Canadian, he himself wanted to explore." As a bar musician, Robertson told Hoskyns, "I came in on a rock 'n' roll train, blues and country music mixed together.... You mix this and that and you get something,... It's just magical when you put it all together."[37]

Robertson has admitted that Dylan's writing influenced him in terms of subject matter, form, imagery, and enigma. "That's the door that he opened," Robertson has said. "But at the same time I was just as influenced [in narrative] by Luis Bunuel or John Ford or Kurosawa. I got this hunger for education and knowledge because I hadn't gone to school since I was 16.... I got into all kinds of mythologies."[38]

Songs on *Big Pink*, such as "Tears of Rage," "I Shall be Released," and even "The Weight," hinted first at religiosity, then—by The Band's second, eponymous album, with "Across the Great Divide," "King Harvest," "The Night They Drove Old Dixie Down"—at the mythology of the American South. That South embraced the Bible Belt's Christianity, with its ethos of "God's gonna get'cha for that,"[39] undercut by a fierce passion for moonshine whiskey and rockabilly in bottle clubs. There, under Hawkins's tutelage, the Hawks first practiced the substance-induced spirituality of alcohol and drugs.

In Woodstock the Hawks found a retreat where Robbie said they might "hide out and shake off the years of wildness we'd spent on the road."[40] The years 1965 and 1966 largely had been spent touring behind Dylan; 1967 and 1968 saw the heart of a cultural revolution of which Dylan was the reluctant avatar. As he wrote in *Chronicles*, "I had been anointed as the Big Bubba of Rebellion, High Priest of Protest, the Czar of Dissent, the Duke of Disobedience, Leader of the Freeloaders, Kaiser of Apostasy, Archbishop of Anarchy, the Big Cheese."[41] In Woodstock he was the oracle of its Byrdcliffe Colony and internationally popular. Hoskyns wondered, in *Divide*, "what would have become of the Hawks had they never crossed the path of Bob Dylan. Would they have plodded on as a bar band . . . or would they have made the quantum leap to genuine creativity anyway?"[42] Helm later wrote, "We all knew the debt we owed Bob Dylan could never be repaid. We were a bar band when he found us. We'd grown up practicing our craft in honky-tonks and dance halls. We learned everything—songwriting, recording, stage shows—from watching him."[43]

The songwriting influences cut both ways. Hoskyns wrote,

> If those endless nights with Dylan had, in Robbie's words, "broken down a whole lot of the tradition of songwriting before my very eyes," by the same token Robbie and the Hawks had taught Dylan something about American music—about country, about rhythm and blues—that he hadn't properly appreciated before.[44]

One wonders, though, how complete the Hawks' influence on Dylan had been, vis-a-vis country and rhythm and blues. Dylan has spoken in interviews and written in *Chronicles* of his exposure via radio, TV, and movies to numerous musical genres. He was no stranger to Americana. As for country and blues, in the spring of 1969 I revisited Hibbing, this trip accompanied by Echo Helmstrom, Dylan's high-school girlfriend and, by most accounts, inspiration for "Girl from the North Country." She told me that as kids they had stayed up late to hear rhythm and blues and blues broadcasts from distant radio stations, and that Dylan haunted the local record store in search of gems. At her parents' house outside Hibbing, she played me 78s that Dylan had been fascinated by. Titles included Spade Cooley's "Detour," Cowboy Copas's "Candy Kisses," Hank Snow's "Prisoner of Love," something by Pee Wee King and his Golden West Cowboys, and discs by Jimmy Rodgers. Notable in the stack was a recording of Carson

Robison's "Ohio Prison Fire," a song about the 1930 accident that took 322 inmates' lives. An "event" or "protest" song, it might have appeared on Dylan's *The Times They Are A-Changin'*.[45]

"These old records were interesting," Echo told me, "but mostly Bob played his own music. Not stuff he'd written, but things from the radio. He'd sit out front on that swing and play his guitar, or perch on some old stone steps that used to lead up to our front door. The songs he'd play then weren't band songs but quiet ones, sort of country, like what we've been listening to."[46]

Picturing Dylan on Echo's swing, and visiting her family in that rural setting, I couldn't help but think how much Hibbing resembled photographs I'd seen of Bob's property in Woodstock.

The spirituality of *Music from Big Pink*, and the devolution of The Band's hipster stance, were obvious. Dylan's songs there, about anger, grief, self-destruction, and release, were cathartic. Robertson's songs were complementary to Dylan's—particularly "The Weight." With its New Testament reference and timeless pilgrimage, Robertson has said that song was "about the impossibility of sainthood."[47] Other songs mention God. "To Kingdom Come," has as a partial refrain, "Me I cried out God, you dared me in the dark."[48] Robertson's "Caledonia Mission" had spiritual overtones, and the narrator of Manuel's "In a Station" seemed to be addressing God. Each of these songs has a pastoral feel. But it would not be until the group's second album that its musical commitment to rural life would become clear.

Hoskyns has remarked in *Ain't in It for My Health: A Film about Levon Helm*, that "Robbie discovered the South" through Levon, and that Helm resented Robertson, in his songwriting, not just for having monopolized copyrights of songs that he felt The Band created together but for having co-opted Levon's way of life. Levon felt, Hoskyns argued, that, "You took what I am and made money off of that."[49] Though again, one questions the degree to which Dylan also may have influenced Robertson. Not only was Bob from a rural town, Hibbing, with strong unions, but he was also obsessed with the Civil War. In *Chronicles* he wrote of having spent days at the New York City Public Library, reading newspaper accounts of the 1855–65 period. He wrote,

> I wasn't so much interested in the issues as intrigued by the language and rhetoric of the times.... There was a difference in the concept of time, too. In the South, people lived their lives with sun-up, high noon, sunset, spring, summer. In the North, people loved by the clock.... In some ways the Civil War would be a battle between two kinds of time.... Back there, America was put on the cross, died

and was resurrected.... The godawful truth of that would be the all-encompassing template behind everything that I would write.[50]

Despite The Band's Canadian roots, the language and rhetoric of their second album could not be more reminiscent of the postwar American South. It fit both a back-to-the-land impetus raging in late-1960s America and the burgeoning lifestyle, among hipsters, of Redneck Chic. The latter was most evident in the music of artists such as The Byrds, The Flying Burrito Brothers, Emmylou Harris, The Great Speckled Bird, and other Gram Parsons-inspired entities. The Band were a sepia-tinted, coarse-bearded, undertaker-garbed variant of this tradition, one whose music, oddly, was branded as country rock. Their sound was less revolutionary than counterrevolutionary, and they were criticized for their conservatism. "We were rebelling against the rebellion," Robertson said. "It was an instinct to separate ourselves from the pack."[51] Nevertheless, *Time* magazine subtitled its 1969 cover story on The Band, "The New Sound of Country Rock." Robertson wrote that "we never thought of ourselves in those terms, but I guess that's what happens when you write a song about the American Civil War from a southern point of view."[52]

In rural Woodstock, Robertson, as principal songwriter for *The Band*, had seemed to have transported himself to the agrarian South—of both the nineteenth and twentieth centuries. "The Night They Drove Old Dixie Down" is the purest reflection of this displacement. It was a lament not just for Dixie, but for contemporary America.

Because of injuries suffered by Danko in a drunken car wreck, The Band were unable to tour behind *Big Pink*. It was not until April 1969 that they returned to the road. The concerts and shows they played (including Woodstock and *Ed Sullivan*) were far removed from Hawkins's bar circuit, but the toll they took emotionally on the group were substantial. "A major heroin scene began to surround the picture," a girlfriend of Helms said in his memoir. "They were very dangerous times for *all* of us."[53]

"We got into it because it was there, and it was free," Helms would write. "It was fun when it started, and then it became a problem."[54] Robertson suggested in *Testimony* that other than an early sniff, heroin passed him by. But he wrote that by 1969, "Levon, Richard, and Rick had started some serious 'chippying' around with heroin. You could feel it: out of reach, out of touch, a cold and dark disconnect."[55] It was a period Robertson would come to know as "the Darkness."[56]

Levon said that drugs weren't the whole problem, that "drugs were just part of the black mood that settled upon us." He and Robertson were arguing, and "questions of artistic control" became paramount.[57] Robertson, who had grown up in an alcoholic family, found himself working around the heroin addictions of Helm, Danko and Manuel. And, by his account, doing substantial caretaking.

Manuel, already an alcoholic, had the strongest habit, and the lyrics Robertson wrote for him in *Stage Fright*'s "The Shape I'm In" are sadly ironic: "Out of nine lives, I spent seven / Now, how in the world do you get to heaven? / Oh, you don't know the shape I'm in."[58] And in "Daniel and the Sacred Harp," a parable of music lost to greed, he wrote, "So to his father Daniel did run / And he said oh father what have I done? / His father said, 'son you've given in, you know you won your harp, But you lost in sin.'"[59] In "Saved," Manuel sang as reformed singer, now a street-corner preacher. As Robertson later remarked,

> This was the first time that writing songs was painful for me.... I wrote "The Shape I'm In" for Richard to sing, "Stage Fright" for Rick, and "The W.S. Walcott Medicine Show" for Levon—all with undertones of madness and self-destruction ... At the time, there was talk that if you wanted to play like the angels, you had to dance with the devil—that heroin was a gateway to music supremacy. That myth was yesterday, but the power of addiction was still in full force.[60]

Musically, *Stage Fright* was a return to the past, to The Band's honky-tonk roots and Hawkins's questionable example. It was seen as the group's first rock and roll album, and its best seller, topping the charts at number five. But Helm was not pleased. The magic of The Band, in his view, "was pretty much over. It ended with that second album."[61]

The group's ability to perform deteriorated, and Robertston's caretaking of his friends increased. They were backsliding. "The mental state of the group was not serious at that time," Robertson said.[62] Finally he threw up his hands and retreated to where The Band were headed emotionally: their youthful experience playing bars. Levon remembered someone saying, "Why don't we just do our old nightclub act?"[63]

The result was 1973's *Moondog Matinee* (named for disc jockey Alan Freed's teen radio frolic), with Elvis's "Mystery Train," Clarence "Frogman" Henry's "Ain't Got No Home," Fats Domino's "I'm Ready," and the Platters' "The Great Pretender," which might have been a set the Hawks had played in 1964. Artistically and spiritually they had relapsed to their comfort zone—that of bars and their devilishly cute and self-destructive routine.

They found a house in Zuma Beach that had been a cowboy bordello, "with little motel-like rooms" and corrals for horses, and built a studio there.

"The guys and I were in search of a new clubhouse," Robertson told Hoskyns. "It felt like we were a street gang that had a place to go every day. We were like the Dead End kids. We'd all go down to the studio and shoot pool, play music, talk and figure things out.... We *did* work, in a kind of punk way. We were a bunch of punks again."[64] They called the place Shangri-La, after the 1937 film about a lost paradise. Big Pink it was not. But they recorded *Northern Lights—Southern Cross* there and would produce other people's work in the studio for years thereafter.

The Band toured with Dylan in 1974. I attended a concert in that series at Washington's Capital Center, fixed in my memory as one of the best I've heard. The group with Robertson would produce six more albums before he quit, with phenomenal panache, after Martin Scorsese's *The Last Waltz*. That film, shot at San Francisco's Winterland Ballroom on Thanksgiving 1976, is high on the list of great rock documentaries, and Robertson's comments therein are noteworthy. "Sixteen years on the road, and the numbers start to scare you," he said. "I couldn't live with 20 years on the road. I couldn't even discuss it." What was implied, if not stated, was the impossibility of life there with his bandmates' addictions—many acquired during gigs. "The road has taken a lot of the great ones: Hank Williams, Buddy Holly, Otis Redding, Janis, Jimi Hendrix, Elvis. It's a goddamn impossible way of life."[65]

It spun out of control for Richard Manuel in March of 1986. He, Helm, Hudson, and assorted replacements for Robertson were on what they'd innocently dubbed the Death Tour—a series of dates at "relatively small clubs" in Florida, Helm remembered. "It was a lot of traveling and not much dignity." The Band's and Dylan's former manager, Albert Grossman, had died, and "Albert's death really got to Richard.... I don't think Richard knew who to turn to anymore when things got bad." They'd reach a club, set up, and ask Manuel, "'Hey, Richard, how's the piano?' Richard would pantomime hanging himself."[66]

He'd had a period of sobriety but had resumed drinking and drugging. On March 3 they arrived at what Helm described as "an upscale fern bar called the Cheek to Cheek Lounge"[67] outside Orlando. After a decent-enough show, Manuel thanked Hudson "profusely for 25 years of good music and appreciation." In Helm's motel room, he talked late with Levon, who reported that "he wasn't too angry or depressed, although he complained about the piano over at the lounge, and we did commiserate together on the hard touring conditions and the lack of respect it implied. He told me, 'Levon, nothing hurts like self-doubt.... And playing these little joints after playing in Japan,'" where they'd had a successful tour, "'you just feel you're slipping.'"[68]

Helm was awakened by Manuel's wife's knocks and screams later that morning. Manuel was in the bath, hanging from a shower fixture. "Richard had buckled his belt around his neck and looped the other end around the curtain rod," Helm wrote. "Richard looked ghastly." He and Danko carried him to a bed and attempted resuscitation. But he was dead. "It was so sad and terrible to see this sweet, sad friend end like this."[69] Manuel was forty-two years old.

"I think he finally just got mad enough at the way things were that he sacrificed himself to shake things up," Helm said. "Richard had had a bellyful, and so he went right ahead and done it."[70]

After his funeral, The Band recommenced its Death Tour.

Hudson, Helm, and Danko each pursued solo projects and worked as The Band, producing three good albums—*Jericho, High on the Hog,* and *Jubilation*—until Danko's death in 1999. Helm worked in bars, briefly fronting one in New Orleans—Levon Helm's Classic American Café—until his death in 2012. The group's addiction to bars stayed with them.

Robertson later admitted that "over the years, Levon and I did a lot of foolish things, and probably could have wound up in prison for some of it. In the end, we did a whole lot more beautiful things."[71]

Helm's life remained about bars. As he wrote, on the final page of *This Wheel's on Fire*: "the main thing that still gets my juices flowing is to get over to the venue on the night of the job. . . . The man that's running the joint knows we're coming, and he invites me in and helps me set up my stuff. We play some music, and then he pays us. That's the only way I ever wanted it."[72]

Notes

1. Levon Helm with Stephen Davis, *This Wheel's on Fire*, Chicago Review Press, 1993, 48.
2. Martin Scorsese, *The Last Waltz*, Columbia Pictures, 1978.
3. Helm, *This Wheel's on Fire*, 42.
4. Ibid., 9.
5. Scorsese, *The Last Waltz*.
6. Helm, *This Wheel's on Fire*, 55.
7. Ibid., 89.
8. Helm, *This Wheel's on Fire*, 120.
9. Ibid., Jacket Cover.
10. Helm, *This Wheel's on Fire*, 43.
11. Ibid., 48–49.
12. Robbie Robertson, *Testimony*, New York: Crown Archetype, 2016.
13. Helm, *This Wheel's on Fire*, 54–55.
14. Robertson, *Testimony*.
15. Helm, *This Wheel's on Fire*, 55.
16. Robertson, *Testimony*.
17. Ibid.

18. Robertson, *Testimony*.
19. Helm, *This Wheel's on Fire*, 57.
20. Norman Mailer, *Advertisements for Myself*, Cambridge, MA: Harvard University Press, 1992.
21. Bob Dylan, "It's Alright Ma (I'm Only Bleeding)," Lyrics, *Bringing It All Back Home*, Dwarf Music, 1965.
22. Helm, *This Wheel's on Fire*, 53.
23. Robertson, *Testimony*.
24. Ibid.
25. Helm, *This Wheel's on Fire*, 90.
26. Helm, *This Wheel's on Fire*, 111.
27. Ibid., 112.
28. Ibid., 114.
29. Ibid., 129.
30. Bob Dylan, *Chronicles: Volume One*, New York: Simon & Schuster, 2004.
31. Scorsese, *The Last Waltz*.
32. Toby Thompson, *Positively Main Street: Bob Dylan's Minnesota*, Minneapolis: University of Minnesota Press, 2008, 161.
33. Ibid., 82.
34. Helm, *This Wheel's on Fire*, 150.
35. Rob Bowman, *Liner Notes, Music from Big Pink*, Capitol, 2000.
36. Helm, *This Wheel's on Fire*, 165.
37. Barney Hoskyns, *Across the Great Divide: The Band and America*, New York: Hal Leonard, 2006.
38. Bowman, *Liner Notes*.
39. George Jones and Tammy Wynette, Lyrics, "God's Gonna Get'cha for That," *George Jones and Tammy Wynette's 16 Greatest Hits*, Sony BMG, 1999.
40. Bowman, *Liner Notes*.
41. Dylan, *Chronicles*.
42. Hoskyns, *Divide*.
43. Helm, *This Wheel's on Fire*, 301.
44. Hoskyns, *Divide*.
45. Thompson, *Street*, 149.
46. Ibid., 151.
47. Bowman, *Liner Notes*.
48. Robbie Robertson, "To Kingdom Come," Lyrics, *Music from Big Pink*, Capitol, 2000.
49. Jacob Hatley, *Ain't in It for My Health: A Film about Levon Helm*, directed by Jacob Hatley, 2013, Amazon Video.
50. Dylan, *Chronicles*.
51. Bowman, *Liner Notes*.
52. Robertson, *Testimony*.
53. Helm, *This Wheel's on Fire*, 184.
54. Ibid., 196.
55. Robertson, *Testimony*.

56. Helm, *This Wheel's on Fire*, 209.
57. Ibid., 209.
58. Robbie Robertson, "The Shape I'm In," Lyrics, *Stagefright*, Capitol, 2000.
59. Ibid., "Daniel and the Sacred Harp."
60. Robertson, *Testimony*.
61. Hatley, *Ain't in It for My Health*.
62. Rob Bowman, *Liner Notes*, Moondog Matinee, Capitol, 2001.
63. Helm, *This Wheel's on Fire*, 235.
64. Hoskyns, *Divide*.
65. Scorsese, *The Last Waltz*.
66. Helm, *This Wheel's on Fire*, 294.
67. Helm, *This Wheel's on Fire*, 294.
68. Ibid., 295.
69. Ibid., 295–96.
70. Ibid., 296.
71. Robertson, *Testimony*.
72. Helm, *This Wheel's on Fire*, 304.

Chapter 2

THE DAY THE MUSIC LIVED

How Bob Dylan and The Band Paved the Way for Southern Rock

CHRISTINE HAND JONES

"American Pie," Don McLean's epic ballad of American music and innocence lost, tells a popular narrative: by the end of the 1960s, rock and roll, along with all the counterculture's hopes and dreams for a better nation, was nothing but so much rubble on the side of the highway. To illustrate that narrative, the song includes two references to Bob Dylan. First, McLean mentions a "jester" in a James Dean coat who sings "in a voice that came from you and me"—an allusion to the title conferred on Dylan as "the voice of a generation."[1] In the next glimpse of this jester-without-a-cause, he wears a cast, apparently watching the drama of the 1967 Summer of Love unfold without him while he recuperates from the infamous motorcycle accident that took him out of commission in late 1966. By positioning Bob Dylan on the sidelines, McLean implies that Dylan's accident and temporary disappearance from public life were early symptoms of rock and roll's inevitable demise, which, in "American Pie," climaxes in a Satanic victory at the ill-fated 1969 Altamont Speedway Free Festival, which descended into violence. After that disaster, all three members of the Holy Trinity skip town altogether.[2] But that vision of Dylan on the sidelines, leaving others to make the music of his generation, was just a convenient myth. The real Bob Dylan was alive and kicking and making more music in 1967 than he ever had before. And he wasn't alone.

In the summer of 1967, America was a country on fire, but Bob Dylan and The Band sought refuge in a cool basement in upstate New York, jamming to traditional folk tunes and writing dozens of new ones. This collaboration ignited a fire of its own: a creative crucible melding folk, blues, country, rock and roll, and the best of emergent pop together into the prototype for a new genre: southern rock. Southern rock is a difficult genre to define precisely because it is such a musical hybrid. The first ingredient of southern rock is Americana, which is itself a hybrid of styles. Amanda Petrusich defines Americana as "traditional folk music, a symbiotic swirl of folk, bluegrass, country, gospel, blues, and classic guitar-and-vocals emoting. It is twentieth century, indigent, mostly rural music that is often connected with poverty and usually written on an acoustic guitar."[3] Americana provides the musical basis for the "southern" part of southern rock; and blues-based, electric-guitar-driven rock and roll, along with what Scott Bomar calls "a generous side serving of jazz-inspired improvisation"[4] provides the "rock" part of the recipe. So crucial is the inheritance of American rock and roll to southern rock that Scott Bomar hesitates to even distinguish southern rock from the music of its rock and roll forbears such as Elvis Presley and Jerry Lee Lewis.[5] Those artists' southern fusions of country and western with rhythm and blues already contain southern rock's basic ingredients. Here, another distinction is in order. Some people distinguish southern rock from country rock on the basis of subject matter—where country rock simply melds country and rock styles, southern rock "promotes a collective [southern] identity," with southern themes and southern pride.[6] However, the distinction between these two genres is not always clear. For example, Stephanie Schafer classifies the band Alabama as southern rock, while placing Lynyrd Skynyrd, who wrote the song "Sweet Home Alabama," as country rock.[7] Scott Bomar, on the other hand, classifies Lynyrd Skynyrd as southern rock.[8] Since the musical makeup is identical, I prefer the term southern rock, especially given The Band's affinity for southern subject matter. Nevertheless, the term country rock appears frequently in discussions of both Dylan and The Band, and I may occasionally use the term here.

Whether we call it country rock or southern rock, the musical experimentation leading to that Americana-blues-rock hybrid is on full display in Dylan's collaborations with The Band in 1967. Americana forms the foundation of their work. While the popular music of the counterculture added louder guitars, more complex sonic exploration, and flights of psychedelic fantasy, Dylan and The Band returned to the simple chord progressions, rootsy instrumentation, and modal melodies of southern folk and blues music. They borrowed from a southern-gothic lyric tradition that mixed magic, biblical and religious tropes, and outlandish characters into a strange, fairy-tale version of the American South. But they were not entirely immune to the currents of popular culture. To these traditional folk elements, they added electric guitar and organ, Beatles-inspired harmonic exploration, and their own rhythm and blues backgrounds, along with Dylan's poetic lyric explorations and The Band's diverse musical experiences.

The resulting musical mélange came closer to that old-time rock-and-roll feeling than anything on popular radio in 1967, and their collaborative work helped Dylan stage a successful comeback in 1968 with the album *John Wesley Harding*, while also helping The Band come into their own on their debut, *Music from Big Pink*. By analyzing key songs from their *Basement Tapes* collaboration as well as songs from *John Wesley Harding* and *Music from Big Pink*, I hope to better understand the mutual influence of Dylan and The Band on each other, and to untangle the musical threads that would go on to influence southern and country rock in the 1970s. Far from sitting on the sidelines, watching others try and fail to keep rock and roll alive, together, Bob Dylan and The Band blasted down genre boundaries and created a new way for a changing world to rock.

A DECISIVE MUSICAL MASH-UP

Time magazine famously said that the meeting between The Band and Bob Dylan was "the most decisive moment in rock history."[9] The reason, says William Bender, for *Time*, is "that rock thereafter began to make increasing use of the modal harmonies then prevalent in folk music."[10] Those "modal harmonies" are rooted in a modal scale—that is, a scale built around a different note than the western "do" or "tonic." Where popular American music up until that point had still been largely diatonic, the folk movement brought modal scales into popular consciousness. When Dylan went electric, he kicked off a widespread trend of setting folk tunes to a rock beat with rock instrumentation, effectively pioneering folk rock. But the folk rock that Dylan played without The Band, known then as the Hawks, was different from the new sounds he made with them. So even before their *Basement Tapes* collaborations, the sound that Dylan and The Band made together changed the course of popular music, paving the way for other artists to more fully fuse the genres of folk and rock together by writing new rock songs using those folk modes.

The members of The Band came with a surprising amount of organic folk music experience. Drummer Levon Helm absorbed folk music through his Arkansas roots. As music critic Barney Hoskyns notes, family musical gatherings were a key component of Helm's upbringing. At these gatherings, mandolins, fiddles, guitars, and whiskey were all passed around, with everyone taking a turn playing a "singularly bluesy kind of Country and Western."[11] But the rest of The Band—all Canadians—had more grounding in the sounds of the American South than their Canadian upbringing might suggest. Bassist Rick Danko came from a family of tobacco farmers who had moved to his part of Ontario during the Great Depression, carrying their Carolina music with them.[12] Pianist Richard Manuel and organist Garth Hudson had both heard southern sounds in Southern Baptist hymns before being exposed to the blues.[13] And guitarist Robbie Robertson, the city boy of the group, was enamored with stories of the American South. Though not raised in the traditions of the folk world, his love of rhythm and blues and rock and roll cultivated a curiosity bordering on obsession with all things related to southern life and music. Eventually, Robertson used his love of southern culture and writing to "hold a mirror up to America, reminding it—and the rest of the world—of its own forgotten essence."[14]

Dylan's folk experience came more through nurture than nature. Folk music was not an important part of Dylan's Hibbing, Minnesota, upbringing. Young Dylan (still known as Robert Zimmerman in those days) was far more interested in rock and roll. But after high school, Dylan discovered the world of American folk through the *Anthology of American Folk Music* (also called the "Harry Smith Anthology") and through other old folk recordings.[15] Dylan says that the first time he heard the Leadbelly song "Cottonfields," it "transported me into a world I'd never known. . . . Like I'd been walking in darkness and all of the sudden the darkness was illuminated. It was like somebody laid hands on me."[16] At that point, he became obsessed with Woody Guthrie and followed Guthrie to New York City, where Guthrie was hospitalized for Huntington's disease. At Guthrie's bedside and in the coffeehouses of Greenwich Village, Dylan learned at the feet of working folk singers and topical songwriters. He copied their singing styles, accents, guitar picking, and melodies, until he mastered folk music and transformed it into something fresh in his own songs. In 2007, Dylan called those songs his "lexicon and . . . prayer book,"[17] and he studied those texts with religious fervor. Ten years later, he ruminated on his folk education in accepting his Nobel Prize in Literature: "By listening to all the early folk artists and singing the songs yourself, you pick up the vernacular. You internalize it. You sing it in the ragtime blues, work songs, Georgia sea shanties, Appalachian ballads, and cowboy songs. You hear all the finer points and you learn the details."[18]

Dylan's carefully studied folk fusions, combined with The Band's down-home folk education, formed much of the "southern" part of what would later influence southern rock. The "rock" part of that equation came from good, old-fashioned rock and roll. Dylan had long been a fan of rock and roll music. Although he had made his name as a folk artist, his childhood dreams had revolved around the music of Elvis Presley, Buddy Holly, and lesser-known rhythm and blues artists. He dressed like James Dean's *Rebel without a Cause* character (as referenced in "American Pie") and learned guitar and piano. In a high-school talent show, a teenage Dylan played rock and roll piano and made so much noise that the school principal brought the curtain down on the act.[19] Today, Dylan remembers Buddy Holly's music as "the music that I loved—the music I grew up on: country and western, rock and roll, and rhythm and blues. Three separate strands of music ... intertwined and fused into one genre."[20] In some ways, Dylan saw himself as the second coming of these rock and roll greats. He felt "related" to Buddy Holly, and when he saw Holly play live, he had an odd, born-again experience, wherein Buddy Holly looked him "right straight dead in the eye, and he transmitted something."[21] Shortly thereafter, Holly died, and the way Dylan tells it, something in Holly's spirit transferred to him in his passing. These tales of the teenage Dylan reveal that he was no stranger to rock and roll. The Band, however, contributed real rock and roll credibility to Dylan's music: they had lived the rock and roll fantasy that teenage Dylan had only played at.

In a signal that stretched all the way up from Arkansas through Ontario, WLAC AM radio blasted the same pre-Elvis rhythm and blues sounds into the young ears of all the future members of The Band.[22] Over time, they each picked up those rhythm and blues skills, but Robbie Robertson in particular fell in love with the rough, bluesy sounds of the Deep South.[23] Eventually, they all put their skills to use for Ronnie Hawkins, an American rockabilly performer who began touring in the Toronto area in order to escape direct competition from the likes of Elvis Presley.[24] Even with Buddy Holly dead, Chuck Berry in prison, and watered-down pop versions of rock and roll hits dousing the genre's fire, Ronnie Hawkins and his band, the Hawks, blazed on. In 1960, as young Dylan moved from the Midwest to make it in New York City's burgeoning folk world, The Band remained deeply rooted in the rough-and-tumble sounds of rock and roll music.

Where The Band brought hard-won, real-world credibility to the folk-rock music that Bob Dylan had worked so hard to develop, Bob Dylan brought poetry and artistry to The Band's fledgling songwriting skills. Only a few years into his career, Dylan was already seasoned at shattering expectations and looking at the world in unusual ways. In the interview for The Band's 1970 *Time* cover story, Robbie Robertson explained the shock of Dylan's lyrics: "We were used to singers who opened their mouths and went 'Whop-bop-bop-lu-bop,' but Bob decided to say something while his mouth was moving, and it was interesting to see how easy it came to him."[25] Spending time in the studio and on tour with Dylan exposed The Band to a depth and style of writing that surely affected their own work in the years to come.

In teaming up with Robbie Robertson and most of the members of The Band for his world tour of 1965–1966, Dylan found the right group to realize his folk-rock visions on the road. Martin Jacobi posits that "this tour was important primarily because it brought the electric Dylan to the world, but also because on it Dylan greatly enhanced his ability to play with a supporting band."[26] As active, touring musicians, The Band brought experience and discipline to Dylan's performances. Robbie Robertson describes one of their first rehearsals with Dylan as "messy," as Robertson attempted to follow Dylan's meandering performance style and translate it into signals that the Hawks could follow.[27] But as they continued to work together, they developed a musical camaraderie and began to form a unit. Dylan, for his part, brought a sense of freedom and spontaneity to The Band's performances. Robertson writes of those early days that he enjoyed "the level of intensity this collaboration brought," admiring Dylan's singing style and the way Dylan "wasn't too fixated on details or fussy about how tight [they] were."[28]

The Band also added a dash of authenticity to Dylan's folk and rock personas. In many ways, The Band embodied a younger Dylan's aspirations. Where Dylan was middle class, most of the members of The Band came from difficult, working-class lives. Where Dylan had once invented stories of riding the rails across the South, Woody-Guthrie style, The Band really *had* spent years of hard life on the road, playing in dive bars and sketchy clubs. Because of those hard times, they had earned their "Woody Guthrie" stripes in a way that Bob Dylan could only pretend to, notwithstanding Dylan's whirlwind education in the first five years of his musical career. Soon enough, though, both Dylan and The Band would be old veterans of the road and its harsh lessons. On the 1965–1966 tour, they kept up a stressful touring pace in which they learned to play through boos and jeers. The stress took its toll. Robertson recalls, "As thick as our skins had become throughout the tour, the negative reaction at the Albert Hall made us angry."[29] Because they were responsible for the electric guitars and drums, much of the hostility was aimed at the Hawks themselves. But Bob Dylan stood by them.[30] Making music under such pressure strengthened the bonds between Dylan and The Band, so that after Dylan's motorcycle crash and temporary retirement, they were in a perfect position to take musical risks.

The curious can find various accounts of the circumstances surrounding Dylan's motorcycle accident in the summer of 1966 in multiple Dylan biographies and studies.[31] Dylan himself recounts the experience as a spiritual rebirth.[32] Certainly, the crash laid the groundwork for a musical rebirth. Immediately after Dylan's crash, both Dylan and The Band laid low. As far as people knew, Dylan neither performed, wrote, nor recorded. He kept The Band on retainer but didn't rehearse with them. Mostly, he stepped into the role of a family man in his home in Woodstock, New York.[33] The Band spent their time recording demos as they prepared to step into the spotlight apart from Dylan as the next artist on Columbia's label lineup. During this time, The Band began to hone their songwriting skills and veer away from the rhythm and blues sound that had characterized their previous work as the Hawks.[34] Sid Griffin singles out the half-written song "Beautiful Thing" from the autumn of 1966 as a strong preview of the sound they would develop in *The Basement Tapes* and in their future work as The Band.[35] But it was not until they joined Dylan in Woodstock in 1967 that they began to develop their distinctive sound in the free, relaxed atmosphere of small-town life, away from the pressures and deadlines of the road and the studio—and away from the chaos of America in 1967.

BASEMENT CULTURE

1967 stands as a crucial year in the 1960s, both for music and for American culture. It was a year marked by the extremes of love and war. On the one hand, the counterculture movement began to spill over from its small hippie communities into the American mainstream. The Beatles released *Sgt. Pepper's Lonely Hearts Club Band*, a landmark album that not only brought the high-seeking, love-making ethos of the counterculture into the suburbs, but also brought sophisticated, symphonic, and psychedelic sounds into the Top 40. On the "war" side, tension surrounding the Vietnam War grew both at home and overseas. In June of 1967, President Johnson moved nineteen-year-olds to first pick in the draft, leading to an increase in antiwar sentiment. Meanwhile, the conflict abroad continued to escalate, culminating in the bloody Tet Offensive at year's end. To add to the sense of unease, a different kind of war broke out in American streets as the face of the civil rights movement shifted from peaceful protests to riots.[36] Secluded in Woodstock, New York, however, The Band and Bob Dylan lived in an America of the past, defined only by its music.

From their home studio, first in a room in Dylan's house and eventually in the basement of Big Pink, Bob Dylan and The Band played old songs and wrote snippets of new ones while Dylan played the role of musical mentor with his peers. They played for fun, with no set agenda, as Robbie Robertson explained to Greil Marcus:

It was all a goof. We were playing with absolute freedom; we weren't doing anything we thought anybody else would ever hear, as long as we lived. But what started in that basement, what came out of it—and The Band came out of it, anthems, people holding hands and rocking back and forth all over the world singing "I Shall Be Released," the distance that all of this went—came out of this little conspiracy, of us amusing ourselves. Killing time.[37]

As they killed time together, they jammed to the many folk tunes Dylan knew and to the songs of Johnny Cash and Hank Williams as Dylan squeezed all the great country and folk songs, as well as many obscurities, from his absorbent mind. Robbie Robertson remembers, "You could hardly name a song he didn't know all the words to, and you didn't have to ask twice."[38] Steeped in this history, the group wrote new songs, with the same use of pentatonicism,[39] rough textures and open harmonies found in the field songs and mountain music on the Harry Smith–era recordings that younger Dylan had devoured in his early folk days. To those simple but potent folk structures, they added a Beatlesesque experimentation as they borrowed chords from other keys and explored chromatic and modal harmonic structures that expanded the harmonic palette of typical folk music. This combination of Americana with the pop-rock style of the sixties created a new, unique blend, containing all the key elements of southern rock.

An excellent example of this unique combination is the Rick Danko and Bob Dylan cowrite "This Wheel's on Fire," which later appeared on *Music from Big Pink*. On the "official" *Basement Tapes* LP, "This Wheel's on Fire" features two guitars, bass, piano, drums, and organ: a typical set-up for The Band. The organ would sound just as much at home spilling from the rafters of an old church as it does moaning through the reel-to-reel tape. And almost as if to support that spiritual connotation, all the vocals and instruments have extra reverberation. The song's chord progression is spooky and unusual; the verses spiral down from A minor to B diminished 7 before moving through a more typical minor folk progression.[40] In my own discussion of Bob Dylan's explorations of apocalypse, I covered this song in depth. That analysis is worth quoting here for its discussion of the song's music:

> The dark atmosphere of the music on the verses to this song adds to the sense of looming apocalypse. On the chorus, however, the mood shifts; Dylan's vision of a wheel on fire, about to "explode" is, like Ezekiel's, one of Divine revelation. Fittingly, when the voices of The

Band come together on the F major chord over the word "fire," the tension begins to lift, and as their voices unite in a crescendo on a G major chord over the word "road," the fiery wheel that they describe seems to roll closer and closer to the listener. This anticipation is rewarded when, in the final line, "This wheel shall explode," the harmony, too, explodes into a shimmering A-major chord. Such a vision of world's end is beautiful and unexpected as the looming clouds of Divine judgment created by the brooding instruments and downward tending harmony of the verse suddenly part to reveal a rainbow of bright organ, crashing cymbals, an exuberant bass line, and above all, the triumphant, transcendent voices, exulting in the A major triad. Dylan's visions of destruction may have been inherited from the harsh fundamentalism of the folk world, but on *The Basement Tapes*, the result is not fire but glory.[41]

In this passage, I interpret the music of "This Wheel" as another layer of ambiguity in Dylan's overall apocalyptic vision. Others have seen the song's unusual music as one of The Band's rare nods to the trends of psychedelic music.[42] But in light of the various backgrounds and traditions that Dylan and The Band brought together, "This Wheel's on Fire" stands as a prime example of how those diverse musical backgrounds combined to produce a new musical hybrid. Garth Hudson's organ playing brings a high-church, classical influence to bear on the song's folk-rock foundation. Adding the vocal and instrumental timbres of the rest of the group into the mix creates a complex fusion of genres and tones unlike anything else in popular music at the time. So unique is "This Wheel's on Fire" that it could stand as the apotheosis of those basement collaborations. It is no wonder that the song is one of a handful of collaborations from that time to make it onto The Band's debut album, *Music from Big Pink*. It is also no wonder that neither Dylan nor The Band ever reproduced anything similar to it again. In its musical and lyrical visions of fire and glory, "This Wheel's on Fire" represents the dramatic height of The Band's and Dylan's combined powers.

Lyrically, "This Wheel's on Fire" takes its place beside several other songs from *The Basement Tapes* that depict all the strangeness of traditional folk music. In an interview with Ralph Gleason, Dylan describes it this way:

The main body of it (folk music) is just based on myth and the Bible and plague and famine and all kinds of things like that which are just nothin' but mystery and you can see it in all the songs—roses growin' right up out of people's hearts and naked cats in bed with, y'know, spears growing right out of their backs and y'know seven years of this and eight years of that and it's all really something that nobody can really touch.[43]

The strange spirit of carnivalesque collage that Dylan describes is so prominent a feature of old folk music that Greil Marcus wrote an entire book on the phenomenon. He terms the style "the old, weird, America," and he traces the style through Harry Smith's *Anthology of American Folk Music*, which he believes forms not only "a backdrop to" but also "a version of" Dylan and The Band's *Basement Tapes*.[44] In "This Wheel's on Fire," that "old, weird" quality comes through in an odd juxtaposition of contemporary and biblical images. The lyrics constantly call on the unnamed "you" to whom the song is addressed to remember particular details from the past: a piece of lace knotted sailor style, a packed bag, a promise to meet. These bits and pieces function as fragments of memory that, in hindsight, become signs, along with that ambiguous reference to the biblical prophet Ezekiel's wheel, of a doomed relationship.

Dylan employs similarly strange folk lyric techniques throughout his early writing, characterized by the "chains of flashing images"[45] prominent in "A Hard Rain's A-Gonna Fall" and "The Chimes of Freedom." He takes his tendency toward weird collage even further in his mescaline-fueled rock years, just before his days recording *The Basement Tapes*. One of Dylan's favorite techniques in those years was bringing a motley cast of historical, biblical, and literary figures together into a vaguely mythical location and tying them together in a peculiar, loose narrative. "Highway 61 Revisited"[46] is a perfect example of this sort of approach. In that song, Abraham and Isaac rub shoulders with Louis Armstrong, Mack the Knife, and a shady southern figure named Georgia Sam—all characters taking part in a grotesque apocalyptic vision spread out across US Highway 61. In Dylan's day, the real Highway 61 passed through Duluth, near his hometown of Hibbing, Minnesota, but in Dylan's song, Highway 61 becomes the site of faith-killing, a home for fugitives, a dumping ground, a bed of incest, and a theater of war. Throughout the song, fiction and fact, history and legend, past and future blur together into a frenetic fever dream.

That dream had its foundations in those "old, weird" folk songs, and Dylan carried that bizarre vision right into his writings with The Band in upstate New York. Many of the songs on *The Basement Tapes* represent the "Odds and Ends" that one of the tracks is named for. For example, "Clothes Line Saga" literally tells the tale of a clothes line. Another song, "Lo and Behold," depicts a strange journey to San Antonio by way of Pittsburgh and

Tennessee. The narrator, nicknamed "Moby Dick" by a stranger, is on a quest for revelation—a "lo and behold"—that neither love nor money can provide. The narrative itself has little to no cohesion. He buys his love "a herd of moose," travels by coach and Ferris wheel while dreaming of buying a truck, then finally drives that moose herd all the way back to Pittsburgh, feeling fed up by the whole enterprise.[47]

These patchwork ballads feature whoops and hollers and exuberant playing, creating a zany, party feeling that pulses through all the recordings that eventually formed *The Basement Tapes*. The joyful jam "Million Dollar Bash"[48] exemplifies the festive atmosphere, with the gleeful shouts of a barn dance punctuating this song about a huge party. The guest list to the "Million Dollar Bash" includes odd characters with names like "Turtle," "Silly Nelly," and "Jones" who engage in comical eccentricities, culminating in the narrator's own strange mishap: he looks down at his wristwatch and somehow hits himself in the face before he can make it to the bash. These lyrical and musical experiments illustrate the sounds of a relaxed group of friends having a party of their own. It is telling that at their most at ease, they drew freely from old American folk sources. Liberated from the pressures of the public or a label, Dylan and The Band took those folk sources and they played with them, rearranged them, added to them, and transformed them into a prototype of southern rock.

DYLAN'S QUIET COMEBACK

Bob Dylan emerged from those remarkable 1967 basement sessions with a sparse, acoustic country album, *John Wesley Harding*. In February of 1968, Dylan chronicler Ralph Gleason began his review of the album with these words: "We can all relax now. Bob Dylan isn't dead."[49] What Ralph Gleason may not have known was just how much Dylan's resurrection owed to his friends in The Band. In his review, Gleason sounds relieved that Dylan has returned from a near-grave with a different sound and perspective, and he highlights Dylan's new calm and happy demeanor. He describes *John Wesley Harding* as "a warm, loving collection of myths, prophecies, allegories, love songs and good times," and his words about the song "I Dreamed I Saw St. Augustine" ring true for the entire album. He calls the song "a major work, a moral dilemma conceived in rock 'n roll and R&B rhythms and played as a C&W [country and western] tune." Of the lyrics, Gleason notes that although the songs still ring with the power of Dylan's poetry, these songs contain "less harshness and more fluidity."[50] All of Gleason's observations could easily apply to The Band's first album; their good influence on Dylan shines softly both in *John Wesley Harding*'s lyrics and music.

Spending time with The Band inspired Dylan's new sound and style. Those weeks of pounding out strange song after strange song alongside his musical brothers seem to have honed Dylan's sense of narrative and character. Many of the songs on *John Wesley Harding* read like short folk tales, with one protagonist on a mini-quest in three verses. Longer works like "The Ballad of Frankie Lee and Judas Priest" have none of the mixed-up qualities of the songs from *Highway 61 Revisited* or *Blonde on Blonde*; we may not know exactly who or what Frankie Lee and Judas Priest represent, but the language and the story remain clear across the song's eleven verses.[51] Even a song like "All Along the Watchtower," which takes place *in medias res*,[52] or which Dylan has said could be read "in a rather reverse order,"[53] maintains a sense of unity with its tale of a joker and a thief commiserating over the signs of a coming storm.[54]

It is also possible that all that time listening to Robbie Robertson's interest in the stories and legends of the old South as well as Levon Helm's real tales of life in Arkansas influenced Dylan's subject matter on *John Wesley Harding*. When asked in a 1968 *Sing Out!* interview where he got the inspiration for "I Pity the Poor Immigrant" and other songs from that time, Dylan squirmed and averted the question, saying, "To tell the truth, I have no idea how it comes into my mind.... The songs don't painfully come out. They come out in a trick or two or for something that you might overhear. I'm just like any other songwriter, you pick up the things that are given to you."[55] Dylan famously "picked up" influences from all over the place, from Blake and Rilke to Woody Guthrie and Ramblin' Jack Elliot, and determining direct influence from his pals in The Band would be a difficult task. Still, the contrast between Dylan's earlier folk albums and *John Wesley Harding* is telling. Dylan's early folk albums feature protagonists taken straight from the pages of the newspapers, such as "The Ballad of Hollis Brown" and "The Lonesome Death of Hattie Carroll." Later, his rock albums overflowed with historical and literary figures thrown together into outlandish collages such as those found on *Highway 61 Revisited*. By contrast, on *John Wesley Harding*, Dylan writes about the "real" legends from history. That he wrote these songs during and after several weeks spent swapping songs and stories of the South with his bandmates is surely no coincidence.

The title character of the album's eponymous lead track, John Wesley Harding, was a famous Texas gunfighter. Gleason calls the title song "a ballad, a tale of a TV Western hero living outside the law and a friend to honest men."[56] That Dylan fictionalized Harding's life is of little account; his version of events only adds to the legend. Dylan mixes the fictional with the historical in a similar way in "I Dreamed I Saw St. Augustine." The Augustine Dylan portrays is partly Augustine of Hippo and partly some combination of other church fathers and Christian martyrs.[57] As in his larger collage works, Dylan fuses fact and fiction in these simpler songs, but they ring with the "truth" of legend—of the storyteller who got a few details wrong in the retelling, but whose version of events becomes part of the canon. Even the album's liner notes contribute to that sense of magic and legend fusing with reality, with a zany tale of three lame and poor kings who come to a man named Frank for the key to unlock Dylan's latest album. Amid interludes from a prophet named Terry Shute and Frank's nagging wife, Frank enacts a strange ritual that ends in his punching through a window, after which the three Kings leave, healed, whole, and rich.[58] It's the kind of strange tale that would be as much at home in a Brothers Grimm tale as in a David Lynch scene, and together with the country sound of the album, the brief story evokes a fairy-tale version of the South. The tale's strangeness certainly connects to the "old, weird America" of *The Basement Tapes*, but its uniquely southern surreality, grounded in familiar southern characters, comes much closer to the plane of reality than Dylan's previous, drug-induced dream sequences. The Band, it seems, helped bring Dylan back down to Earth, or at least reignited Dylan's affinity for southern folklore.

In other songs like "Drifter's Escape" and "I Am a Lonesome Hobo," Dylan puts on the voice of southern vagabonds, and in "The Ballad of Frankie Lee and Judas Priest,"[59] Dylan delivers an intricate tale of such hobos and drifters. These characters seem both real and fantastic, living in a world of magic realism, where either Paradise or Purgatory might await in "the home across the road." Gleason explains these songs as "myths and legends . . . and maybe even parables on the edge of time."[60] But again, these myths and legends maintain a foundation in the reality of the poor, the unjustly accused, and the cheated, with whom Dylan blatantly identifies in "Dear Landlord" and "I Pity the Poor Immigrant."[61] All these mournful songs of the disenfranchised develop the theme Dylan began in the basement with "I Shall Be Released," a song that tells of a prisoner's longing for freedom.[62] The Band's beautiful rendition of that song on *Music from Big Pink* provides one of the most overt stylistic and thematic connections between *John Wesley Harding* and The Band's debut.

THE WEIGHT OF DYLAN

Both in its music and its lyric, *John Wesley Harding* functions as a stripped-down preview of the style that would come in The Band's *Music from Big*

Pink. Gleason noted Dylan's interesting mix of rhythm and blues and country and western, and an even more potent and original fusion of these sounds would come together in The Band's debut. *Rolling Stone* called the new music "country rock," saying "With *Music from Big Pink*, The Band dips into the well of tradition and comes up with bucketsful of clear, cool, country soul that wash the ears with a sound never heard before. *Music from Big Pink* is the kind of album that will have to open its own door to a new category."[63] In his memoir, *Testimony*, Robbie Robertson discusses the early listening sessions of The Band's premiere album. Time and again, people reacted as if to something brand new. Their manager, Albert Grossman, apparently played the music for "everybody who came through his office or home for the next three months" just to see the looks on their faces and make them "guess who they were listening to."[64] Dylan loved the new sound. Robertson reports that Dylan "stood up and said, 'That was SO good. You did it, man, you did it.'"[65] *Music from Big Pink* signaled The Band's independence from their famous friend and mentor. Aside from three Dylan covers or cowrites and a cover of the classic "Long Black Veil," all the songs on the album are originals. At one point, Dylan offered to sing background vocals on the record, but then graciously backed out, acknowledging the need to let The Band do their own thing.[66] Instead of contributing to the recording, he donated a painting for the album cover that depicts all six of them jamming away in the basement. That album cover provides a powerful metaphor for Dylan's involvement in the album. Like the fourth figure in the fire in the biblical account of Shadrach, Meshach, and Abednego, Dylan stands as the invisible sixth band member, and his influence—even when uncredited—is palpable.

The Band's most enduring song, "The Weight," almost didn't make it onto their debut album. Apparently, writer Robbie Robertson thought it was a throwaway song, partly because of its simplistic chord progression.[67] That "throwaway" song became one of the most important songs of the 1960s. "The Weight" intrigues with its evocative, quasibiblical lyrics, its quirky cast of characters caught in a convoluted narrative, and its instantly singalong chorus: "Take a load off, Fannie."[68] The song appears in the decade-defining film *Easy Rider* and has inspired countless cover versions. Although The Band later produced a critically acclaimed body of work, this single song from their first album is still the one most people remember when they think of The Band. Perhaps to highlight the song's importance and originality, as well as to separate The Band from their mentor, most commentaries overlook Dylan's impact on "The Weight," but his influence is apparent to the careful listener.[69] The song's length, style, and chord progression all reflect Bob Dylan at his mid-1960s peak. The song's surreality and its collage of crazy characters owe a debt to Dylan's cluttered mid-sixties folk-rock ballads as well as those basement sessions. Last but not least, the song's biblical imagery and messianic undertones also take a page from Dylan's book.

The simple chord progression of "The Weight" reflects The Band's dual inheritance of folk tropes and Dylan's unique writing. Robbie Robertson has said that the song does not "have a very complicated chord progression," calling it "just kind of traditional."[70] That simple chord progression in the verses (I, iii, IV, I) shares its pattern with Dylan's "When the Ship Comes In."[71] That progression is common enough in folk music, but it was almost unheard of in late sixties popular music. "The Weight's" unconventional structure also indicates Dylan's influence. Even if long, sprawling narratives were already part of the folk tradition that both Dylan and The Band inherited, only Dylan was so bold as to put that tradition into practice in popular music. Dylan's early and mid-sixties songs break all boundaries of the standard three-and-a-half-minute pop song. Robbie Robertson recalls his early days of performing with Dylan, thinking, "How in the world does this man remember all the words to his songs?" He goes on to comment, "With Bob this was a feat above and beyond, not only because of the complexity of his lyrics but also because some of his songs seemed to contain more verses than the Bible."[72] Those who covered Dylan's songs often cut out verses for the sake of time. For example, The Byrds' version of "Mr. Tambourine Man" plays only one out of Dylan's four penned verses, bringing the song down to a more palatable two-and-a-half minutes.[73] While "The Weight" perhaps pales in comparison with Dylan's eleven-minute-and-sixteen-second ballad "Sad-Eyed Lady of the Lowlands" (which Robertson helped to produce),[74] "The Weight" nevertheless exceeds the bounds of most pop songs of the day. Like their mentor, Dylan, where other pop writers would have limited themselves to two verses, two choruses, and a bridge, The Band kept playing. "The Weight" clocks in at four minutes and thirty seconds with five verses and five choruses. It is difficult to imagine any band that did not come of age with Bob Dylan attempting something so unusual for their debut record.

The song's subject matter and cluttered cast list also reflects Dylan's influence. Robbie Robertson penned the song's lyrics, inspired by the surrealistic films of Luis Buñuel and "memories and characters from [his] southern exposure."[75] "The Weight" tells the tale of a failed quest for sainthood, and Robertson wrote it in a single sitting.[76] Peter Aaron acknowledges Robertson's debt to Dylan, but says that Robertson was not interested in writing the "epic, wordy, labyrinthine style" that characterized Dylan's pre-basement songs.[77] But if Robertson failed to catch Dylan's tendency toward collage while barreling through his wild folk-rock fantasies on tour in the mid-sixties, that penchant for pastiche certainly took hold while they were holed up in their makeshift basement studio in upstate New York, churning out all the "odds and ends" that formed *The Basement Tapes*. The lyrics of "The Weight" share similarities with both periods.

Like Dylan's quasimythical Highway 61, from the song "Highway 61 Revisited," "The Weight" takes place in a real US locale: Nazareth, Pennsylvania, as Robertson tells it,[78] but Nazareth, the hometown of Jesus to any casual listener. Like Dylan before him, Robertson transforms an ordinary American place into a scene of legend and magic. In this symbol-laden town, the nameless narrator encounters such diverse characters as "Carmen and the Devil," "Miss Moses," "Crazy Chester," and ordinary folks like "Anna Lee" and "Miss Fannie."[79] Several of the odd characters mentioned in the song were based on some of Levon Helm's real-life acquaintances from Arkansas. "Crazy Chester" came right out of Helm's Fayetteville experience, remembered as "a happy-go-lucky Fayetteville eccentric who wore capguns on his hips and thought himself the local keeper of the peace."[80] "Luke" may have referred to "early Hawks guitarist Jimmy Ray 'Luke' Paulman," and "Anna Lee" was someone Helm knew from Turkey Scratch, Arkansas.[81] These "real" people meet up with other mythical and fictional characters, burdening the narrator with various tasks until he completely loses track of his mission, and together, they sing that catchy chorus one more time: "Take a load off, Fannie." Having already examined similar styles from Dylan's earlier work, this wild combination of truth and fantasy in an off-kilter story populated by a collage of biblical, mythical, and actual characters should sound rather familiar.

Since "The Weight's" chord progression, structure, length, and interesting lyric style all owe a debt to Bob Dylan, it also seems likely that the song's central theme, "impossibility of sainthood,"[82] could be read differently in light of Dylan as well. Doomed or thwarted narrators on an absurd quest appear often on *The Basement Tapes*—even in those songs we've already examined, such as "Lo and Behold" and "Million Dollar Bash." Another variant on that theme in Dylan's writing occurs when Dylan introduces a narrator or main character who takes on some messianic role or mission. His songs with a messianic theme begin early in his career but pick up speed considerably during *The Basement Tapes* sessions and come to a head during his born-again years.[83] Many songs from *The Basement Tapes* employ messianic imagery or ideas. Two stand out for the oddness of their messianic vision and their similarity to "The Weight."

The first is "Quinn the Eskimo," which became a huge hit for Manfred Mann and which Dylan later released on his *Self-Portrait* album. The song revolves around the wait for the arrival of the title character, Quinn. He never actually arrives in the song, but we are guaranteed that the promised land awaits in his arrival, which will see everyone "jump[ing] for joy," sleeping soundly, and literally flocking to him ("all the pigeons gonna run to him").[84] "Open the Door, Homer" is another *Basement Tapes* song that rings with messianic longing. The song's title recalls Jesus's words in the book of Revelation: "Behold, I stand at the door, and knock: if any man hear my voice, and open the door, I will come in to him, and will sup with him, and he with me."[85] The messianic implications grow stronger in the song's last stanza, when the narrator encourages Homer to both "forgive" and "heal the sick."[86] Oddly, the recorded version gives this would-be messiah a different name: Richard (perhaps in reference to The Band's Richard Manuel, who would have been present at the time).[87] Either way, both songs paint an ambiguous vision of a Christ figure that, when combined with the overtly religious overtones of many of *The Basement Tapes* songs, may add an interpretive layer to "The Weight."

The nameless narrator of "The Weight" is not only a man on a thwarted mission for goodness—he's also a man with a message to "take a load off" and "put the load right on me." Such a message evokes Christ's "Come unto me, all ye that labour and are heavy laden, and I will give you rest."[88] And indeed, our narrator repeatedly bears the weight of everyone else's burdens, until his bags "are sinking low" and he returns to "Miss Fannie, who sent me here with her regards for everyone."[89] In this metaphor, "Miss Fannie" becomes an unusual version of God the Father, but the overall oddness of the messianic vision is no stranger than the savior found in Mighty Quinn, an Eskimo, who makes pigeons come running. Dylan's variations on the messiah trope are unique, and even if the messianic connection to "The Weight" isn't perfect, there are enough corollaries to Dylan's quirky Christ figures to reveal an absorption, on Robertson's part, of the kinds of practices Dylan favored.

While "The Weight" is not the only evidence of Bob Dylan's influence on The Band, this song stands out; of all the songs on *Music from Big Pink*, "The Weight" sounds the most like The Band's signature style. According to Robertson, Bob Dylan was impressed and surprised the first time he heard the song, and he congratulated Robertson for the achievement.[90] In "The Weight," Robertson as writer and The Band as collaborators took the lessons of the basement and transformed them into something new. "The Weight" represents Robertson's coming of age as a writer, but it would be foolish to believe that he could have come up with such a song without having spent so many days churning out songs with Bob Dylan.

SOUTHERN AMERICAN PIE

The exact threads of Bob Dylan's and The Band's musical tapestry cannot be untangled. While Peter Aaron notes Dylan's key role in exposing The Band to real folk music and poetic lyrics, the members of The Band were already steeped in folk tradition before meeting Dylan.[91] Aaron also highlights The Band's importance in making Dylan more of a team player due to their collaboration.[92] Though Dylan was a renowned songwriter before The Band, already possessing the raw materials of folk and rock that he needed, it is impossible to say what he would have done with those materials without that precious time spent working with his friends on the basement sessions. Likewise, The Band were a group of highly skilled musicians, already working on some original material before they began working with Dylan. But the speed with which they learned to write and collaborate and the artistic freedom and musical development that they gained in Big Pink may not have happened any other way. The astounding musical output for each artist after their collaboration reveals deep debt on both sides.

For their part, The Band took the best of the sonic exploration popularized by psychedelic rock and used it to create darker, stripped-down sounds that set the listener free into a kind of southern fairy tale. Far from letting rock and roll die, they pulled it up from its grave and gave it a new kind of life by reminding the nation of the musical foundation of their beloved musical genre. Bob Stanley argues, of Dylan and The Band's influence on the development of southern and country rock, that "The stream of country influence on post-Beatles pop became a flood after Bob Dylan's touring band, then known as the Hawks, spent 1967 in Woodstock," calling their influence "instantaneous."[93] Scott Bomar posits that the collaborative work of The Band and Bob Dylan helped to set the stage for all of southern rock, starting with the Allman Brothers Band in 1969.[94] Indeed, one of guitarist Duane Allman's earlier claims to fame was playing guitar on Aretha Franklin's cover of "The Weight,"[95] so in that small way, The Band's music was directly instrumental to the development of the Allman Brothers. The influence does not stop there. Bob Stanley lists several artists and bands who began to fuse country with their rock and roll following that summer in the Woodstock basement, including Crosby, Stills, and Nash's country-leaning folk, the Rolling Stones' country-flavored "Honky Tonk Women" and "Country Honk," the Byrds' country-rock album *Sweetheart of the Rodeo*, and even Elton John's album of southern sounds and stories, *Tumbleweed Connection*.[96] The Band's music took America away from the shiny, mod-pop, psychedelic flights of fancy and back down dusty roads. While neither The Band nor Bob Dylan were ultimately immune to the societal pressures that eventually "killed" the music, their unique 1967 collaboration lived on long after *The Last Waltz* and helped to revive a dying music and culture, thus paving the way for southern rock to shine in the 1970s.

Don McLean released "American Pie" in 1971. His song centers around the fifties and sixties and the rise and fall of rock and roll. The Dylan in his song is a parody of James Dean, and, if not dead like that 1950s icon, just as irrelevant. But McLean spoke too soon. That junk heap of a motorcycle came roaring back to life, this time with a country flair and a band of brothers. Today, the impact of Dylan's and The Band's work is visible every time a new Americana group dons depression-era suspenders and fedoras for their album cover—not to mention in the musical fusions we now take for granted. Barney Hoskyns explains The Band's career as one that "spans the entire course of American rock and roll from rhythm and blues to retro rockabilly," calling their music "the most soulful, haunting music ever made about America."[97] That description paints The Band as the answer to McLean's lament. In The Band's music, we can hear the whole story of rock and roll unfold and end, not in cynicism, but in hope that reverberates every time we press play.

Notes

1. Don McLean, writer, "American Pie," recorded May 26, 1971, in *American Pie*, Don McLean, United Artists, 1971.
2. Ibid.
3. Amanda Petrusich, *It Still Moves: Lost Highways and the Search for the Next American Music*, New York: Faber and Faber, 2008, 5.
4. Scott B. Bomar, *Southbound: An Illustrated History of Southern Rock*, Milwaukee, WI: Backbeat, 2014, xiv.
5. Ibid.
6. Stephanie Schäfer, *"Cashville"—Dilution of Original Country Music Identity through Increasing Commercialization*, Hamburg: Diplomica Verlag, 2012. http://ebookcentral.proquest.com/lib/dalbapt-ebooks/detail.action?docID=1035426.
7. Schäfer, "Cashville."
8. Bomar, *Southbound*, 101–28.
9. William Bender, "Down to Old Dixie and Back," *Time*, January 12, 1970.
10. Ibid.
11. Barney Hoskyns, *Across the Great Divide: The Band and America*, Milwaukee, WI: Hal Leonard, 2006, 24.
12. Ibid., 16.
13. Ibid., 18–24.

14. Peter Aaron, *The Band FAQ: All That's Left to Know about the Fathers of Americana.* Milwaukee, WI: Backbeat Books, 2016, 25.

15. Elijah Wald, *Dylan Goes Electric!: Newport, Seeger, Dylan, and the Night That Split the Sixties,* New York: Dey St., 2015, 43–53.

16. Bob Dylan, "Bob Dylan- Nobel Lecture," Nobelprize.org, June 5, 2017.

17. Jon Pareles, "A Wiser Voice Blowin' in the Autumn Wind," *New York Times,* September 28, 1997, Arts section.

18. Bob Dylan, "Nobel Lecture."

19. Wald, *Dylan Goes Electric!,* 40–41.

20. Bob Dylan, "Nobel Lecture."

21. Ibid.

22. Barney Hoskyns traces the influence of this single radio station in his in-depth discussion of The Band's musical beginnings in *Across the Great Divide,* 7–28.

23. Ibid., 15.

24. Ibid., 37. Apparently, Conway Twitty gave Hawkins the tip to go to Canada.

25. Bender, "Down to Old Dixie and Back."

26. Martin Jacobi, "Bob Dylan and Collaboration," in *The Cambridge Companion to Bob Dylan,* ed. Kevin J. H. Dettmar, Cambridge, NY: Cambridge University Press, 2009, 69–79.

27. Robertson, *Testimony,* 178.

28. Robertson, *Testimony,* 178–79.

29. Ibid., 240.

30. Ibid., 241.

31. Sid Griffin does an especially thorough job piecing together various accounts of the accident itself: Sid Griffin, *Million Dollar Bash: Bob Dylan, The Band, and the Basement Tapes* (London: Jawbone Press, 2014), 33–45. While there are several other notable Dylan biographies, two of my favorites are Robert Shelton, *No Direction Home: The Life and Music of Bob Dylan,* New York: Da Capo Press, 1997; and Dylan's own creative memoir, Bob Dylan, *Chronicles: Volume One,* New York: Simon & Schuster, 2004.

32. Mikal Gilmore, "Bob Dylan Unleashed: A Wild Ride on His New LP and Striking Back at Critics.," *Rolling Stone,* September 27, 2013.

33. Sid Griffin, *Million Dollar Bash,* 45–46.

34. Sid Griffin provides insight into this period in *Million Dollar Bash,* 46–58. Robbie Robertson's memoir, *Testimony,* is also useful: 257–68.

35. Ibid., 50.

36. Mark Lytle, *America's Uncivil Wars: The Sixties Era: From Elvis to the Fall of Richard Nixon,* New York: Oxford University Press, 2006, 217–39. It is also worth noting that peaceful protests and riots coexisted throughout the civil rights movement of the sixties, but the summer of 1967 marks major riots in Newark and Detroit that gained national attention.

37. Greil Marcus, *The Old, Weird America: The World of Bob Dylan's Basement Tapes,* New York: Picador, 1997, xx.

38. Robertson, *Testimony,* 272.

39. That is, five-note scales common to folk and nonwestern music, as opposed to the seven-note scale common to most Western music.

40. Bob Dylan, "This Wheel's on Fire," in *The Basement Tapes*, Columbia, 1975.

41. Christine Hand Jones, "Bob Dylan and the End of the (Modern) World," PhD diss., University of Texas at Dallas, 2013, 213.

42. Peter Aaron, *The Band FAQ*, 44.

43. Ralph Gleason, "Bob Dylan: The Children's Crusade," *Ramparts Magazine*, March 1966, 31.

44. Greil Marcus, *The Old, Weird America*, 88.

45. Bob Dylan, quoted by Ralph Gleason, "Bob Dylan: The Children's Crusade," 30; Also, Allen Ginsberg uses this term to describe Dylan's poetry in "On Reading Dylan's writings," from *First Blues: Rags, Ballads and Harmonium Songs, 1971–74* reprinted in *The Dylan Companion*, eds. Elizabeth Thomson and David Gutman, Da Capo Press, 2001, 147–48. This quotation about "chains of flashing images" is cited often, though sources differ on its first use. Some say Dylan said it of himself; others attribute it to Ginsberg, but since the phrase appears in scare quotes in the Ginsberg poem, it seems as though Ginsberg is quoting someone else, possibly Dylan. Either way, the phrase has been quoted and requoted by virtually everyone who has written about Dylan, sometimes with attribution, sometimes without.

46. Bob Dylan, "Highway 61 Revisited, in *Highway 61 Revisited*, Columbia, 1965.

47. Bob Dylan, "Odds and Ends," "Clothes Line Saga," and "Lo and Behold," in *The Basement Tapes*, 1975.

48. Dylan, "Million Dollar Bash," *The Basement Tapes*.

49. Ralph Gleason, "Dylan Has Returned with 'John Wesley Harding': So John Wesley Harding Has Been on the Turntable for a Few Days Now and This Is a Preliminary Report," *Rolling Stone*, February 10, 1968.

50. Gleason, "Dylan Has Returned with 'John Wesley Harding.'"

51. Bob Dylan, "The Ballad of Frankie Lee and Judas Priest" in *John Wesley Harding*, Columbia, 1967.

52. Mike Marqusee, *Chimes of Freedom: The Politics of Bob Dylan's Art*, New York: New Press, 2003, 238; Bob Dylan, "All Along the Watchtower" in *John Wesley Harding*.

53. Bob Dylan, interview with John Cohen and Happy Traum, *Sing Out!* October/November 1968, in *Dylan on Dylan: The Essential Interviews*, ed. Jonathan Cott, London: Hodder, 2007, 122.

54. Bob Dylan, "All Along the Watchtower."

55. Bob Dylan, interview with John Cohen and Happy Traum, *Sing Out!*, in Cott, *Dylan on Dylan*, 128–29.

56. Gleason, "Dylan Has Returned With 'John Wesley Harding.'"

57. Bob Dylan, "I Dreamed I Saw St. Augustine," in *John Wesley Harding*.

58. Bob Dylan, *John Wesley Harding*, liner notes.

59. Bob Dylan, "Drifter's Escape," "I Am a Lonesome Hobo," and "The Ballad of Frankie Lee and Judas Priest," ibid.

60. Gleason, "Dylan Has Returned."

61. Bob Dylan, "Dear Landlord" and "I Pity the Poor Immigrant," in *John Wesley Harding*.

62. Bob Dylan, "I Shall Be Released," in *Music from Big Pink*, Capitol, 1968.

63. Alfred G. Aronowitz, "Friends and Neighbors Just Call Us The Band," *Rolling Stone*, August 24, 1968.

64. Robertson, *Testimony*, 310.

65. Ibid.

66. Hoskyns, *Across the Great Divide*, 163.

67. Ibid., 154–55.

68. Robbie Robertson, "The Weight," in *Music from Big Pink*.

69. Peter Aaron is one exception. He acknowledges that Robertson could not have written "The Weight" without Dylan's influence. *The Band FAQ*, 22, 167.

70. Hoskyns, *Across the Great Divide*, 154–55.

71. Bob Dylan, "When the Ship Comes In," recorded October 23, 1963, in *The Times They Are A-Changin'*, Bob Dylan, Columbia, 1964.

72. Robertson, *Testimony*, 185.

73. Bob Dylan, "Mr. Tambourine Man," recorded April 12, 1965, in *Mr. Tambourine Man*, the Byrds, Columbia, 1965.

74. Bob Dylan, "Sad Eyed Lady of the Lowlands," in *Blonde on Blonde*, Columbia, 1966; Robertson helped in the final mixes for *Blonde on Blonde*. Robertson, *Testimony*, 248.

75. Robertson, *Testimony*, 283.

76. Ibid.

77. Ibid.

78. The location was inspired by the birthplace of Martin guitars in Nazareth, Pennsylvania. Robertson, *Testimony*, 283.

79. Robertson, "The Weight."

80. Aaron, *The Band FAQ*, 35.

81. Ibid.

82. Robertson, *Testimony*, 283.

83. I discuss Dylan's ambiguous Messianism at length in my dissertation: Christine Hand Jones, *Bob Dylan and the End of the (Modern) World*, 239–76.

84. Bob Dylan, "Quinn the Eskimo," in *Self Portrait*, Columbia, 1970.

85. Revelation 3:20.

86. Revelation 3:20.

87. Ibid.

88. Matthew 11:28.

89. Robertson, "The Weight."

90. Robertson, *Testimony*, 310.

91. Aaron, *The Band FAQ*, 166.

92. Ibid., 167.

93. Bob Stanley, *Yeah! Yeah! Yeah!: The Story of Pop Music from Bill Haley to Beyoncé*, New York: Norton, 2015, 290–91.

94. Bomar, *Southbound*, 15.

95. Bomar, *Southbound*, 37.

96. Stanley, *Yeah Yeah Yeah*, 292.

97. Hoskyns, *Across the Great Divide*, 4.

Chapter 3

READING BALDWIN'S "SONNY BLUES" WHILE LISTENING TO THE BAND

CHARLOTTE PENCE

There were no rules. And it just felt right.
—LEVON HELM[1]

I have been researching The Band in preparation for my essay on this foundational, classification-resistant, Canadian American group. In 2004, *Rolling Stone* ranked them #50 on its list of greatest artists of all time. A quick sweep of just a few of their honors includes the Grammy Lifetime Achievement Award and inductions into the Canadian Music Hall of Fame and the Rock and Roll Hall of Fame. My college students know them best as that group that backed Bob Dylan, but they didn't back Dylan so much as they collaborated with him. They were, and have always been, their own thing.

As I'm listening to The Band, I am also prepping for my graduate creative-writing class focused on different strategies for the "I" in poetry, nonfiction, and fiction. We are reading James Baldwin's classic "Sonny's Blues" about two brothers' response to institutionalized and individual racism in 1950s Harlem. The nameless narrator in this first-person story and his brother Sonny choose different paths: the narrator serves in the military so that he can attend college and become a math teacher, diligently grasping the slow rungs up that American ladder. Sonny, however, goes the route of jazz and heroin. Both choices take the brothers to the same spot: a project in Harlem, living together and having to deal with the world and its faults. Whereas the narrator's rage manifests as a concealed "great block of ice" that "got settled in my belly and kept melting there slowly," Sonny uses his music to openly confront his despair.

While reading the story, a quotation about music stops me cold:

All I know about music is that not many people ever really hear it. And even then, on the rare occasions when something opens within, and the music enters, what we mainly hear, or hear corroborated, are personal, private, vanishing evocations. But the man who creates the music is hearing something else, is dealing with the roar rising from the void and imposing order on it as it hits the air.[2]

At that moment, I realize I am that listener. I have never really heard the deadening-finality of the bass drum's beat before the lines "I pulled into Nazareth, was feeling 'bout half-past dead"; I have never really heard the acceptance of loss in the finger-picking opening of "Atlantic City"; I have never really heard The Band.

• • •

In the Baldwin story, lack of sound equals a lack of life. Simply put, silence equals death. The story also suggests that people can be alive yet emotionally dead, unable to hear what is happening around them. I first noticed the use of sound when the narrator describes his daughter's death from polio. The mother, Isabel, recalls the moment their daughter fell and was unable to breathe: "Isabel says that when she heard that *thump* and then that silence, something happened in her to make her afraid."[3]

Silence, however, is removed at the story's end when the narrator finally understands why it is his brother plays. The narrator, like many at that time, feared what jazz would mean for his brother—what the life of jazz would mean. Garth Hudson from The Band put it this way in *The Last Waltz* in 1978: "There is a view that jazz is 'evil' because it comes from evil people, but actually the greatest priests on 52nd Street, and on the streets of New York City, were the musicians. They were doing the greatest healing work. And they knew how to punch through music, which would cure and make people feel good."[4] Sonny, in "Sonny's Blues," was doing just that: healing others and himself. Music was providing a way to fight death. It is and was a stay against oblivion.

• • •

One of The Band's most famous persona songs, "The Night They Drove Old Dixie Down," is a stay against oblivion—an attempt to remember a region as it will never be again.

To be honest, the song about the last days of the Civil War makes me uncomfortable. I struggle to see that war as anything other than one group that was for the evil machine slavery and one group that was against it. People tell me it is more complicated than that, and I'm sure they're right. Still, I struggle to feel sympathy for those who view the South's loss as the end of something wonderful. It was the end of an era, certainly, but an era that existed on the whip-welted black backs of others. I have been surprised that others aren't more uncomfortable with this song and view it as an extension of support for institutional racism. In a lot of ways, I don't want to listen to this song's speaker. I feel like the narrator in "Sonny's Blues" when a friend of his brother's, a heroin user and panhandler, approaches him: "Look. Don't tell *me* your sad story, if it was up to me, I'd give you one."[5]

But two aspects to the song make me listen, and keep listening. The first pull of the song is the separation between the singer and the speaker in the first line: "Virgil Kane is the name, and I served on the Danville train."[6] Immediately, the singer distinguishes himself from the speaker with the proper noun of Virgil Kane with its short i's and long a's, all of which create a twangy assertion of self and region. The other aspect of this song that impresses me is the song's authenticity. Even though I know intellectually that the character is fictional, I feel as if Virgil Kane is by my side, chopping wood with calloused hands and attempting to communicate to me his side as a poor, white southerner: a sense of failure. The two ideas of authenticity and separation work in harmony and build toward that chorus between Levon, Richard, and Rick that rings out like the mournful bell that it is.

And in that lonesome chorus, in that elongation of the word "night" with the long "I" insisting that I listen, I do feel something that intellectually I don't want to feel: empathy for the protagonist's suffering. I feel the sense of frustration of the train tracks being torn up—again—and the sense of destitution that comes from the line: "In the winter of '65, we were hungry, just barely alive."[7] I see the soldiers as what they were: another group of people being caught up and used up in this awful enterprise. In the powerful chorus that is sung with energy rather than timidity, the depth of the sorrow comes out. "The night they drove ol' Dixie down / and the bells were ringing"[8] is followed by that weird la-la-la that sounds all at once mocking, mournful, and majestic. And it is. Finally, through the sounds of the chorus, I get what intellectually I have trouble understanding. Not only did the Confederacy lose the war, but they also lost a sense of identity, honor, and beliefs about their place in the world—not to mention the daily struggles regarding loss of family, friends, homes, and income. As Virgil Kane explains, "Ya' take what ya' need and ya' leave the rest / But they should never have taken the very best."[9]

• • •

I am supposed to be writing on The Band's use of persona, and so I will write on persona. It is:

A mask.

A false face.

An ancient distinction.

We know the term, but we stumble if asked to give a definition because all the definitions sound slightly off.

According to J. A. Cuddon in *A Dictionary of Literary Terms*, the term derives from the dramatis personae and denotes "the 'person' (the 'I' of an 'alter ego') who speaks in a poem or novel or other form of literature."[10] It's the type of definition that clouds more than clears. So, we try again.

A character.

A social role.

A personality projected in public.

It is supposed to be decidedly not the writer, but perhaps what trips us up is the question: who is the writer to begin with? With which self is the writer writing that day? Essentially, definitions of persona feel inadequate because self-identity is inadequate and continually in flux.

Still we need some facts, something conclusive, which lists can provide. Famous personas include the Duke in Browning's "My Last Duchess"; Virgil Kane of "The Night They Drove Old Dixie Down"; Eminem's Slim Shady; the truck driver of "Up on Cripple Creek"; Gulliver of *Gulliver's Travels*; the farmer of "King Harvest." Fiction writing, as opposed to songs and poems, use persona most of the time, but in that genre it's simply a character like the well-known Humbert Humbert in *Lolita*.

Awareness seems key to the definition of persona. For example, the writer needs to be aware that they are creating a persona different from themself for the persona to be considered a persona.

In my graduate class, we have talked extensively about how a successful use of persona is determined by three things.

1) The distinction between writer and persona—and how quickly and clearly the author makes it.
2) How authentic the persona feels.
3) The writer remaining, somehow, a player in the drama. The best writers of persona cannily mine the relationship between the writer, the speaker of the text, and the reader.

・・・

The last point is a tricky one, especially for a fiction writer. How do writers remain players in their first-person dramas? In other words, what is the role of the creator within the creation? As James Joyce explains so well, "The artist, like the God of the creation, remains within or behind or beyond or above his handiwork, invisible, refined out of existence, indifferent, *paring his fingernails*."¹¹ In "Sonny's Blues" the narrator is not Baldwin, yet the story feels true, especially with its locale of Harlem, home to Baldwin and the narrator. And that feeling of truth, of authenticity, is key to a compelling listening or reading experience.

Baldwin's novel *Go Tell It on the Mountain* (1953) is known for his blending of the narrator with the author. Fiction writers call this "autobiographical fiction." The book focuses on a young man growing up in Harlem grappling with his father, religion, sexuality, and race. Baldwin later said that "*Mountain* is the book I had to write if I was ever going to write anything else. I had to deal with what hurt me most. I had to deal, above all, with my father."¹²

An old interview with Baldwin from the *New York Times* in 1979 feels quite relevant to today. The questions reveal assumptions and challenges writers of color face. Baldwin, however, rises above everyone's epoch. The interviewer summarizes that Baldwin's "fiction has often been attacked, notably by younger black writers in the 1960's, as too personal, too patently a working-out of inner conflict at the price of distorting the realities of race and racial conflict in America."¹³

One exchange is especially worth quoting:

Q. You feel, then, that the writer should become involved, that his work should reflect his involvement?

A. I certainly can't imagine art for art's sake . . . that's a European approach, which never made any sense to me. I think what you have to do, which is the difficult thing about a writer, is avoid slogans. You have to have the [guts] to protest the slogan, no matter how noble it may sound. It always hides something else; the writer should try to expose what it hides.¹⁴

• • •

Sometimes when I'm listening to The Band, I sense that their songs are trying to pull certain people—or impulses—out of hiding. Take "Up on Cripple Creek," for instance, The Band's fifth song on their second album. The Hohner clavinet being played with a wah-wah pedal helps give this song a fun, feel-good feel. And it does what The Band do so well: mixing influences from funk, roots, bluegrass, and country. Yet, at the center of this light-hearted song about a truck driver visiting a young woman in her town of Lake Charles, Louisiana, are some darker elements: a man bored with his life who finds enjoyment via distraction. Whatever Bessie provides with her "doughnut in [his] tea"[15] isn't going to be permanent. And then there is the question of the speaker's fidelity. Is he cheating on his wife with Bessie?

> So I guess I'll call up my big mama
> Tell her I'll be rolling in
> But you know, deep down, I'm kinda tempted
> To go and see my sweet Bessie again.[16]

Many have wondered who is "big mama." The speaker's wife? Others suggest that big mama could be the affectionate nickname truck drivers give the dispatcher over the CB radio.

Robbie Robertson, cleverly, hasn't denied or affirmed if the speaker in this persona song is committing adultery. When asked about this in an interview with Bill Janovitz, Robertson focused on this idea of revealing what is hidden. "We're not dealing with people at the top of the ladder; we're saying what about that house out there in the middle of the field? What does this guy think, with that one light on upstairs, and that truck parked out there? That's who I'm curious about.... Just following him with a camera is really what this song's about."[17] The goal of the song then, according to Robertson, is not to judge but to reveal. The role of the songwriter is simply to see what is there, record it, and fade into the background.

What strikes me about this song is a quality of authenticity. When I'm listening to it, I feel as if I'm listening to the unedited thoughts in this trucker's mind. Many outward conversations about affairs veer toward confession or repentance. But in this song, there is none of that. Instead, we have the reasons someone might commit adultery: escapism, emotional support, and entertainment. This direct chorus cuts through all apologies and explains the trucker's attraction to Bessie: "If I spring a leak, she mends me. / I don't have to speak, she defends me. / A drunkard's dream if I ever did see one."[18] Even with that last line, the speaker tosses out alcoholism without the usual condemnation. Here, in this moment of the song, the listener and the speaker both engage in something duplicitous—and enjoy it.

If this song were identifiably one of the singers, I don't think the listener would be able to tap his feet to the beat in the same way. The distinction between the singer and speaker (since it's clear The Band are not a group of truck drivers) allows a certain emotional distance for everyone involved. We know this song is made up. But at the same time, it feels real, as if we have entered that unmade bed in the house out in the middle of field with a rig in the drive.

• • •

Ultimately, what persona provides the writer—and as such the reader—is a lack of commitment. This mask the writer dons allows him/her to say things that otherwise might be considered taboo, impolitic, or thorny. In other words, the mask serves more as a cloak of artistic detachment. And this detachment, this shout out to the reader that what is being created is made up, allows both reader and writer to explore alternative perspectives without committing to them. While the persona is a means to explore the self, "It prevents the poet from being hurt by self-exposure or being led astray by the limitations of her own vision; it is a means for expressing anxieties and frustrations."[19]

• • •

One aspect of The Band's use of persona that fascinates me is how they define themselves within a world of persona. Other than Levon Helm, the talented group is from Canada—not the roots and ruggedness of the South that their lyrics embody. What's more, each musician is an expert at more than one instrument, allowing a fluidity of roles amongst the players just as their songs allow a fluidity of personas. (Supposedly, the guy credited with forming The Band, Ronnie Hawkins, competed with other groups in town by poaching their best musicians.) In one of the many paradoxes of persona, the multiple masks their individual songs occupy allow a collective persona for The Band as a group that is as hard-scrabble and home-grown as their dramatis personae.

This sense of role-playing, though, is a complicated one, according to psychologists who see persona as a conduit between the conscious and unconscious parts of the psyche. As the editors of *The New Princeton Encyclopedia of Poetry and Poetics* explain, "Jung opposed the persona, the self a person assumes in order to play a social role, to the anima, a person's true inner being."[20] The idea of the self is complicated because the self does not remain static. Hence the spate of terms that follow: "The inner and outer; the hidden and the overt; the individual and the social; reality and appearance; the authentic and the put-on; the true self and the persona."[21] Despite the ever-shifting quicksand of identity concepts, behavioral psychologists value the importance of role-playing for personal growth and for public situations.

However questionable any sense of the true self might be, one thing is clear. The personas The Band creates help to define them—while simultaneously differentiating them from their creations. The Band are not the Confederate sympathizer Virgil Kane. The Band are not the adulterous, bored truck driver. The Band are not the farmer suckered by the union.

Yet, The Band, in their compassion with these characters and the wholeness with which they created them, sometimes employing research to better understand a time or place, became a part of these personas. Some theorists maintain that poetry's role, and by extension a song's role, is ultimately an attempt to resolve an identity crisis. Readers are invited in to tease out questions of authenticity and separation. And somehow, through all these conversations about lines between selves, a whole emerges.

• • •

A passage in "Sonny's Blues" addresses what it is that singers, good singers, can do. Sonny has just returned from an errand and passes by a small group singing on a street corner. "The revival was being carried on by three sisters in black, and a brother. All they had were their voices and their Bibles and a tambourine,"[22] which will soon turn into a collection plate. He tells his brother, "Listening to that woman sing, it struck me all of a sudden how much suffering she must have had to go through—to sing like that. It's *repulsive* to think you have to suffer that much."[23] Suffering, though, is a necessary part of this connection between the singer and the listener. When else do we allow ourselves to sit and experience whatever it is the person before us wants us to experience? A singer, though, like a preacher or a poet, possesses a unique privilege that society refuses to grant many people—and that privilege is a passage into the listener's internal psyche, which is often guarded by Cerberus and Saint Peter both.

The narrator describes it this way: "As the singing filled the air the watching, listening faces underwent a change, the eyes focusing on something within; the music seemed to soothe a poison out of them; and time seemed, nearly, to fall away from the sullen, belligerent, battered faces, as though they were fleeing back to their first condition, while dreaming of their last."[24]

A healing has emerged on this street corner, a healing that can emerge from the fractured pieces of identity the bard chooses to present. The true self and the assumed mask interact and inform each other to perform a type of public healing.

• • •

One of The Band's most remarkable songs for its use of persona is "King Harvest (Has Surely Come)." In this song, the listener experiences a rare occurrence, but an important one: the skillful emergence of the writer into the dramatic monologue by way of that haunting, subdued chorus sung by Richard Manuel and Levon Helm.

The songwriter credited is Robbie Robertson, although Levon Helm claims this story of an impoverished farmer was a collaborative creation. The song begins with its chorus delivered in gravelly, subdued tones before we hear the speaker of the song announce himself in the first verse. Like many of The Band's persona pieces, they are quick to delineate between self and speaker: "I work for the union 'cuz she's so good to me / I'm bound to come out on top / That's where she said I should be" (lines 3–6).[25] Immediately, listeners discern that this speaker is with the union and not yet successful because the verb tense of "bound" denotes unactualized reward.

The effusive way the speaker describes the union, which might have been historically based on the Trade Union Unity League's organizing drives that created collective bargaining units for sharecroppers from 1928–1935, alerts the listener that the speaker is either idealistic, desperate, or both. The farmer, as we learn through the song, has lost his barn to a fire, his horse to madness, and his crops to drought.

One of the many interesting elements to this song is the timeline; the songwriters end the song before this man's harvest, which the third changing chorus alerts us is almost here: "Scarecrow and yellow moon, / and pretty soon a carnival on the edge of town."[26] What's more, at this moment, the desperate farmer doesn't tell us what is happening now to him; instead he recalls what has happened to him in the past: "And I can't remember things bein' that bad."[27]

Is he going to be as successful as he claims he'll be? We don't know because the song ends before that information, which is a telling move. I'd argue that listeners do indeed know the outcome. The chorus tells us everything. The chorus is sung by Richard Manuel and Levon Helm, and contradicts the energetic melody found in the verses. Instead, Manuel and Helm lower their voices and distinguish that they are not the speaker by the change in melody, vocals, and tone. So then, who are they in this chorus?

Some believe that the chorus reflects the inner thoughts of the farmer. In other words, the chorus represents the speaker's fears. But what is happening here is a rarity in a persona song: the writer speaks in the chorus, breaking down that fourth wall, that conceptual barrier between any creative work and its viewers.

In that juggling of three balls—the writer, the speaker, and the listener—The Band figure out that their voices could serve the role of an ancient Greek chorus. In Classical Greek dramas, actors composed the chorus, and their role was to comment upon the pivotal moments in the play through song, movement, dance, facial expressions and/or recitation. The Band use the technique in this song as their voices become the Greek chorus. With the assertion of themselves, they also assert their opinion on the situation, which differs from that of the main speaker. There will be no bounty nor relief for the farmer. In "King Harvest (Has Surely Come)," a title that even uses parentheticals to undercut the speaker's assertion, the song beautifully juggles all necessary parts—the writer, the speaker, and the listener.

• • •

One period of the persona's heyday was the Victorian era from 1837 to 1901. This was also the period when novels found their land legs through works by George Eliot, Charles Dickens, Jane Austen, Thomas Hardy, and all those other novelists to whom we now owe so much. It's no surprise that persona poems were popular during this time because poetry had to do something to compete with this relatively new genre that was running away with people's imaginations (and reading time). Famous personas include Elizabeth Barrett Browning's novel in verse *Aurora Leigh*, which is a Bildungsroman of a female poet who is not Barrett Browning. Other examples include Robert Browning "My Last Duchess" and "Soliloquy of the Spanish Cloister" whose influence can later be seen in contemporary works such as "Daffy Duck in Hollywood" by John Ashbery, "Lady Lazarus" by Sylvia Plath, Berryman's *Dream Songs*, and a number of poems by great persona practitioners such as Patricia Smith, Carol Ann Duffy, and Ai.

The Victorian personas often emerge more as dramatic monologues with the character speaking to someone in the room or out loud. In his blog, poet Reginald Shepherd explains that "by revealing a character in the context of a dramatic situation (a 'soul in action'), a dramatic monologue provides knowledge not just about the speaker's personality, but about the time, the setting, key events, and other characters involved in the situation at hand, even if they are not present."[28] One could say The Band write in the style of dramatic monologues: they are performing on stage to an audience—which is the ultimate listener. But is the audience a player in the drama? In the case of "King Harvest," I think the answer is yes.

Social, technological, and scientific changes complicated how Victorian readership viewed the first-person "I," which was so prominent during the previous Romantic period. Loss of religion and therefore the need for the writer as secular cleric, increased awareness of a writer's obligation to society, and popularization of realist fiction that strives for scientific objectivity all contributed to a decline in a personal "I." In other words, people wanted their poet to also be their priest. To always be the wise one, the thoughtful one, the sitting-under-a-tree one. The problem is writers know they are not better than their readers. Hence, the persona allows a certain amount of latitude.

One aspect important to this discussion is the Victorian era's growing binary between public and private. With industrialism, work shifted to being conducted in a public space such as a factory or workshop instead of one's private fields. This resulted in an awareness of what is private and public, with one manifestation being a new emphasis on housing having public and private rooms, such as the "public" living room and "private" bedroom. Legendary literary critic Terry Eagleton explains that people had to "learn new temporal rhythms and bodily habits, different perceptual skills and styles of emotional response."[29]

Another way to look at the anxiety surrounding less privacy in the Victorian era is to consider a bus or subway commute. Simply, the less space one has, the greater the need to create a sense of privacy, be it in a physical barrier such as a wall or a figurative barrier such as holding up a newspaper on a subway car and inserting ear buds. Or more appropriate to this discussion, with more public roles, one needs an intellectual barrier that can be nimble enough to provide personal details at one moment and allow the writer to hide personal facts and feelings the next.

Persona or dramatic monologues do just that: allow the writer to explore what he otherwise would not be able to say if he has to only write about the self. The Band, through their use of persona, allow everyone to feel the darker disappointments that polite society dictates are not prudent to share.

I cannot help but think of how the narrator in "Sonny's Blues" describes watching his brother play at the end of the story and how it relates to The Band:

> They were not about anything very new. He and his boys up there were keeping it new, at the risk of ruin, destruction, madness, and death, in order to find new ways to make us listen. For, while the tale of how we suffer and how we are delighted, and how we may triumph is never new, it always must be heard. There isn't any other tale to tell; it's the only light we've got in all this darkness.[30]

• • •

The beginning quotation from "Sonny's Blues," with its assertion that the only people hearing music are the ones creating it, are the ones attempting to impose order on the void, haunts me. The passage goes on to say, "What is evoked in him, then, is of another order, more terrible because it has no words, and triumphant too, for that same reason. And his triumph, when he triumphs, is ours."[31] The combination of "terrible" and "triumphant" gives pause, not because of its inaccuracy but because of its truth. When Garth Hudson rumbles his wit through the Lowrey organ; when Richard Manuel slides from his soulful baritone to delicate falsetto; when Levon Helm drums the downbeat and backbeat while simultaneously singing off those two beats—all of that is a triumph because it achieves some new sense, a reaching beyond how we understand music, something more like a thunderstorm, or a turn in a story we never saw coming. The songs articulate the emotions we can't see but that rule us nonetheless. We know that inevitable disappointment when the speaker in "King Harvest" bemoans his burning barn, decimated crop, and demented horse, and sings about the king harvest surely to come that everyone, including the union man proselytizing hope, knows will not come. The singers' voices with their low, mournful o's in "blows" and "come" embody the terrible and triumphant. At that moment, someone sings as someone felt. And that is perhaps the only triumph for this farmer, perhaps the only triumph at all.

Notes

1. Levon Helm, "Interview," *Classic Albums, The Band*, Eagle Rock Entertainment, 2005.
2. James Baldwin, "Sonny's Blues," *Going to Meet the Man*, New York: Dial, 1965, 137.
3. Ibid., 127.
4. Scorsese, *The Last Waltz*.
5. Baldwin, "Sonny's Blues," 106.
6. The Band, "The Night They Drove Old Dixie Down," recorded September 1969, track 3 on *The Band*.
7. Ibid.
8. Ibid.
9. The Band, "The Night They Drove Old Dixie Down."
10. J. A. Cuddon, *A Dictionary of Literary Terms: Revised Edition*, New York: Penguin Books, 1982, 501.
11. James Joyce, *A Portrait of the Artist as a Young Man*, London: B. W. Huebsch, 1916, 252.
12. "Daily Trivia: James Baldwin." Accessed May 18, 2014: https://ijustliketoread.word press.com/tag/james-baldwin/
13. John Romano, "James Baldwin Writing and Talking," interview with James Baldwin, *New York Times*, September 23, 1979.
14. Romano, "James Baldwin Writing and Talking."
15. The Band, "Up on Cripple Creek," recorded September 1969, track 5 on *The Band*.
16. Ibid.
17. Robbie Robertson, "Song Review," *AllMusic*, review of "Upon Cripple Creek," by Bill Janovitz, Accessed August 21, 2018: https://www.allmusic.com/song/up-on-cripple-creek-mt0011252707.

18. The Band, "Up on Cripple Creek."

19. Alex Preminger and T. V. F. Brogan, *The New Princeton Encyclopedia of Poetry and Poetics*, New Jersey: Princeton University Press, 1993, 901.

20. Preminger and Brogan, *The New Princeton Encyclopedia of Poetry and Poetics*, 901.

21. Ibid.

22. Baldwin, "Sonny's Blues," 128.

23. Ibid., 132.

24. Ibid., 129.

25. The Band, "King Harvest (Has Surely Come)," recorded September 1969, track 12 on *The Band*.

26. The Band, "King Harvest (Has Surely Come)."

27. Ibid.

28. Reginald Shepherd, "A Few Thoughts on the Dramatic Monologue," *Reginald Shepherd's Blog*, http://reginaldshepherd.blogspot.com/2007/07/few-thoughts-on-dramatic-monologue.html.

29. Terry Eagleton, *The English Novel: An Introduction*, Hoboken, NJ: Wiley-Blackwell, 2004, 143.

30. Baldwin, "Sonny's Blues," 139.

31. Ibid., 137.

Chapter 4

BIG SOUND FROM BIG PINK

JEFF SELLARS

Music from Big Pink is the "record that changed everything."[1] One of the reasons it changed everything was its unique soundscape. In this brief essay, I want to try to weave some of the history of *Music from Big Pink* together with some particulars of the recording of the album—focusing on its sound. I also hope to place the album in context by, very briefly, recapitulating the cultural setting. While there aren't many details about the exact recording techniques and equipment, we can try to piece some things together from the very few mentions of recording equipment and techniques we do have, taken primarily from autobiographies recounting the sessions.

Additionally, the sound of the group is not only attributable to the recording techniques of the engineers, the producers, or the equipment. Also, as a practical matter, The Band did help dictate some of these recording techniques, as we will see. However, just as important, the members of the group were unique musicians. As Al Kooper noted, "People still say about other bands, 'That sorta sounds like The Band,' and I always reply, 'Yeah, sorta!' But no one else has ever had the writing, arrangement or similar vocal prowess to really compete with it."[2] Indeed, there is a distinct sound combination created by the members of the group. So, I want to acknowledge this special feature of the group at the outset. However, the recording techniques do play a large part in not only the nature of the music but also in its influential reach—those recording techniques are a big part of what made *Music from Big Pink* a record that changed everything—and a record from which many artists try to crib. And this is why I want to focus my attention on the sounds of the album.

Furthermore, The Band's contemporaries demonstrate this influence—for example, in the Beatles' *Get Back/Let It Be* sessions, where they looked to "get back" to their roots by recording with no overdubs (a rule they then subsequently broke), a reflection of The Band's *appearance* of recording everything live. George Harrison had hung out with The Band before the recording of *Let It Be*: "I had spent the last few months of 1968 producing an album by Jackie Lomax and hanging out with Bob Dylan and The Band in Woodstock, having a great time."³ The method for recording the *Get Back/ Let It Be* sessions mirrored The Band's style—for example, having all of The Band members in the same room, playing with, against, and off of each other. This, of course, worked to varying degrees, as can be witnessed in the film *Let It Be*. George Harrison also noted that he always liked Robbie's guitar style and that he had "quite a bit of time with The Band."⁴ He was jealous of Robbie's freedom in writing for different voices as well, something he did not get to experience until he formed the Traveling Wilburys.⁵ Also, in general, the Traveling Wilburys' sound, writing techniques, and communal atmosphere owe something to The Band's approach.⁶ Levon Helm also wrote about Harrison's support for The Band: "George Harrison . . . complained that EMI released *Music from Big Pink* in England in a single sleeve instead of the double-fold jacket of the American version. . . . George was an advocate for us, being quoted in the British press about how *Music from Big Pink* was *the* new sound to come from America and everybody better pay attention."⁷

Eric Clapton has cited The Band's influence on him—specifically for prompting him to leave Cream and pursue other musical styles. Of course, his complicated relationships with his band members helped him move on as well, but he was also searching for alternative avenues for musical creativity. He came upon *Music from Big Pink*, and it changed him.

> I heard [*The Basement Tapes*] first from a friend in London called David Lipenhoff. He told me about this band who had been called The Hawks and how they were now hanging out with Dylan. I'd missed all that because I wasn't a big fan of Dylan at that time. But I heard *The Basement Tapes* and it sounded like they'd jumped on to what I thought we ought to be doing. That was what I wanted us to sound like and here was somebody else doing it. After that another friend played me *Music from Big Pink*. It shook me to the core.⁸

Contemporary bands also took inspiration by using The Band's recording techniques (sometimes cribbing from them directly and sometimes tweaking them to their ends). For example, artists like Wilco and Fleet Foxes borrow the recording and song grammar laid out by The Band, particularly in the use of echo, instrumentation, and natural acoustics. The Band's unique stylings lend themselves to a back-to-basics recording technique, with an emphasis on musicianship and capturing the natural sounds of voices and instruments (though, of course, special effects and overdubs appear in their recordings). Artists that borrow from The Band's stylings and recording grammar are numerous—artists as diverse as Elton John, Elvis Costello, Led Zeppelin, Black Crowes, Counting Crows, Phish, My Morning Jacket, and Death Cab for Cutie. However, the primary drive here is not to look at those who have been influenced by *Music from Big Pink* or The Band in general; it is to look at the album itself to see some of what made it so influential. I will not have space to look at each song, so I want to get a general picture of the background and the sound landscape of the album, picking just a couple of songs that are indicative of the album's sound as well as their recording studios and bring in details where I can.

Music from Big Pink was recorded early in 1968 and released July of that same year. The "Big Pink" referenced in the album title was a small house that worked as a "clubhouse" where The Band could rehearse and write music: it was a "pink ranch-style house in the middle of a hundred acres—a ridge of mountains, a good-sized pond, and nothing but space and wilderness all around."[9] Robbie Robertson had a recording engineer look at the house. The engineer advised Robertson that it would make for the worst sound imaginable—but Robertson was happy breaking conventional recording rules.[10] Big Pink was set up for recording and rehearsing by Robertson and Garth Hudson with "half a dozen Norelco mics . . . a couple little Altec mixers and two speakers for playback listening. . . . Garth got a pair of headphones so he could adjust the levels on the mics through the mixer. We plugged the main vocal mic into my guitar Echorec machine."[11] Although the album title and cover suggest otherwise, the songs were not recorded in the basement of Big Pink but were recorded on four-track and eight-track machines at A&R Studios in New York and Capitol and Gold Star Studios in Los Angeles. However, Big Pink had a considerable influence on The Band's approach to writing and recording. The Band wrote the songs there and recorded material (known as *The Basement Tapes*) with Bob Dylan. Robbie Robertson noted how the playing layout influenced The Band:

> Playing music in a circle in the basement or on an acoustic set in the living room was having a big effect on our musical approach: it was a balance of vocals and instruments. If you couldn't hear properly, somebody was too loud and out of balance. This approach was as old as music but had very little to do with the way a lot of people were playing those days. Louder was becoming king . . . but we evolved to a place where loud music was like greasy food, not really good for you.[12]

The images that accompanied the album contributed to the myth of The Band's "persona," and it was a precursor to the times ahead—this quasi-commune retreat to the mountains, this turn to simpler living. As Tom Pinnock notes,

> On the inside cover of the record they looked like a gang of turn-of-the-century train robbers: sombre suits, short hair, a palpable air of unbreachable unity. The beards weren't groovy, but rather the unkempt face furniture of the mid-west sharecropper. Even their name—a mere afterthought which nonetheless spoke volumes—was a cultural anomaly, its plain understatement resonating in the age of Quicksilver Messenger Service and Frumious Bandersnatch. Everything about *Music from Big Pink* was radically antithetical to the prevailing mood of the times.[13]

Levon Helm also speaks to this uniqueness: "We wanted *Music from Big Pink* to sound like nothing anyone else was doing. This was our music, honed in isolation from the radio and contemporary trends, liberated from the world of bars and the climate of the Dylan tours."[14]

However, as original as The Band were, one should contextualize Pinnock's claim that "everything about *Music from Big Pink* was radically antithetical to the prevailing times."[15] Yes, The Band were different in many ways from current music radio trends and the popular cultural scene of 1967–1968. However, there are antecedents present within the culture of the time that inform this change—a culture that The Band certainly helped inaugurate into the mainstream—but *Music from Big Pink* did not just drop from the sky. Pinnock quotes from Robbie Robertson to this effect as well, noting that the culture surrounding Big Pink was a transforming one: "Woodstock was a lovely, low-key little art colony . . . Once we were up there, there was a real feeling of artistic freedom in the air. It had its own thing and everybody gravitated to it. We went on a mission to find a place where we could work and which could be our little clubhouse, and then Rick found Big Pink."[16] There is also the mention of the mountain music surrounding and enveloping them—as well as Bob Dylan's influence.

> "It was a combination of mountain music and spirituals, and we started to get an appreciation for harmonies that we would hear from Johnnie & Jack, or the Louvin Brothers," admits Robertson. "Mountain music! And we were up in the mountains, so it all seemed like it fit together. There was something so pure about it. It was pure

American—and so is rock'n'roll. It all came together, but when you're in it, you don't dissect it, you're following your gut feelings." They were also reacting to changes in Dylan's writing. The quicksilver edge of Blonde on Blonde had been replaced with a phantasmagorical mix of woody traditional textures and words centering on myth and fable, often apparently imparting some coded moral lesson. The bleed between the basement songs and Big Pink is a fine one. "Some of those songs got incorporated into what we were doing," confirms Robertson. "Richard wrote 'Tears of Rage' with Bob, Rick wrote 'This Wheel's on Fire' with Bob, I was off writing songs like 'To Kingdom Come,' 'Chest Fever,' 'Caledonia Mission,' and it was all starting to come together."[17]

Additionally, the culture in general was moving from the psychedelic, highly adorned, overtly produced music of 1967 to a more "back to basics" approach. The Beatles started moving away from their psychedelic-laced music of 1967 (with *Sgt. Pepper's* and *Magical Mystery Tour*) to a more straight approach in *The Beatles* (or White Album)—again, influenced by living and writing most of the tunes from the album in a communal setting while visiting India with the Maharishi Mahesh Yogi. By the time we get to the *Get Back/Let It Be* sessions, the change has taken full effect. Moreover, we see this change in approach, too, in the beginnings of musical communities of this time in San Francisco, for example in the Grateful Dead and other bands living and making music communally in Haight-Ashbury.

The Band reflects aspects of the cultural zeitgeist, even as they push it forward in real ways. The communal nature of writing and recording *Music from Big Pink* was at the very least a quasi-commune response to the general commune culture floating around at this time. According to Timothy Miller, the "latter months of 1967 through the first few years of the 1970s saw a frenzy of commune-founding that dwarfed what had gone before."[18] While noting that the "whys" can be subjective, Miller offers a few answers of his own, as well as one from Philip Slater.

Disgust with the direction that American culture had taken—especially the worship of the almighty dollar—has something to do with it. Psychedelics had something to do with it. The war in Vietnam had something to do with it. Philip Slater argued . . . that American culture had "deeply and uniquely frustrated" three basic human desires—for community, for engagement, and for dependence—and the sixties represented an attempt to overcome that long-felt but little-articulated frustration and to meet those basic drives of the human spirit.[19]

The general historical push of the times was building—the Summer of Love pushed into the political confrontations of 1968 (the siege of Chicago and other political protests). For some, this led to disillusionment with political approaches and, in turn, led to a potential alternative for living off the grid.[20] In many ways, *Music from Big Pink* was a response to the general fatigue of the times. Levon Helm noted that the move to Big Pink was in part a response to the prevailing atmosphere of the times,[21] and Robbie Robertson also notes this.[22] While never losing its political edge, the album is subtle in its reproach—it moves away from direct political protest songs to nuanced critiques in songs like "Tears of Rage," "Chest Fever," and "The Weight." With the Woodstock Festival just around the corner, it is no wonder that living and working in the area would influence the members in ways both immediate and veiled. But the heightened ethos of the Summer of Love also led to a reflective period amid the fervent idealism. Of course, the general sentiment of hippie culture was still present, and would be for years after, but the breakdown of some of those ideals was already present within the youth culture promoting it—this is due to various factors, of course, such as the political confrontations mentioned above, the Vietnam War, and general disillusionment with the possibilities of creating a world community of love.[23] The Band found themselves reflecting on this moment as well, finding and creating a new way forward, yet still holding to some of the larger values of the cultural zeitgeist, altering and contextualizing them where necessary: ideals of community, love, freedom, resistance, and pacifism. Out of this reflection comes a new way to do things, a new sound, and a new album. It manifests both physically, in their "remove" to Woodstock and Big Pink, and musically in their departure from, and alteration of, what had gone before.

In The Band's song imagery, the particular becomes the universal: that is, the closer they got to their experience, the more weighty and expansive their music and lyrics became. In contrast, the idealistic push of the Summer of Love is a paradoxically narrowing attempt to speak to humankind in general—to speak into existence one kind of universal ethic where people "come together as one in love and community." The Band represents a shift (or at least a reworking) of this ethic—allowing an individual perspective to breathe and expand into a potential larger story. This move is, in one way, more insular—it comes from direct, particular experience. However, in the process, there is a generalizing effect that allows that individual story to become "our" story. So, the population of characters they knew (Luke,

Anna Lee, Crazy Chester) become symbols for us to recognize, interpret, and apply to our lives. The protest is still there—they were "rebelling against the rebellion" in their way:[24]

> When I think about that album, I still have to laugh about how close the songs were to our lives. The characters that appear in the lyrics—Luke, Anna Lee, Crazy Chester—were all people we knew. The music was the sum of all the experiences we'd shared for the past ten years, distilled through the quieter vibe of our lives in the country. There was a whole movement toward country values in America in those days, as young people searched for different ways of surviving during the Vietnam era. That's in there too.[25]

Even the opening track was an act of rebellion for them: "'Tears of Rage' opened the album with a slow song . . . We were deliberately going against the grain. Few artists had ever opened an album with a slow song, so we had to."[26] Their personal experience moved into the recording studio. However, capturing all of this personal history in the recording of the album was a decidedly different process than was usual at most studios:

> "They had the drums go over here, they spread us all out so there was no leakage," remembers Robertson. "We were just doing what we were told because this huge room was famous for getting a fantastic sound. After a while we said, 'We can't do this. We've got to get in a circle like the basement, we've got to play to one another. We're speaking a language. This doesn't work.' The engineer is like, 'What? What are you talking about?' But he said, 'All right, let's give it a shot, but it's not going to sound too good.'" They formed a tight circle and switched to Electro Voice RE15 mics "that don't pick up much unless you're right on them. We put them on everything, because they served our purpose."[27]

The Band's approach changed the recording process from the inside, making the studio into a makeshift Big Pink to suit the players and the songs. The group was arranged together in the big A&R studio:

> We cut upstairs in that big studio on top of A&R, which had a very live sound. I'd set up in the middle of the room. There was a sound-booth against the wall, which is where Garth placed some of his speakers, so it would be a little muffled, the way he liked it. The piano'd be there,

and Rick and Robbie would sit on folding chairs, with their amps beside them. That was the way we did it. There were sound-baffles around the drums, and John would kind of lean over them to discuss different drum ideas and strategies because he took it seriously and wanted a solid, professional record.[28]

As noted earlier, The Band recorded *Music from Big Pink* at A&R Studios (in New York) and Capitol Studios and Gold Star Studios (both in Los Angeles). "Tears of Rage," "Chest Fever," "We Can Talk," "This Wheel's on Fire," and "The Weight" were recorded at A&R, while "In a Station," "To Kingdom Come," "Lonesome Suzie," "Long Black Veil," and "I Shall Be Released" were recorded at Capitol Studios and Gold Star Studios.

A&R Studios used four-track recorders on an Ampex 300 machine, and for "these sessions, everybody was recorded live on two of the four tracks, the horns were put on the third track, while the fourth track was reserved for vocals and tambourine."[29] The studio at A&R is famous for its design—particularly its height, which gives it a distinct resonance. As previously mentioned, the opening track of the album sets a new tone meant to buck trends of starting albums with fast numbers. The album begins in "quiet" manner, but this slow number builds on emotional impact rather than sheer volume or pace. Bob Dylan wrote the song, but The Band put their indelible mark on the track, making it their own—through their instrumentation, and especially their unique vocals. Rick Danko's searing voice cuts right through the track. There is an immediacy to his plaintive wails: he is reaching to the top of his range, communicating a distinctive vulnerability; his performance sounds as if we are about to catch him break down in tears himself.

Robbie Robertson notes the recording setup: "We were recording everybody live onto three tracks, with one track left to overdub horns. Final decisions in the sound and balances had to be made now.... I made some tone changes on my amp ... We recorded 'Tears of Rage' two more times, back to back."[30] This was somewhat unusual for a professional recording setup, and he notes the uniqueness of the overall sound.

It was hard to believe that breaking the rules in the unusual way we had set up the studio could produce something that sounded this magical. Richard's voice and piano were sterling. Rick's harmony vocal was loose and soaring, while his bass playing was like warm chocolate. Levon's tuned down drums gave a thunderous heartbeat to the track. Garth's church organ could bring tears to your eyes. I found a new sound and guitar style with a subtlety to it that rebelled against all rock-raging guitar slingers across the land. . . . Then John overdubbed euphonium/high school horn and Garth played sax for our Salvation Army horn section effect. Beautifully sad. Now we were discovering what our new music could conjure up. . . . I knew we were making music unlike anybody else.[31]

The low drone of the horns at the end of the first chorus, continuing through the remaining verses, is an indication of the unique instrumentation that follows with the rest of the album. Just as *Sgt. Pepper's* solidified the use of classical instrumentation in popular rock music,[32] so too did The Band solidify a certain use of "country" or "folk" instrumentation (though, again, antecedents are detectable).

Levon's unique drum sound, which Robbie mentions above, was described by Levon as a take-off of Ringo's drum tuning: the track's "moaning tom-tom style of drumming" was parallel to what Ringo Starr was doing "at the same time. You make the drum notes bend down in pitch. You hit it, it sounds, and then it hums as the note dies out. If the ensemble is right, you can hear the sustain like a bell, and it's very emotional."[33] It is fascinating to think of this influence working back and forth—with the *Get Back/Let It Be* sessions subsequently cribbing off The Band, the sounds feeding and building off each other.

The big room at A&R helps the heavy, thick drums. The toms, in particular, give off a deep sound. The slap of the drumsticks on the skins fills the ear, and the sluggish drum fills resonate. Levon's vintage drums (Ludwig Slingerland and Gretsch) give this sound a unique quality, and the warmth of the room adds texture. The height of the room gives that depth on the bottom end, on the floor, and allows for the top end of the sound to float upwards and stay lively—one gets a direct sound from the mics with a faint recombining of the echo dancing above in the heights of the room.

"The Weight" demonstrates this room sound as well. The engineers recorded the song on four-track at A&R, with Levon's voice and drums on one track.[34] Rick's voice (who takes over lead vocals from Levon during the "crazy Chester" portion) was on one track along with an acoustic guitar and bass.[35] Again, the heavy toms on the intro demonstrate the effects of the A&R room wonderfully: the low, deep tones combined with the high, lively echo floating on top. The Band tried to record live as much as possible—and effects were recorded live, directly on the tape as opposed to adding them later.[36] This was done to "paint a fuller picture" by committing to the sound and making overdubs and atmosphere conform to this initially recorded sound.[37] Recording this way was more about making a song than making just "tracks."[38] Amazingly, the song almost did not make the album. As Levon Helm noted, "We recorded the song maybe four times. We weren't sure it was going to be on the album, but people really liked it."[39]

Arguably, one of the most memorable and original aspects of "The Weight" is its vocal arrangement: the three-part harmony build-up in the chorus is superb, but the arrangement of different voices in the verses is fascinating too. Robbie Robertson describes it thus:

> I began singing the chorus to "The Weight" over and over to the guys, trying to convey the staggered vocal idea I had. . . . Garth's piano playing was dynamic and joyous in the key of A, a bit tricky for a piano man, but not for Garth. Levon would sing the first three verses, and I thought it would be interesting to have Rick, with his down-to-earth sound, sing the "Crazy Chester" verse. . . . I asked Richard to try a little falsetto turnaround melody to go with his organ part.[40]

We hear the alchemy of rhythm and blues, country, roots music, and rock and roll working in this track. The groove of the drums and bass in particular recall the best rhythm and blues grooves of the time: Levon's stuttering snare pattern augments the groove and a slight deep-hall, slap-back echo adds to the syncopation. Rick's high, country harmony on the last verse is a emblematic straining country vocal cry that is further evidence of The Band's influences coming out to play on this track.

In contrast, "I Shall Be Released" was recorded at Capitol Studios in LA, where they had eight-track machines and the famous echo chambers. Robbie Robertson noted how this song is an example of the live element coming into the studio. While working live, The Band would organically arrange their harmonies—with everyone hitting the notes they could hit—and "I Shall Be Released," is evidence of this. Richard sings the lead vocal and moves from the melody in the verses to the high harmony in the choruses (where Rick takes over the melody).[41] The Band are laboring together here, covering for each other, making the music work and sound the best it can by interchanging harmonies between members. These peculiar vocal arrangements give all of the songs a distinct sound—unsettling, confusing at times, and challenging to work out who is hitting what note when.

One of the most exciting sounds on this track comes partially from a mundane but ingenious source: "The drum sound was me playing the snares of an upside-down drum with my fingers."[42] It gives the track's percussive sound a marching effect. Additionally, the famous Capitol echo chambers give the song a second notable feature. The echo chambers at Capitol Studios are thirty feet underground. There are eight of them, trapezoidal in design, and they contain speakers pumping in sounds with microphones placed to capture those sounds coming from the speakers reverberating in the chambers. This can give a cathedral effect. Of course, other bands have used this for noticeable impact—bands like the Beach Boys, with Brian Wilson at the helm, used these chambers to make their unforgettable music. But it is interesting to note the distinctiveness of The Band's use—it does not sound like Phil Spector or the Beach Boys. Particularly in "I Shall Be Released," Levon's strumming of the snare, Richard's vocals, and Garth's oceanic organ make the swirling wash of the echo chambers a revelation: it pushes the instruments into separate space rather than creating the "wall of sound" that Spector made and Brian Wilson tried to emulate. However, one must not underestimate the playing of Garth. The "windlike sound is Garth playing organ with one hand and manipulating the stops with the other,"[43] and Garth's atmospheric organ sound certainly adds a cinematic, imagistic ambiance to the song, one that is accentuated by the echo chambers. Robbie Robertson claimed that Garth's style of playing was not done much before Garth did it—and that it is difficult to hear what he is playing exactly, or even at times what instrument is making the peculiar noise.[44] Garth's equipment also added to this soundscape—with his use of the Lowery FL model and the Hammond B2/B3 series. But it was his playing style that made the equipment sing.[45] As with the opening track,[46] Bob Dylan wrote the closing track of *Music from Big Pink*. The song was a "prisoner's lament that Bob had sung on the basement tapes and Richard sings in his falsetto voice."[47] And, again, we hear The Band make this song their own—in particular with Richard Manuel's fragile vocal delivery and deceptively simple piano playing, particularly the piano intro with octave play and falling notes.[48]

These seemingly deceptive musical elements and recording techniques can add to the notion of an utterly "live" affair. This "live," "down-home" feel of the album is dazzling and is a unique achievement in rock history. However, the myth of completely "live off the floor" should be guarded against:

> Music from Big Pink was one of the first albums that sold the myth of "live off the floor" recordings. With people picturing this music being recorded in the basement of that pink house, inevitably the assumption was that the songs were done in minimal takes, with all of them in one room banging it out effortlessly. But The Band was all about creating a great sound, and they were more interested in achieving this by any means possible rather than adhering to unnecessary standards such as everything being a strictly collaborative, live effort in the studio.

The important thing here is not to assume that they were above using the latest studio tricks to achieve their purpose, and this included a lot of vocal and instrumental overdubbing.[49]

Nevertheless, the approach to this record was different from popular music records that immediately preceded it. While dreaming up *Music from Big Pink*, Robbie Roberson was "harping to John Simon that it had to have a unique sound, a flavor of its own."[50] Robertson played John Simon various records to give a sense of this new sound, "tracks from Chess Studios in Chicago, Sun Records in Memphis, Cosimo's Studio in New Orleans, Muscle Shoals in Alabama, and Gold Star in Los Angeles."[51] Of course, The Band were not the first to try a "live off the floor" approach. One can find this approach riddled throughout recording history, especially pre-overdubbing recording history. Or, as Robertson writes, it is "as old as music" itself.[52] Despite this method being typical for many pre-overdubbing era recordings, The Band have a unique atmosphere—and another element that gives these recordings that unique atmosphere is the use of the same microphone type to record many different kinds of instruments. Often different microphones are used to record different instruments: e.g., a particular microphone is used to record vocals; or a series of mics are used to record the drums. On this record, we have specific mic use combined with live recording techniques, and the use of Electro-Voice RE15 mics made close-range sound isolation possible and gave the album an individual and tight soundscape.[53]

The RE15 microphones allow for an exciting interplay between sounds—they give distinct isolation in combination with overlap and leaking of other instruments and sounds. We can, for example, get a little leaking of the drums squeezed into the bass guitar sound—and vice versa, so that in a song like "The Weight" we can still hear the individual, distinctive notes of the bass guitar but mixed in with the deep ringing, low tones of the bass drum and toms. And the use of the RE15 microphone is no small detail for the reconstruction of the album's sound. The microphone is a dynamic cardioid, and cardioids are often used to limit other sounds from creeping in from other directions. When aimed at its source, it is reasonably effective at rejecting those other sounds due to its heart-shaped (hence "cardioid") polar response. This gives it a distinctive feature, and it was often used to record speech due to this specific feature. The RE15 has a rejection (i.e., limiting of the sound from other directions) at 150 degrees, whereas many other cardioids of its type have a rejection at 180 degrees. So, it cuts out other sounds a bit more. This type of microphone would allow The Band to be recorded in one room while keeping some sense of the distinctiveness of individual instruments—preventing too much leakage between different instruments. However, it would still give some leakage, and this balance between the leakage of other sounds and individual sounds is a main feature of the album as a whole.

In "Chest Fever," some of this strange alchemy can be heard in the stereo spread in the drums and organ, with the sounds leaking over to both sides of the track at times (and the echo dancing around as well). For the organ, Garth Hudson used his Leslie cabinet and added some extra material for the intro of the song:

> For his legendary introduction to "Chest Fever," Garth explained to Terje Mosnes: "We had the song all done, but John Simon wanted an intro. We put the Leslie cabinet, a 145, in a small cubicle and opened it up completely. I played the first three notes from Bach's *Toccata and Fugue in D minor* and then I improvised. The intro is longer than what you hear on the album. John edited it down." He has confirmed this since, speaking to Seth Rogovoy: "The sound on 'Chest Fever,' that was a 145 Leslie cabinet," though it does seem that in 1969 a pair of model 147RV's were employed instead—presumably one for each organ keyboard.[54]

The RE15 microphones also give a tightness to the bass and guitar. This can be heard in "Chest Fever" as well: the thunkiness of Rick's bass and the wirey guitar of Robbie are largely a result of these microphones.[55] When The Band went to record in the "traditional" way, it did not work for them. They were separated by sound-baffling, listening to each other through headphones, and the vibe was not right. Robbie Robertson recounts,

> I put down my guitar on the floor and went into the control room. "This doesn't work, John. Sorry, but we can't record like this. . . . We can't make music with an isolated setup . . . We have to see one another. We have to read one another's signals. That's how we play—to each other." . . . I laid out a floor plan.[56]

The directness of the microphones and the directness of the approach to recording mixes with the directness of the times—the music and culture of the period was moving away from the distant, abstract, psychedelic to the honed, sincere, and back-to-basics approach. And while the focus on paring down the adornments of the mid- to late-1960s was just beginning to take root in rock culture at the time, The Band were the first to solidify this new approach to recording. There is an interplay of culture making and culture mirroring happening in these recordings.

Music from Big Pink was both a reflection of its time and a catalyst for change. The album reflects the process of culture participation as well as culture creation: great artists both reflecting their time and sign-pointing to new directions. Just as the Beatles took the zeitgeist of the mid-1960s culture and pushed it forward (with *Revolver* and then *Sgt. Pepper's* through to *Magical Mystery Tour*), so too did The Band capture the spirit of the late 1960s to create something new. Just as *Sgt. Pepper's* brought about a host of imitators and continuations of the album's ethic (*Their Satanic Majesties* by the Rolling Stones, *Ogdens' Nut Gone Flake* by the Small Faces), so too did *Music from Big Pink*. The album ushered in a variety of imitators and creators in line with this new ethic of music making. In the time following *Music from Big Pink*, we see some big bands of the day move in The Band's direction: the Beatles with the *Get Back* sessions; The Rolling Stones with *Beggars Banquet*, moving back to basics after the high of their mid-sixties work. All of this is summed up by Roger Waters's assessment—that *Music from Big Pink* was just as influential and game-changing a record as *Sgt. Pepper's Lonely Hearts Club Band*: "After *Sgt. Pepper*, the next record that changed everything was *Music from Big Pink* because of the way in which it was recorded. Particularly Levon's drum sound, and the way the drums were recorded. But also the way they harmonized. . . . and the way it was put together—again—changed everything. . . . You heard that record and went, 'Wow!'"[57]

Notes

1. Harold Lepidus, "Roger Waters talks about influence of Bob Dylan and The Band in New Interview," *Bob Dylan Examiner*, January 18th, 2012, http://www.examiner.com/article/roger-waters-talks-about-influence-of-bob-dylan-and-the-band-new-interview.

2. Tom Pinnock, "The Band, Bob Dylan and *Music from Big Pink*—the Full Story," *Uncut*, July 31, 2015, http://www.uncut.co.uk/features/the-band-bob-dylan-and-music-from-big-pink-the-full-story-69989#mvtU7okxgBDU8iu6.99.

3. The Beatles, *The Beatles Anthology*, Chronicle Books, 2000, 316. Also, as mentioned in the introduction, Paul was certainly listening to The Band during 1968, and this can be seen in his improvisational vocal ad lib of lyrics from "The Weight" (during the Beatles' semi-live performance of "Hey Jude" on the *Frost on Sunday* show, October 2nd, 1968). Paul gives a knowing smile/look to George (who doesn't see it) as he sings it as well. Paul's improvisation can be heard in this video around the 6:19 mark: https://www.youtube.com/watch?v=A_MjCqQoLLA.

4. George Harrison, "Interview," *Classic Albums, The Band*, Eagle Rock Entertainment, 2005.

5. Ibid.

6. This can be seen explicitly in the documentary, *The True History of The Traveling Wilburys*, where one can watch the Wilburys performing, writing, and recording together. (A copy can be found here: https://www.youtube.com/watch?v=OU-7GX8s0dA.) One sees a community of musicians, working together as equals, recording and writing in a way that resembles The Band's idea of a musician's community.

7. Helm, *This Wheel's on Fire*, 177–78.

8. Eric Clapton, "Interview," by Tom Pinnock, *Uncut*, November 30th, 2012.

9. Robertson, *Testimony*, 267.

10. Ibid., 268.

11. Ibid., 269–70.

12. Robertson, *Testimony*, 282.

13. Pinnock, "The Band, Bob Dylan and *Music from Big Pink*."

14. Helm, *This Wheel's on Fire*, 165.

15. Ibid.

16. Pinnock, "The Band, Bob Dylan and *Music from Big Pink*."

17. Ibid.

18. Timothy Miller, *The 60s Communes: Hippies and Beyond*, Syracuse, New York: Syracuse University Press, 1999, 67.

19. Ibid.

20. Miller, *The 60s Communes*, 68.

21. "There was a whole movement toward country values in America in those days, as young people searched for different ways of surviving during the Vietnam era" (Helm, *This Wheel's on Fire*, 166).

22. Of the years leading up to the recording of the album, he remarks, "There was a different tone in the air. The war in Vietnam was looming larger in our lives as American involvement deepened. As we had planned, our friend Connie B. married Levon to keep him from being drafted" (Robertson, *Testimony*, 109).

23. For example, this can be seen in complications of drug addiction present in the Summer of Love phenomenon (not to mention other social issues percolating in "love" culture of the time). As just one example of this, Jennie Rothenberg Gritz writes about Joe Samburg's photographs of the area and time, "Joe was part of it all, but he was also slightly outside of it, watching everything through the lens of his camera. Years later, when he was a highly regarded professional photographer—after he'd settled down and raised three children (including the comedian Andy Samberg)—he showed me some of his early portraits from Telegraph Avenue. They've been in my mind's eye ever since, a counterpoint to all the popular images of peace signs, daisy chains, and Aquarian circle dances. The reality Joe saw was very much like the one the Atlantic author described: hordes of kids who had been lured to California by utopian ideals and then settled into a life of sex, drugs, and lethargy" ("The Death of the Hippies: The photographer Joe Samberg Remembers How Drugs Destroyed the Telegraph Avenue Scene," the *Atlantic*, July 8, 2015). Joan Didion's essay "Slouching Towards Bethlehem" (also the title her 1968 book, published by Farrar, Straus and Giroux) details some of the problems with the "utopian" vision given to the Summer of Love, especially her harrowing depiction of a young child given LSD by her parents. For a slightly related overlap, one may also be interested in reading Alexa Clay's

essay on utopian communities and why they fail, entitled "Utopia Inc," found here: https://aeon.co/essays/like-start-ups-most-intentional-communities-fail-why.

24. Helm, *This Wheel's on Fire*, 166.

25. Ibid.

26. Helm, *This Wheel's on Fire*, 166.

27. Pinnock, "The Band, Bob Dylan and *Music from Big Pink*."

28. Helm, *This Wheel's on Fire*, 165.

29. *The History of The Band*, http://theband.hiof.no/history/part_5.html, from Rob Bowman, "Life Is a Carnival," *Goldmine* magazine, July 26, 1991, vol. 17, no. 15, issue 287.

30. Robertson, *Testimony*, 298.

31. Robertson, *Testimony*, 299.

32. Though there are, of course, antecedents in the Beatles' music as well as numerous other recordings from other musicians.

33. Helm, *This Wheel's on Fire*, 166.

34. John Simon, "Interview," *Classic Albums, The Band*, Eagle Rock Entertainment, 2005.

35. Ibid.

36. Ibid.

37. Ibid.

38. Helm, "Interview."

39. Helm, *This Wheel's on Fire*, 167.

40. Robertson, *Testimony*, 299–300.

41. Robbie Robertson, "Interview," *Classic Albums, The Band*, Eagle Rock Entertainment, 2005.

42. Helm, *This Wheel's on Fire*, 169.

43. Helm, *This Wheel's on Fire*, 169.

44. Robertson, "Interview."

45. As we have just noted, it was somewhat of a mystery to the members of The Band exactly what Garth did, and other musicians have echoed this sentiment: "The work of Garth Hudson has long been a mysterious and largely undocumented chapter. Not knowing how he does what he does is part of his magic, of course. Much of his playing seems to defy transcription, even apparently simple phrases are blurred and unresolved. His legendary solo improvisations drift from one idea to the next like a dream sequence, or as though someone kept fast-forwarding some strange movie soundtrack, skipping through the scenes. The timing, seemingly unhinged, is dragged and drawn out with elegant perfection." ("Garth's Gear—The Classic Years," by Kerrin, http://theband.hiof.no/articles/ghs_keyboards_knz.html).

46. Richard Manuel also cowrote "Tears of Rage." Bob Dylan wrote the lyrics and Richard Manuel wrote the melody.

47. Helm, *This Wheel's on Fire*, 169. Bob Dylan gave praise to The Band's rendition as well: "At the end of 'I Shall Be Released'—one of the most beautiful tunes Bob had written during our time in the basement—he stood up and said, 'That was so good. You did it, man, you did it.' Coming from a dear friend, one of the greatest songwriters ever, and our fearless leader, Bob's enthusiasm and words meant the world to the boys and me" (Robertson, *Testimony*, 310).

48. Artist Bill Payne has an interesting write-up about his experiences of tracking down and playing Richard Manuel's piano: "Somewhere between 1967 and 1969 . . . Richard Manuel and Garth Hudson went on a search for a piano. The quest led them to New York, Chicago, and other places in the United States and Canada. They tried out a dozen or so pianos in the process, according to Johnny Lee. . . . Based on that information, I placed a call to Garth Hudson and had a brief conversation about what transpired. . . . [The] search ended (or began and ended) in Poughkeepsie, NY, at Vincitore's Hudson Valley Piano Center. Garth remembers the two of them going there and that Richard picked out the piano. The Steinway Richard chose was from the 'L' series, measuring just under six feet, Steinway's smallest concert grand—otherwise known as a baby grand. I would imagine that one of the features Richard and Garth were looking for was something small enough to haul around on tour (which Garth confirmed) and, of course, possessed a wonderful tone and touch." The write-up can be found in its entirety here: https://billpaynecreative.com/writing/richard-manuel/.

49. Chris LeDrew, "*Music from Big Pink*: Myth Debunked, Genius Retained," *On Stage Magazine*, May 9, 2013.

50. Robertson, *Testimony*, 293.

51. Ibid.

52. Ibid., 282.

53. For those interested, the description of the Electro-Voice RE15 is as follows: "The Electro-Voice RE15 is a dynamic cardioid mic created especially for the most exacting professional applications. Emphasizing a major technological breakthrough, the RE15 features a degree of directional control so effective that frequency response is virtually independent of angular location of sound source. The result is a microphone that generates no off axis coloration, yet provides greatest possible rejection of unwanted sounds. A super cardioid, the RE15 provides its greatest rejection at 150° off axis. (Typical cardioids provide greatest rejection at 180°.) This assures greatest rejection in the horizontal plane when the microphone is tilted in its most natural position—30° from horizontal (as on boom or floor stand). An easily operated 'bass-tilt' switch corrects spectrum balance for boom use and other longer reach situations" (https://www.electrovoice.com/binary/RE15%20Engineering%20Data%20Sheet.pdf).

54. Kerrin, "Garth's Gear—the Classic Years," The Band website, accessed October 12, 2017: http://theband.hiof.no/articles/ghs_keyboards_knz.html.

55. This is not to say, of course, that Rick's and Robbie's equipment did not play a part in their sound. For a look at Rick's basses, one may want to read the write-up in *Bass Musician* magazine, found here: Rob Collier, "How to Danko: A Lesson in the Style of Rick Danko," *Bass Musician* magazine, https://bassmusicianmagazine.com/2012/04/how-to-danko-a-lesson-in-the-style-of-rick-danko-by-rob-collier/. Similarly, for a look at just some of the guitars that Robertson used through the years, one may want to look at his interview with *Vintage Guitar* magazine, found here: Dan Forte, "Robbie Robertson: The Many Sides Of," *Vintage Guitar* magazine, http://www.vintageguitar.com/11786/rockin-robbie-robertson/.

56. Robertson, *Testimony*, 297.

57. Lepidus, "Roger Waters talks about influence of Bob Dylan and The Band."

Chapter 5

"CAUGHT IN THE SPOTLIGHT"

The Band's Performance Anxiety in *Stage Fright*

JUDE WARNE

> The basic result of all this was to make The Band easier to listen to, less outrageous, and less fun.
> —GREIL MARCUS[1]

After several years supporting Ronnie Hawkins and Bob Dylan, The Band asserted themselves as an independent act with two consecutive album releases: *Music from Big Pink* in 1968 and *The Band* in 1969. Both left deep and well-defined footprints on the musical community of the late 1960s. The Band's sound was one of egalitarianism and of old Americana-ism, despite their mostly Canadian roots. The records required intellectual attention and sophisticated listening; they held weight, uniqueness, and value, carrying The Band to the top wave of the musical ocean. But what comes after success? Stage fright.

On their third album, *Stage Fright*, The Band ask their listeners to dive into a full-on crisis of confidence—the type that abounds once success has been reached. In this state, there is an abundance of every kind of vice, the devouring of which is up for grabs and subject to the morality and conscience of the individuals exposed to them. The more one has, the more one wants—and The Band are no different.

Had achievement, notoriety, and glittered-up fame caused The Band to be "less fun?" What exactly would a "less fun" record sound like? *Stage Fright*, according to music journalist Greil Marcus.[2] But maybe the responsibility of maintenance that accompanies the achievement of success *is* less fun. The wool has been pulled away from The Band's eyes in *Stage Fright*, and they are forced to deal with reality. They are no longer able to cushion themselves with the dream of "making it," because they have made it. Now they just have themselves, which includes the presuccess identity as well as the postsuccess one and the reality that surrounds it. Reality is imperfect. To comprehend imperfection and accept it requires strength, fortitude, and a high level of confidence. Could the members of The Band muster enough of these qualities to grow and climb the ladder rungs to artistic immortality? Or would they ruin themselves? *Stage Fright*, as an aural organism of its own independent volition, seeks to find out.

The album was recorded in the early summer of 1970 at the Woodstock Playhouse, right near to where The Band resided in upstate New York. The studio space was isolated and somewhat cold and alienating. Communal closeness created during the second-album sessions, experienced in the intimate self-made studio at Sammy Davis Jr.'s home in Hollywood, felt very far away. On *Stage Fright* a young Todd Rundgren served as engineer, and legendary Glyn Johns was responsible for much of the final mixing.

The cultural malaise that had ushered in the 1970s—the disappointment that the hippie dream of the previous decade had failed, that the Manson Family murders and Altamont Free Concert killing catastrophe of 1969 had quashed it for good—was a constant undercurrent of almost everything directly following. Drug experimentation that had allowed for some good, some bad over the course of the 1960s seemed to have gone a bit sour, or grown weightier as of late. Heavy stuff—heroin—had found its way into The Band's orbit by the *Stage Fright* sessions. Robbie Robertson's songwriting, which had played a prominent role in The Band's first two albums, now dominated the new record's track list out of creative necessity. Fellow band members took increasingly less interest in the songwriting discipline. The coherent brotherhood of composing and creating that The Band had established themselves with, the magic that the group suggested via their working together as one unit, seemed to have—for the moment—vanished. The ultimate high of a first hit of heroin—the pleasured rush and intense relief from dis-ease forever impossible to reproduce, no matter how a user might try—mimicked the first hit of an immense artistic win The Band had experienced with their first two albums. And The Band chased the thrill just the same on its third trip in *Stage Fright*.

"Try to understand, I just wanna feel good all the time," urges Levon Helm's narrator in the album opener "Strawberry Wine." He is trying to rationalize his own wild behavior, to explain why he is the way he is—why he has forsaken all else, even his woman, for the sweetly seductive numbness that his strawberry wine provides. Other people—lovers, especially—can be reliably unreliable in their effects on us. They may provoke frustration, admiration, desire, or worst of all, they can ignore us, whether on purpose or accidentally. That reality—and risk—places a lot of power in the hands of others. Alcohol, though, is dependable. It has the ability to make one "feel good all the time." All one has to do is drink it.

Most people want to "feel good all the time"; it is a natural human desire to seek pleasure and contentment. But perhaps it isn't a reasonable wish in the realm of the mortal, corporeal world. Truthfully, if all a person feels is *good*, how can he distinguish it as such? The possibility of feeling bad gives feeling good its strong and warranted value. The singer with this desire—to "feel good all the time"—is unreasonable, and no doubt has felt good so often that feeling anything *less than* good feels wrong and in need of correction. In this song, strawberry wine is the corrector. The choice to sing of strawberry wine, too, provides an additional saccharine and devilish quality to the song. Helm's protagonist doesn't just want wine, with its wondrous effects aplenty. He is greedy; he wants *sweet* wine. He wants it all.

The rock and roll lifestyle, in part, is built upon the core values of excess, indulgence, and pleasure. Artists, and musicians specifically, are a unique bunch. They are creators who live outside the organized world in order to comment on it. They make many of their own rules, allow a lot, and are tolerant of a lot. They give the world at large a good deal of room. In turn, they demand the same treatment for themselves; they demand proverbial square footage. But too much room is sometimes as hazardous as not enough. Room is space; space is freedom; freedom demands responsibility; responsibility demands confidence. Do The Band have confidence by the time they set out to record their third album? They should, as they've achieved critical and commercial success with their first two offerings. And what's left can be evened out with an instant confidence-builder: strawberry wine. Though, in all probability, the specific beverage is a stand-in for any artificial pleasure-deliverer, strawberry wine represents the kind of perceived corrector to which an addicted, self-esteem-deprived person might be persuaded to give all of his money and time—which could otherwise be devoted to his lover, his art, or anything remotely productive.

Any sort of success, too, can imply that one deserves to feel good because he has achieved something; he is in constant celebration mode. Celebrate enough, and it soon becomes the norm. The celebration—the postperformance high—must then be maintained. The only problem is that everyday life is more neutral, milder, and at times disappointing, frustrating, and annoying. The performer, feeling any of these emotions postsuccess, feels unnatural in these everyday moments. To compensate, the strawberry-wine quotient switches into 24/7 consumption mode.

The album's second track, "Sleeping," is mood-heavy, contemplative, and reflective. Sung by Richard Manuel, who cowrote the song with Robbie Robertson, its lyrics seem to be the product of a quiet and solitary, strawberry wine–less series of perceptive moments. The song articulates a wistful yearning to return to a calmer time of innocence. The line "For the life we chose, in the evening we rose, just long enough to be lovers again" suggests the singer's reconciling with the existence that he has made for himself. This existence is largely nocturnal, alluding to that of the touring musician, reclaiming his own full life force every evening in front of an audience. The word choice of "lovers," too, shines light on the necessary intimacy of artistic colleagues, forged in nightly performances onstage with one another, escaping just long enough—ninety minutes or a few hours at most—to provide release. Then there is the return to the solitary, to the realization of one's loneliness, to the harsh remembrance of the fact that "the world was too sore to live in."

The retreat from society and the communal acceptance that the artist's life provides, shine brightly in "Sleeping." "Where else on earth would you wanna go? . . . why would we wanna come back at all?" The melancholy melody and romantically resigned piano work—descending, almost mournful notes—tell the tale of one who has woken up from the dream and only now realizes how sweet the dream was. "I'll spend my whole life sleeping," the protagonist swears. But what has he awakened from? What reality has he woken up to find?

The Band have awakened from the innocence of prefame, when they may have been able to glorify what success, recognition, and artistic achievement could be. Hence they were able to dream—and bask in the freedom of that ability. In pursuit of their success, The Band sought to thrive as Ronnie Hawkins's band the Hawks, to grow and soar as Bob Dylan's backing band, and to come into their own as The Band. They then released the brilliant records *Music from Big Pink* and *The Band*, which garnered acclaim and awe from nearly every contemporary musician of the day, as well as from critics and fans. Over the whole course of their journey of becoming, The Band stared at the burning starlight of their desire, fixated on what they wanted to achieve. How good it would feel once they arrived there.

Now it's *Stage Fright*. Now the dream is over and the reality is here. The Band has "turned from the sun, [to see] everyone searching," and as suggested by the song's title, there is "Time to Kill" now—to pause, rest, and reflect. There is time to take a look around, only to find that feeling successful feels very similar to dreaming of success. The Band seems to discover that the core of a person remains the same, no matter what; that each person is still searching and still doesn't have answers. They find that perhaps it felt better to live in dreamland. Now The Band knows too much.

The Band's members have, in part, become innocents again; they have shaken hands with their child-dreamer selves. "Time to Kill" is a manifestation of the exorbitant joy that accompanies success. Success has been achieved, and good times are in order. Now everyone can sit back and relax—but *can* they?

"Time to Kill" begins as an account of time spent, many roads covered, and many trails burned. Danko's narrator has been through a lot; he has worked hard, and it has paid off. Now, he and his girl have an abundance of time to themselves. "Don't know what we've got," he says, "but it feels like a lot," implying an instinctual need to hold fast to whatever success the singer has achieved. With achievement comes fear of losing it, and fear that everyone around wants to steal it from the achiever. "Be careful what you wish for" seems to be a resounding lesson as well. He has everything that he ever wanted and ever could want, yet pause and paralysis run rampant. Now what?

Now, the individual insists upon being content—for the time being. He acknowledges that he has accumulated a great deal of experience along his trail in the physical world. Since he met his lady, his understanding of his own life and of the world around him has changed. He no longer possesses an insatiable thirst for variety and newness. He has found the Good Thing and is ready to lie low and enjoy what he has made for himself with the person he loves most. Yet one can't help but feel the relentless uneasiness that chips away at the entire run of "Time to Kill." "We've got everything; it's perfect!" the echo seems to articulate—except it can't be perfect. Nothing is. Something *has* to be wrong with this idyllic picture postcard of a description.

There is the sense too of the intense awareness—on the part of both the song's narrator and The Band at large—of a consistent uneasiness pervading everything. He is insistent that all is well now, that the future looks bright because the present is bright. He seeks to permanently possess the unreliable pure pleasantness of the moment in order to make it certain for himself: "Gonna bolt the door, don't know what we've got, but it feels like a lot, we don't need no more." When life is going well and flowing smoothly, it's best not to wonder *why* exactly—or to look too closely at the reality at hand. Otherwise, chinks in the armor could be found. Worriers know that there is always one issue or two left to worry about, no matter how lovely all other matters may be, and sooner than later, the troublesome issue takes over the worrier's entire outlook. The good that is there is then rendered irrelevant.

The narrator's girl in "Time to Kill" is desperate too: "My love wants to have her fortune read, and I know that she's in a hurry. / If we go along the straight and narrow, you don't even have to worry." She wants to know what will happen to her and her man; she wants to know *now*. The unending supply of free time and its limitless possibilities, afforded by success and space, have unnerved her.

Still it is the upbeat, rousing, seductively melodic music that steers this track, and that makes up the listener's emotional conclusion. "Time to Kill" encourages us to enjoy ourselves, and over the course of the song, we try to. Whether we succeed at this or not is up to each individual, but at least we are left with the knowledge that we *should* be enjoying.

"Just Another Whistle Stop" summons both the exhilaration of the performing artist's one-night-only existence and the numbing, devaluing repetitiveness of it. Still, though this is the reality of The Band's life at the moment, and the reality of the life they have known, the song's protagonist (voiced by Manuel) begs the listener to stay. "If you don't quit till we reach the top, I'd be much obliged to you." As frustrating as the artist's audience may become to the artist, he knows that he needs it in order to stick around. The interdependent relationship between artist and audience is impossible to deny. The most successful artists come to terms with this truth at some point in their evolution.

"Pay no mind to what they say—when they're bitter, they talk that way," Manuel's narrator comforts us. The "they" in this instance could be any group of jealous naysayers—critics, fellow rock groups, or disapproving passersby. Once again, it is clear that The Band are aware of these doubting voices, though they might try to ignore them as they continue down their artistic path. Notoriety and attention, such as the kind The Band have garnered, draw positive and negative people. To release any sort of artistic output, the artist lays himself bare naked—to be torn apart or crowned regal, whatever the current climate will permit. This type of risk demands intense confidence, and of the most sensitive souls imaginable, those who deal in the vulnerable realm of emotionality on a constant basis. It's quite a conundrum, but one that stands as the basis of the artist-audience mechanism. One hopes that as the artist's career gains momentum, as success expands, that his confidence will follow suit. Many times it does, sometimes to a detriment. But always, *always*, the "lonely kid" holds permanent residence in the artist's memory— the kid who remembers everything he ever did, bad and good; the kid who measures and judges the worth of the self.

Another song in which the narrator attempts to relate to his own innocence is "All La Glory." Here it comes in the form of what seems to be a father-child relationship; the father relives his own youth through that of his young child. It is almost as though The Band's recently intensified success has made them feel certain that their innocence has evaporated for good. Any chance that they ever had at reclaiming it has disappeared. Qualities that maintained a pathway to innocence, or the memory of it, may have been earnestness, personal integrity, work ethic, optimism, faith, goodness, or a clean spirit. The Band were in the game for the music, for the joy of creating. In the words of Traffic, "When playing music for the people seemed to be enough."[3]

Now The Band have money and everything that it can buy. Now they are "loved" by thousands of fans, but not for who the members really are. They are loved for their talent, for their status, and for their image. This is instant attraction and lust, with onlookers projecting all their desires onto The Band, even if the group can't deliver satisfaction. They become Christ figures, artist martyrs, selfless Statues of Liberty with open arms willing to bleed themselves dry of human emotion on stage nightly so that we don't have to.

The Band's members feel far from the simpler desires of their childhood, when a big day was determined by whether they were able to feel free and to do everything they'd wanted. Now they have grown "tall like a prison wall" and are trapped at the heights they have reached. There is no going back, neither to childhood, nor to anonymity where pressure was nowhere to be found, when no one wanted anything from them. They are stuck on top, far away from the crowds to whom they play, and they are most lonely.

In "All La Glory," The Band articulate the limits of experience—that even though one may have accomplished and achieved a great deal, there is still more to know and feel. Life is glorious to the song's child character, but it is also glorious to the singer-narrator. Even with the accumulation of earthly years, one's quotient of the unknown seems to stay the same.

Experience may bring a person scenes of many colors and leave him with memories of varying degrees of wildness, but it does not answer every last question. *Why am I here? What can all this lead to? Does it matter?* It's almost as though the members of The Band, or anyone for that matter, expect experience to deliver feelings of finality, or certain knowledge. This, they think, will bring them confidence—the lack of which partly drove them to success in the first place. But it doesn't, the realization of which is a bit disarming.

Still, the singer-narrator is hopeful: "Before the leaves all turn brown . . . you will find the harmony," he tells his child. His own leaves have not yet all turned brown, but he is optimistic that harmony exists at the end of every person's road. For now, for this child, it is just the beginning, but the singer-narrator is stuck in his adulthood, stuck on the "second story." The point at which he finds himself in his life seems to have a stranglehold on him. This fits aptly within the paranoia in which the album *Stage Fright* is doused. "All La Glory" is one of the lighter moments on the record, a moment that looks toward the future, to the next generation. Even if the singer-narrator does not understand life in its totality, perhaps his child might. Still, he is uneasy; still, he must venture forth and continue to perform, with or without his accumulated anxiety—the sort that existed prior to success and the sort that was accumulated with success seeming to have massed into a package deal. Only time will tell if The Band can handle the weight of it all.

The B side of the album begins. "The Shape I'm In" depicts a man beside himself, dealing with an intense case of personal unrest. He is so beside himself, in fact, that he won't even let the listener of his song's story understand what he is going through. "Oh, you don't know the shape I'm in." He does spend a good deal of energy attempting to articulate it. Does he ever truly succeed? Perhaps he is in too emotional a state to do so logically or comprehensively.

The man mentions several things that seem to have gone wrong for him. First, there's the issue of his lady. Where has she gone to? He has no idea and asks "has anybody seen" her. One gets the sense that before anyone has a chance to respond, even if anyone *has* seen her—it doesn't matter. The man won't stay long enough to hear an answer; he has already flown off down the road, a victim of his own mad fever. He plans to "go down by the water," but he won't be able to jump into it—he'll be too busy looking for his "maker."

"Out of nine lives, I spent seven," the man continues to sing. He is very, *very* spent, and has no idea how "you get to heaven." But he must propel himself forward, in his mad frenzy, unable to lie still, unable to relax. "I just spent sixty days in the jailhouse," he continues on, with all the pent-up energy of a recently released prisoner. His crime was his nomadism, his freedom, and "having nowhere to go."

This track seems to be The Band's coming to terms with whether or not a person, an artist, can have it all and maintain his own sanity. The man in "The Shape I'm In" is faced with unending decisions to make, decisions that he seems to fear may be the defining moments of his life. He is under pressure, he is under the gun that he and his conscience have loaded. One cannot, in his view, both save his own neck and save his brother. No, he must choose between the two. With such a demand before him, how can he relax?

It is obvious that this song is one of confusion, anxiety, and fear. The specific instances detailed over the course of the track are all manifestations of the singer's generalized feelings. But how has the singer, here Richard Manuel, reached such a state? How has The Band reached it? Is the "shape" in question good or bad?

There is a plethora of truths available in the universe, and it is up to individuals to choose those to which they can attach themselves. The mere act of choosing can cause the chooser to feel uneasy. Perhaps the singer is so frenzied because he is experiencing a period of intense self-definition, which can become uncomfortable because it demands intense self-evaluation. Such a period could occur following a recent escalation of artistic and financial achievements, which is right where The Band were in 1970.

What kind of band were The Band going to be? What kind of band had they been thus far? What kind of shape were The Band in during the *Stage Fright* sessions? Increased and harder drug use had affected the group's compositional output, its ability to work together easily, and its overall balance of artistic confidence—a temporary state of being that was in part reflected in the youth culture of the time. The same youth culture that had been rattled by the recent previous decade's assassinations, violent episodes, and doomed, complicated involvement in the escalating Vietnam War.

The Band seem to spend the entire artistic journey of the *Stage Fright* album attempting to figure out where they indeed stand. Would stage fright and the seductive refuge that joy-inducing substances offered overtake The Band's pursuit of greatness? Would their baggage, accumulated over years on the road, prevent them from accepting and embracing their critical and commercial success? The record is all but conclusive; it puts forth a variety of considerations and possibilities, but by its end has not explained itself, or even chosen to love itself after staring in the mirror for thirty-five-plus minutes. The album is tentative and transitory—a portrait of a group of guys in flux.

"The W.S. Walcott Medicine Show" presents a tale of seduction via an old-time Americana traveling act. Physical pleasures abound and tempt in the carnivalesque show, urging anyone with "nowhere to go" to come along and see what W. S. Walcott has to offer. The show's contents seem to encompass the full range of life's characters and situations: "saints and sinners . . . losers and winners" will all be present. Such totality suggests a "come one, come all" environment in which anyone and everyone is welcome—"all kinds of people you might want to know." This kind of tolerance is one of the mainstays of the world of rock and roll, The Band's real world. Freedom and individuality are encouraged here because they are the bases of creative expression. But with freedom comes the responsibility to not be completely taken down or taken over by vices, by cheap thrills. And since the medicine show has everything, it has those too. Bystanders and wanderers drawn in by the medicine show's charms had best keep their wits about them or risk being lost to ruin.

The medicine show promises to be a cure-all-ills trip for its attendees. W. S. Walcott can lead them to "the real thing," whatever that might be. His acts include several fascinating characters, familiar archetypes of the carnival experience, who seem to be as dangerous as they are wonderful. There's the "young faith healer" who can make a person right as rain merely through his belief that he can, and through his claimed connection to God. The healer is so talented at making people feel good that he can't resist using his abilities on the opposite sex—"he's a woman stealer." Then there's the bejeweled Miss Brer Foxhole, whose teeth are covered in diamonds and who promises to be "pure gold down underneath." One cannot help but wonder how true these claims are; yes they sound enchanting—but can the medicine show deliver? And at what price?

"Once you get it, you can't forget it," the singer-narrator insists. What, exactly, is "it?" Hunger, desire, need. It almost seems as though the medicine show attendees will become transformed after experiencing it. Beforehand, they were bored, neutral at best, and half-dead. Now that they know what life can be like, now that they know faith healers, gilded women, and "the Klondike Klu Klux Steamboat Band" exist—now that they know what's possible—they know what they want: magic. They want that which lies beyond the comforts and certainties of normal, everyday life and promises the extraordinary. They want to feel good, just like The Band.

The Band have been seduced by the life of the artist. They have fallen for the promises articulated in the W. S. Walcott Medicine Show. Like any vocation, that of the rock and roll musician comes with a certain kind of lifestyle. Those called to the artistic way, as The Band's members were, take on their chosen craft and the corresponding methods of living. From this song, it is clear that the colorful path of the artist, with its cornucopia of characters—some intoxicating, some sinister—incorporates some rough and tumble living. Push a lifestyle away from middle-of-the-road and toward extremes, and one is forced to face both sets of extremes. With the sweet comes the sour. Artistic talent, ego-quenching attention garnered from performing before audiences, and the free pass that delivers one out of the humdrum, soul-killing elements of the average workaday life come with their own set of dangers. When rules and regulations are removed, anything goes—and the fate of the artists, who have chosen to join the circus, the bandwagon, the medicine show, is at the mercy of their own consciences, their own free wills, and those of the others around them. It is of utmost importance not to succumb to the downfalls of pleasure-seeking.

"Daniel and the Sacred Harp" is a song with biblically charged lyrics that also manage to serve as an allegory for the journey from anonymity to success. It opens and closes with an identical verse that addresses Daniel directly, asking him permission to handle and examine his sacred harp. Two characters, Daniel and the objective storyteller (sung by Richard Manuel and Levon Helm, respectively), carry the song from its start to its finish.

The storyteller sings of his surprise at Daniel having received the harp at all. Daniel explains how, since he was not related to the familial line by which the harp was passed down, he had to pay for it with silver and wait for its arrival for three years "from the sea of Galilee." The man who brought it to him intended to ask Daniel for something in return, but Daniel ran off before he could hear what it was, saying, "Take what you may need." He didn't care what it was.

"But the price that Daniel had really paid, he did not even know." What does selling one's soul for success imply? What—precisely—is sacrificed in the transaction? What would have been present in a person before such a transaction, the absence of which evidences the loss of the soul? Compassion, maybe. More likely, such an allegory seems to be a description by other jealous, green-eyed watchers-on who feel in the depths of their beings that "no one could be *that* good, *that* talented, *that* successful—because I'm not." Daniel, or whoever the subject, must be cheating or lying; he must have stolen his talent from something or someone. Such achievement couldn't possibly belong to *that guy*. Not honorably or innocently so.

Daniel even asks his brother for help, but the brother only jests at him, intensely excited about how "Old Daniel's gonna land in jail." One can almost picture the brother rubbing his hands together in satisfaction, wild-eyed, laughing in triumph. It seems biblically fitting, as "no prophet is accepted in the prophet's hometown."[4] As a person, or a band, climbs ladders to successes, it sometimes seems that bystanders of varying degrees of intimacy to the subject are waiting to witness failure. "See?" they crave to point out, "you still are that little kid I knew, no better than I am. You're not that special." Daniel's father at least offers some wisdom: "Son you've given in, you know you won your harp, but you lost in sin." There it is, an "Ask Dad, he knows!" kernel of wisdom. But to what has Daniel given in? To what have The Band given in? What are the core problematic beliefs of the successful person?

Perhaps he feels that he can do whatever he wants *because* he has been successful. This includes acting for himself and himself alone at the risk of hurting those around him, those he loves. It includes, too, missing out on the potential joys of living a more balanced everyday life, the kind of joys that come from basking in the light of consistent and mild jobs well done and having been disciplined enough to achieve something in a steady, reliable, and sober manner. It includes not being present for other people, not present enough to help them. It includes betraying friends and lovers, putting his own needs above those of his counterparts. It includes citing talent and success as reasons for being allowed to behave at his own whims more than others might. It includes having succumbed to the ego monster that squats inside all of us, having waited its whole existence to assume total control over its corresponding self, just needing the appropriate amount of evidence of recognized success to take over.

The song concludes with a bookend of the opening verse, taking the listener back to where he began. But not before Daniel steals away to be alone, to play his harp for his own enjoyment, the way most artists begin their relationship with the appropriate tool of trade. Now, however, Daniel casts no shadow. His true and original self is lost, and he belongs only to his musicality.

"Stage Fright," the album's title track, is the most sincere and true-to-life track on the entire record. As songwriter, Robertson is able to encapsulate and explain the human weakness of insecurity in a mere few minutes. He uses the character of the stage performer, a character close to home for the entire band (here sung by Danko) as a metaphor for life. Robertson himself fell victim to stage fright at The Band's debut Fillmore West concert in 1969, at which point a hypnotist was brought in to help him perform the show, despite the malady. It worked.

Performance anxiety, the subject of which makes multiple appearances amidst the entire album, takes the center ring in "Stage Fright." From the opening lines, the listener is faced head-on with the idea of individual guilt and the role that it plays in a person's journey to success. Robertson targets its source right back to childhood: "Now deep in the heart of a lonely kid, who suffered so much for what he did." What did he do, exactly? It doesn't quite matter, for the feeling is the same. It is enough for the audience to know that, at least once, the individual did something as a kid theoretically worth suffering for. The magnitude of the act matters not; instead, it is the feeling of guilt, here tied with loneliness—as though the loneliness is a byproduct of the subject's mistake—that's up for consideration.

Via "Stage Fright" one gets the sense that the scared children within all of us have much more control over how we feel and react in life than we'd like to admit. The "lonely kid" in question has not been the same since he was given "his fortune and fame." He has been changed by it, and not necessarily for the better. But the inner resistance, or refusal to feel worthy of his success, remains steadfast. The song's protagonist visits a doctor about his condition, who only assures him that he should be fine, as long as he doesn't come clean about who he really is, as long as he doesn't let the lonely kid out to play. The song's protagonist can't let his full-on fear show to the rest of the world, to the audience. To do so would reveal his mortality, his imperfection. The audience would know that he doesn't really know any more truths than they do; he is just skilled at pretending he does.

The most terrifying moment of "Stage Fright," which falls in line with the deal-with-the-devil tale of "Daniel and the Sacred Harp," is the middle eight of the song. The lyrics urge the listener to take the boy's fear seriously and explain how he got to this moment: "For the price the poor boy has paid, he gets to sing just like a bird." When phrased in just this way, the trade of one's soul for performative talent assumes ludicrous proportions. Was it worth it, we wonder?

The line "fancy people go drifting by" serves up another taunt for the stage-frightened to question his own validity and artistic worth. Will these people see through the singer's act—through The Band's act? Not to say that The Band's act is false, but it is performative out of necessity. The musical artist must incorporate a certain amount of theatrics in order to recreate his music for the public, but the very act of performing possesses a degree of falseness. Art is not regular life; it stands apart from it. It's special by definition, and so are the artists who produce it. They are not regular. They do not fit in with mainstream society.

"When we get to the end, he wants to start all over again," the song's chorus insists. One's life is a performance, with a beginning, middle, and end. One's life is, in part, a long struggle with fear and its imposed limitations on success, worthiness, and the scope of enjoyment. "Please don't make him stop . . . let him start all over again," the track concludes. Songs are inextricably linked with time, and "Stage Fright" is no different; when the song ends, all we desire is to play it again, from the beginning.

"The Rumor" concludes *Stage Fright* in an unsettling attempt to achieve some kind of peace. Whether or not the attempt succeeds is left up to the listener to decide. The whining guitar and piano intro, with its notes of unease, bring us into the song's tale. Lyrics form a direct warning to explain what the rumor is—small town talk, up for distortion to anyone who grabs at it. Beware, the lines seem to urge, of falsified stories with the capacity to turn one's opinions of people or events inside out. Gossip is dangerous. The more in the spotlight one is, the more in the spotlight The Band are—which, after two well-received albums, they were—the greater the risk of being a target for false rumors, or for helping to bring The Band's success to the ground. "The Rumor," more than anything, makes palpable The Band's fear of losing their place on top, of being called out for the lonely kids they are and sent back to where they started out, to anonymity.

"Big men, little men turned into dust," we are reminded. The Band "didn't mean to ruin no one," and call upon the merciless bystanders to relate to their humanity and vulnerability before condemning it. Let the sinless take the lead in throwing rocks forth. Though success and talent have lifted The Band above the masses, thus placing the members at a more accessible level for attack, The Band are still human. The members, "big men," will still "turn into dust," just like the "little men" of the audience. "For whether this rumor will prove true or false, you can forgive or you can regret, but he will never ever forget." Who is "he" in this scenario? He certainly exudes omniscience. It may be God, the silent witnessing universe at large, or the individual's true self, the everpresent, conscience-drenched version who tallies every good and ill done to us and done by us.

"Close your eyes . . . let it (the fog) roll away," the chorus instructs us, "open up your arms and feel the good, it's a-comin', a brand new day." The words come across as a line of wishful thinking, with an indeterminate amount of possibility. A person can open up his arms, and the next day will come, but unless changes are implemented in his lifestyle and outlook, how brand new will it be? Now that The Band have "made it," artistically and commercially, after their first two albums, how much more good can come? And even if it comes, *do* The Band deserve to feel it? These are the kinds of questions that can only be answered by the subject alone, in front of a mirror. These are the kinds of questions that require courage and curiosity to even ask. No matter what the results are, no matter how tentative the brand-new-day bits of "The Rumor" are, they do shell out echoes of hope. Despite the gnawing doubts, the lyrics in their written certainty remain. They're here still.

Notes

1. Greil Marcus, "Rock-a-hula Clarified," *Creem*, (June 1971).
2. Ibid.
3. Traffic, "Memories of a Rock N' Rolla," *When the Eagle Flies*, Island Records, 1974.
4. Luke 4:24.

Chapter 6

CHASING THE MUSIC

The Sacred and Profane in The Band's Early Years

JEFFREY SCHOLES

John Burks, in his 1970 review of The Band's third album *Stage Fright* for *Rolling Stone* magazine, asked three emphatic times, "is this The Band's 'religious album'"? He's referring to the biblical imagery and religious themes in the songs on *Stage Fright*; language that is not as easily detectable in the two preceding albums, *Music from the Big Pink* and *The Band*, released in the two preceding years (it's Nazareth, Pennsylvania, for the record). Yet Burks, in his enlightening, rambling, possibly drug-influenced—it was the *Rolling Stone* in 1970 after all—review doesn't let his repeated rhetorical question get in the way of his auditory canal. "Glory is the operative word at this stage of the game. What this third Band record seems to lack is the glory of the first two."[1] Burks is right and wrong about *Stage Fright*. It does lack the glory that he and other countless fans had come to expect from The Band based on their first two offerings. But *Music from Big Pink* and *The Band* and not *Stage Fright* are their most religious albums, and this is one reason why the 1970 album lacked the glory of what came before.

The difference musically was not noticed by Burks alone. Drummer Levon Helm recalls, "*Stage Fright* was when everything changed for us. It was an immense turning point, something that was obvious to anyone who bought and played the record."[2] While *Stage Fright* gained higher chart position sales-wise than *Music from Big Pink* and *The Band*, the album signaled a downward slide on which The Band was never able to gain footing. *The Last Waltz*, a documentary film of The Band's final concert, performed a mere six years after *Stage Fright*, was masterful and triumphant but was also the last gasp of a dying band dredging up the good old days rather than their current material. Many legitimate reasons for the decline have been proffered by critics, biographers, fans, and band members themselves, which range from heroin use to the fame to the money that led to battling egos. Distinct, though related, as these explanations are, they are all symptoms of a single cause: the breakdown of The Band's social unit that worked concomitantly with a distancing from their sacred object: their music.

In this essay that leans heavily on Emile Durkheim's concept of the sacred and the profane, I argue that the music being made for the first two albums possessed a sacred quality for The Band—a quality that began to fade a little before the writing and production of their third album, *Stage Fright*. The sacred and profane character of their music was not imputed to it from a divine source or from some transcendent plane. Rather, its sacredness or lack of it was nothing other than the felt power of how the collective members of The Band did their music and then sent it back to the fans as something "extra-ordinary," as Durkheim would put it. As such, despite a preponderance of religious lyrics in the third album, the first two are the *real* religious albums as they reflect the symbiotic relationship between a close-knit group and the sacred music that it made.

The Band's status as a backing ensemble for Ronnie Hawkins (then briefly under Levon's lead) and then for Bob Dylan for the previous seven years built them into supremely talented musicians, but the frenetic schedule that moved them through big cities, while exciting, became perfunctory and alienating. After Dylan's motorcycle accident ended their travelling temporarily, The Band moved into Big Pink, the secluded house near Woodstock, New York, in 1967. It acted as a kind of monastery where, in Durkheimian fashion, their collective of "all equals" produced an aura that seeped into the music produced there. And if you will, the "totem," the transcendent, sacred object that bound them to their house and to each other, was the music. Touring and the fame that followed altered the way in which they approached their music, and as they slowly moved out of Big Pink and back into a more profane environment, their "collective effervescence" gave way to individualism and selfishness that is reflected in the music they subsequently made.

RELIGION AND MUSIC

Before digging into the support for this claim, a few notes on my approach are necessary for clarification. Many of the scholarly analyses of the relationship between religion and popular music focus on the effects of music on its audience. Music performs a religious function, however defined, and therefore may have a religious dimension. As an example, Robin Sylvan lays out several levels (physiological, psychological, sociocultural, semiological, virtual, ritual, and spiritual) on which music operates religiously in this way. In each of these musical compositions is the phenomenon that registers in the listener and generates an experience. On the "ritual level," all previous levels that facilitate the "transformation of experience" are concretized and structured by music's own ritualistic content to evoke a religious sensibility par excellence. Sylvan's final and most important level, the spiritual, draws on Rudolph Otto's notion of the numinous to argue that music can tap into the spiritual realm and serve as a "revelation of it."[3]

Sylvan's work throws my approach to music, in particular the music of The Band, into contrasting relief in two ways. One, I rely on the production of the music, not its reception, for my evidence of a relation between music and religion. Two, Sylvan's attribution of a spiritual dimension to music comes close to a kind of essentialism—that music has a spiritual essence to it that explains its effects—a position that I reject.

There is no unchanging spiritual core in music (even Gregorian chants or The Band's music) or in any cultural expression or practice. Or when the scholar investigates popular culture, religion is never "found." Rather religion sometimes participates in the interchange of economic, political, social, and geographical forces that work together to produce cultural artifacts. The scholar's task, then, is to observe these artifacts and ask whether religious concepts, beliefs, practices, or worldviews are factors in expressing them in a certain way. In this vein and as Durkheim argues, the "sacred" is built by humans as is the "profane." And lest we are tempted to demand that the divine be actually present to sacrilize spaces and times, Gary Laderman reminds us that that the sacred "is a force to be reckoned with in almost any social situation, even though it cannot be reduced to one essence, like God, or identified by one standard of measurement, like adherence to the Bible."[4]

Following J. Z. Smith and other scholars of religion, Jason C. Bivins similarly resists locating a spiritual essence in music but asks us to "imagine" the religion that relates to jazz music. If "religions sit at the intersection of a wide range of human activities both imaginative and embodied," then the production and product of music must be a place where religions sit.[5] And as I will attempt with a particular era of The Band, Bivins does so with the data of American jazz. "Underlying testimonies of the musicians and the evidence of their practice (communities, performances, compositions), there is an overarching concern with perception, performance, experience, and identity, often construed religiously."[6] Moreover, and related to The Band as a small community and their Big Pink house, "communities bound together not by institutional ties and affiliation with conventional sites of worship, but by more diffuse sacred bonds that shape identity, provide orientation in a larger cosmic frame, and infuse moral sentiments and sensibilities in a larger group" help create religion in this day and age.[7]

One more qualification is merited. There most certainly is a subjective element at play with the assessment of music, as is in all judgments related to aesthetics. Some, no doubt, see little drop off in the quality of The Band's early music; some may hold that the first two albums weren't all that great. Some, myself included, hold that they discovered some of that old magic on their 1975 album *Northern Lights—Southern Cross*. So subjective valuation is inescapable in my own argument. Though not up for debate is that it was The Band's first two albums that put them on the Woodstock stage in August of 1969 and on the cover of *Time* magazine in early 1970.

MUSIC AS SACRED TOTEM

The Durkheimian description of the sacred and the profane, while problematic[8] and not a perfect fit for my purposes,[9] puts forth a helpful conceptual scheme. He writes, "In one world he languidly carries on his daily life; the other is one that he cannot enter without abruptly entering into relationship with extraordinary powers that excite him to the point of frenzy. The first is the profane world and the second, the world of sacred things."[10] These powers are projected and centered on the totem, but it is the totemistic principle that generates the power. The totemistic principle is that the totem gains its power from the group that reveres it, or the reverence for the totem, which *seems* utterly external, is really just reverence for the group itself. "Religious force is none other than the feeling that the collectivity inspires in its members, but projected outside the minds that experience them and objectified. To become objectified, it fixes on a thing that thereby becomes sacred; any object can play this role."[11] And the object's sacredness is maintained because of the collective, equal imputation. "Imputing the emotions to the image is all the more natural because, being common to the group, they can only be related to a thing that is equally common to all."[12]

For the members of The Band (the Hawks until 1968), the sacred attribution to their music occurred concomitantly with their gelling as a group of equal partners. Under Hawkins's leadership (and thumb), the Hawks learned their musical chops as well as how to be professional musicians. Their music, while felt strongly, was primarily technical. It served as a means to make them better technical musicians. Their voluntary break from Ronnie was not only about him "treating the band like shit," but also about the Hawks needing to try their own music because, as guitarist Robbie Robertson thought at the time, "How you gonna stop this train?"

Under Dylan, their solidarity as a band began to take shape around the music that they were making. In fact, they proved to be a solid unit before they joined up with Dylan as they refused to play with him unless Bob took all the members on. True, the Hawks were playing Dylan's songs on stage. But because Dylan was such a massive star, invisibility and anonymity was part and parcel of playing behind him in the mid-1960s. The Hawks were playing Dylan's new, electrified music, which was despised by the folk purists that had come to see Dylan as their high priest. Every night was a battle against the crowd, and Robbie, Garth, Rick, Richard, and Levon began to forge a protective trench around themselves.[13] As Robertson conveys, "It felt good to have our own little army together on the front lines."[14]

Dylan's motorcycle accident in the summer of 1966 forced an immediate retreat from the battlefield. Their general led the Hawks to the Catskills, where they licked their wounds in the basement of Big Pink. Once Dylan recovered, he joined them in the mountains less as a leader and more as a catalyst. "There was a real family feeling between Bob and the Hawks up in the Catskills," Robertson recollects. "He was a very special friend and co-conspirator. We were already survivors from our year of living dangerously on one of the craziest tours in history. Now we had our feet back on the ground and sanity reigned."[15] With Bob and without Bob, the Hawks began to find their own groove apart from the road.

> The move to Big Pink meant, amongst other things, that the Hawks could finally stop running. They could look around and decide what they (not Ronnie Hawkins or Bob Dylan) wanted to do. Dylan kept them on retainer which allowed the group to exist without financial concerns. Levon Helm remembers this moment. "It was the first time in our lives where we had a chance to relax. We'd been on the road nonstop for six years at that point, and for the first time we didn't have to play joints to stay alive anymore . . . Going to Woodstock felt like going home."[16]

In addition, the absence of a clear leader left a vacuum that was organically filled by The Band's members as a unit. Helped by the fact that each were superlatively talented, were all able to play multiple instruments, and that three, not one, shared the lead-vocals role, the Hawks had the enviable problem of everyone being leader, so that no one was. Eric Clapton, no stranger to dysfunctional band dynamics, noticed this immediately when he visited The Band at Big Pink.

I envied the fact that they had that kind of fellowship and brotherhood that went back obviously a long way. I didn't really know what the dynamics of it were at the time. It was quite mysterious about who was the boss. It seemed to shift. It depended on who you were talking to. I mean I thought, when I first met Robbie, that Robbie was the leader of The Band. And then once you hung with them, for a little while, you sensed that there was another kind of power structure going on and that Levon originally had been the leader of The Band and still, in some sense, was the leader of The Band. And then it depended on from there it kind of went to whoever was singing at the time as to who was the leader of The Band. And who was leading on what kind of level. Rick was the leader in having fun. There were all kinds of dynamics going on.[17]

Notably, there was very little drinking of alcohol and no speed—staples in their touring days—going on during their writing and recording sessions at Big Pink. They cooked their own meals and had a house dog named Hamlet. In "The Last Waltz," Hudson fondly reminisced about the quotidian tasks done to keep a home: "That was just a part of a lifestyle that we got to love in Woodstock. You know, we got to like it, you know being able to chop wood or hit your thumb with a hammer. We'd be concerned with fixing the tape recorder and fixing the screen door, you know, and stuff like that. And getting the songs together."[18] They had recording equipment at the house which meant that Big Pink was a self-contained, self-sustaining compound for them. "Living so communally, like in the days of Big Pink, helped pass the ideas around," Helm remembers, "and with the studio right there we were always experimenting, without any deadlines or worrying about the engineer's overtime."[19] And most importantly, they didn't tour or play live for an audience for almost three years. Isolated from the outside world but insulated with the heat from their own creativity, they lived in a kind of cocoon. Helm again: "We wanted *Music from Big Pink* to sound like nothing anyone else was doing. This was our music, honed in isolation from the radio and contemporary trends, liberated from the world of the bars and the climate of the Dylan tours."[20]

They quickly found that in order to play music, they all had to be in a circle so that each could see each other. When they finally went to a New York City studio to make their first album and were asked how they wanted it to sound, The Band, as they were now known, replied, "Just like it did in the basement."[21] Up on the seventh floor of the midtown Manhattan studios of A&R, they required that the engineer's standard requirement that all musicians play and sing isolated from each other be scrapped. They couldn't even play without the interaction!²² Sure, each were individuals and brought their unique personality and ability to The Band, but as much as another rock band of that era and since, The Band played as a true unit during these years.

For their second album, much of the material was written at Big Pink but was finalized in a house in Los Angeles. Not quite the isolated edifice that stood in the woods of upstate New York, but Sammy Davis Jr.'s previous house, which, again, The Band had to themselves. "We had hardly any interaction with the LA music scene and, indeed, rarely saw anyone at all. When a writer from Look magazine showed up near the end of the month, he told us the neighbors were whispering about the grouchy, bearded mountaineers who had taken over Sammy Davis's house. Some kind of cult, maybe."²³ Deliberately sequestered from a country that was undergoing nothing less than the war in Vietnam, the civil rights movement, and the rise of the counterculture that permanently changed America, The Band were able to block off much of the noise that could distract them from the sole task of making *their* music.

How, though, was their music at this time sacred? Helm puts it this way: "Instead of touring, our creative energies went into making this record. It was the way we ordered our lives. We wanted to *chase that music* [italics mine]. We were a self-contained unit."²⁴ It seemed as if the music was separated from them, waiting to be caught—a transcendent sacred that could only be engaged on the immanent plane when The Band moved toward it as a unified front. And when they caught it in the form of a lyric, a chord progression, a solo, a gong, or an album, they didn't exhaust it as more music was always running ahead of them.

They chased and often caught the music, and once secured, however tenuously, that music deployed its power back on the group. "We discovered the songs themselves dictated who would sing and who would play the supporting roles. That was the real pleasure we got out of playing as a group."²⁵ There are two significant parts to this quote by Helm. One, instead of one or more band members or an engineer/producer directing the arrangements, as is the case in most bands, the music told them who would do what. Again, the double-edged sacred item stands outside, leading the players while being created by those players. Two, because music mediated their writing and recording, and no individual could stand out or take undue credit, they experienced true joy or perhaps a form of collective effervescence.

THE DARKNESS

If "lighten" is a word that describes the joyous music making of *Music from Big Pink* and *The Band*, then Robbie Robertson's description of what came next was apt. Helm recalls that Robertson referred to "the *Stage Fright* era as 'The Darkness,' by which he means this period of addiction and dissolution. But I remember that the drugs were just part of the black mood that settled upon us. There were also the issues of artistic control of The Band and the direction we were going in—if any."[26] As is so common in bands who gain quick success, the money and the fame began to get in the way of the pursuit of the common good. This is certainly true of The Band, but blaming self-interest in the form of reckless drug use is too facile. As Helm's recounting indicates, "The Darkness" was caused by the breakdown or "dissolution" of their social unit. Binge drinking by Manuel, pill popping by Danko, and heroin use by Helm didn't help keep them together, admittedly. But other dissolving forces were also at work.

Several members got married and started having children in the late 1960s, which competed with the "family unit" of The Band. After the Woodstock festival, the wooded space that they cherished as remote and unknown was over. Hippies flocked to the area and merchants set up shop there for years to come. Expensive cars were bought by all of the members of The Band. This enabled individual mobility (and multiple car crashes) away from Big Pink. A centrifugal force was further applied with The Band finally going on the road to tour in 1969. No less significant is the jettisoning of a surrogate family member—their producer, frequent guest at Big Pink, and even musical contributor, John Simon, in favor of themselves as producers and the very green engineer Todd Rundgren for *Stage Fright*. Or perhaps The Band simply ran out of gas, as music journalist Don Ignacio surmises:

> They weren't even trying for something of that caliber, since they're both so difficult to top. They're human beings, after all, and they didn't have the energy. . . . According to some reports, they didn't even have enough energy to cope with the amount of popularity they were getting at this point. *Stage Fright* consists of straightforward rock music with exceptional instrumentals, but not-so-exceptional melodies. . . . And that's not to say the melodies are bad, they're just flat sometimes. And the atmospheres aren't so thick and charismatic.[27]

But according to the two most prominent members of The Band, Robbie Robertson and Levon Helm, their competing explanations for the decline, while different, both corroborate a diminishment of their shared sacred, the music. Robertson solely blames drug use and the personal irresponsibility that accompanied it in Helm, Danko, and Manuel for the deterioration in the music—a regression that he alone was trying to stem. Robertson recalls,

"At one time, there was talk that if you wanted to play like the angels, you had to dance with the devil—that heroin was a gateway to music supremacy. That myth was yesterday, but the power of addiction was still in full force. It hit me hard that in a band like ours, if we weren't operating on all cylinders, it threw the whole machine off course. This was the first time that writing songs was painful for me."[28] When Helm purportedly lied to Robertson about his heroin use, "things changed in that moment" for the latter. Robertson further recalls what led to their final break up later in the mid-1970s with a particularly poignant reflection.

> Somewhere in the middle of this storm, even with my own shortcomings, I felt a hand tap me on the shoulder, reminding me to tread lightly and try to protect my brothers. I kept harping to Levon, to Richard and Rick, about finding some kind of sanctuary where we could stop riding so close to the edge. At times we lamented, and other times we rejoiced. But somewhere along the way we had lost our unity and our passion to reach higher. Self-destructiveness had become the power that ruled us. How does that happen? Where did that demon come from? Were we too blind to see?[29]

Alternatively, and expectedly, Helm downplayed the drug use and played up Robertson's deliberate and disrespectful positioning of himself as The Band's leader. It was the opportunistic Robertson plus The Band's (and Dylan's) hard-driving manager, Albert Grossman, who pushed for a hurried release of *Stage Fright*, according to Helm. The Band's appearance on the cover of *Time* magazine in January of 1970 helped speed things along, as Helm recalls. "With just ten songs and running a little over thirty-six minutes, *Stage Fright* reflected the haste to get it to marker to capitalize on our post–*Time* notoriety."[30] In his review of *Stage Fright* in *Rolling Stone*, Burks's comments that the album makes it sound like "the team hasn't had much of a warm-up" before recording. Haste unfortunately makes waste as they were not "allowed" to be meticulous about their music as they had been in times past. "It takes a while to polish a record, but by the time of *Stage Fright* the pendulum had swung, and we were forced to put the polishing rag away. The days when we would *live* with the music were over."[31] Instead the music had become a temporary boarder in The Band's ever-growing house.

Further adding to the social dissolution of The Band, as Helm saw it, was the emergence of a leader when one was not needed. Helm was primarily angry over who was getting the songwriting credits (and therefore the money afterwards). Robertson claimed sole credit on most of the songs—songs that

Helm knew he and others contributed to substantially. In a documentary about his life, Helm heatedly proclaims, "On that third Band record, it was pretty much over. It was obviously a goddamn screw-job. The credits and the money and everything was all screwed up." And once money matters fell solely to Robertson and Grossman, they only gave the fans what they wanted instead of listening to their own desires. "After that, it was 'The Band plays your favorites,' 'The Band live somewhere,' because we couldn't get in there and collaborate anymore. It lasted about five years, but it was over after that second record."[32]

Once the music had become a means to end such as money-making and fame and not an (*the*) end in itself, the center could not hold. When the music was the sacred brass ring, each knew that all had to be leaders and followers in equal shares, otherwise the product would suffer. The minimal drug use during the making of the first two albums not only sealed the members of The Band more closely but also suggests the reverence that they had for the music and its production. The loss of the sacred quality of the music was coextensive with their social bonds weakening, whether through self-indulgence or hierarchy. Robertson's and Helm's respective explanations scapegoat the other so that the pain associated with the group ending is mitigated. But both are unwittingly bearing witness to their music slowly shifting from the sacred to the profane along with the weakening of the ties that bound them together.

As Burks points out, *Stage Fright* contains more explicit references to religion than do the previous two albums combined. But the sacred and amount of religious language may have nothing to do with each other. And in the case of The Band's first three albums, the two are actually in an inverse relationship. The collective effervescence infused throughout *Music from Big Pink* and *The Band* emerged in the form of the staggered, almost sloppy chorus of voices on songs such as "The Weight" and "Jawbone." We hear a jazz-like ensemble in songs like "We Can Talk" and "Rag Mama Rag" where instruments come in and out based on feel rather than on preplanned structure. The social bonding drives the music, and the music reinforces their bonds. With *Stage Fright*, on the other hand, gone are the syncopated harmonies and interweaving instrumentalization.

I conclude with a comparison of the lyrics of "To Kingdom Come" off of *Music from Big Pink* and "Daniel and the Sacred Harp" off of *Stage Fright*, both written by Robertson.[33] The eschatological title of "To Kingdom Come" suggests a cosmic apocalypse, and some of the lyrics gesture towards a foreboding end. But Robertson never directly theologizes but opts for glancing blows, metaphysical hints, biblical intimations of the end times.

Instead of a hellfire and brimstone warning replete with frightening (and banal) images from the book of Revelation, we get a kind of Calvinistic uncertainty about election mixed with a resignation to the authority of karma. Shopworn threats about what happens to those who disobey are traded for a more complex picture of one's fate. There is no need to fear the end when there's "Nothing we can do." Then again, the golden object of God's ire is also staring you in the face. The ambiguity of the eschaton and where we fit in is captured perfectly here.

We find a similar attempt at ambiguity over the state of one's soul in "Daniel and the Sacred Harp," but the effort largely falls flat. Allusions to the biblical Daniel and a harp (no mention of Daniel having a harp in the Bible, but this one comes from the Sea of Galilee) are mapped onto a well-tread Faustian narrative of selling something of value for musical prowess. But instead of addressing the troubling concept of sacrifice whereby one's soul is given in exchange for musical ability, Robertson opts for Daniel merely stealing the harp. With no sacred quid pro quo, the religiosity of the song is reduced to a sin that Daniel committed and its hinted-at wages. Absent in "Daniel" is the mystery of the human condition in the context of ultimate judgment that is present in "To Kingdom Come." While cautious of overstating the difference in the lyrics, I hope to have conveyed that when the sacred music is no longer chased by The Band, the polishing rag is indeed put away, and attempts at capturing the sacred again only come off as the thinly veiled profane.

Notes

1. John Burks, "The Band: Stage Fright," *Rolling Stone*, September 17, 1970.

2. Helm, *This Wheel's on Fire*, 208.

3. Robin Sylvan, *Traces of the Spirit: The Religious Dimensions of Popular Music*, New York: NYU Press, 2002, 40.

4. Gary Laderman, *Sacred Matters: Celebrity Worship, Sexual Ecstasies, the Living Dead, and Other Signs of Religious Life in the United States*, New York, New Press, 2009, xvi.

5. Jason C. Bivins, *Spirits Rejoice! Jazz and American Religion*, New York, Oxford University Press, 2015, 7.

6. Ibid., 8.

7. Laderman, xvii.

8. See Lynn Hunt, "The Sacred and the French Revolution," in Jeffrey Alexander (ed.), *Durkheimian Sociology, Cultural Studies*, Cambridge: Cambridge University Press, 1988, 25–43.

9. Durkheim studied aboriginal tribes in Australia in the early 1900s who used animals and plants as their totems, not musical groups for whom the music was sacred.

10. Emile Durkheim, *The Elementary Forms of Religious Life*, trans. Karen E. Fields, New York: Free Press, 1995, 220.

11. Durkheim, *The Elementary Forms of Religious Life*, 230.

12. Ibid., 222.

13. During the tour, Helm, after being the lead man in the Hawks before joining Dylan, left the group citing his dislike of the music that they were playing in addition to his having to move from the front seat to the back seat once again. He rejoined them at Big Pink a year later.

14. Robertson, *Testimony*, 183.

15. Ibid., 272.

16. Helm, *Across the Great Divide*, 150; 154.

17. Gregory Hall, *The Band*, TH Entertainment, 1995.

18. Neil Minturn, *The Last Waltz of The Band*, Hilldale, NY: Pendragon Press, 2005, 87.

19. Helm, *Across the Great Divide*, 184–85.

20. Helm, *Across the Great Divide*, 187.

21. Ibid., 209.

22. Robertson, *Testimony*, 297.

23. Helm, *Across the Great Divide*, 187.

24. Helm, *Across the Great Divide*, 184–85.

25. Ibid., 187.

26. Helm, *Across the Great Divide*, 209.

27. Don Ignacio, "Stage Fright (1970)," accessed online July 18, 2017: http://donignacio.com/music/bandpage.html.

28. Robertson, *Testimony*, 364.

29. Ibid., 452–53.

30. Helm, *Across the Great Divide*, 215.

31. Ibid., 216.

32. Patrick Doyle, "Levon Helm's Last Years Captured in 'Ain't in It for My Health,'" *Rolling Stone*, April 15, 2013.

33. The complete lyrics to "To Kingdom Come" can be found here: https://genius.com/Passion-pit-to-kingdom-come-lyrics. The complete lyrics to "Daniel and the Sacred Harp" can be found here: https://genius.com/The-band-daniel-and-the-sacred-harp-lyrics.

Chapter 7

HALF PAST DEAD

Remnant Identity in The Band's America

JOSHUA COLEMAN

Despite having only one member from the American South, in the person of drummer/singer Levon Helm, The Band often capture that region in terms of themes, stories, and most important here, characters. Yet these songs easily double as American stories, the South a microcosm of many themes found all "across the great divide." The themes are as diverse as their influences—Bob Dylan, John Lee Hooker, B. B. King, Muddy Waters, and others. The Band's "style" might loosely be described as a combination of boxcar folk, blues, country and New Orleans jazz, all stirred into a pot of rock and roll. Beneath this observation lies a unique ability to create empathetic characters who have been cast out by society; and at times, as will be explored, those who have been *rejected by the rejected*, thereby achieving a personal, impactful critique of broken American structures through those very individuals. By giving close attention to their first two albums, *Music from Big Pink* and *The Band*, we find unusual types of suffering—or sufferers—who, having lost all cultural supports, have created themselves ex nihilo in the face of oppressive and misleading American metanarratives.

One who is left out of a culture that has itself been rendered broken or rejected—or who exists as an oddball within a dismissed subculture— requires that his/her identity come from a peculiar place. Simply put, one cannot lean on the cultural comforts or supports typically involved with becoming a self. The Band's ability to "let suffering speak" makes room for a particularity of character in relation to the listener, one which leaves space for the listener to help create or fill out more precisely who that character is.[1] In capturing such particularity, light is shed upon universal American problems made poignant by the character's situation. Whether it is those who suffer from continued racism—exhibited most obviously by recent instances of police brutality and the rise of white supremacist movements—or whether it is all victims of economic injustice who live revictimized by state-driven origin tales of manifest destiny (ones supported by a certain kind of religiosity), the characters create a sense of community within marginalization for the listener.

Such a person is what Franz Rosenweig referred to as the "remnant" of society, in his case a reference to the outsider status thrust upon Jews throughout much of European history. One of many factors was the inability to inherit land, one common way cultural identity has historically been passed down and absorbed to support one's individual identity. It might be the case that the remnant self is our truest, most unrepeatable identity, making possible an authentic type of communion with others by way of *their* remnant selves in the wake of being ostracized. In the words of contemporary thinker Frank Seeburger:

> [Eric] Santner comes to the insight that it is only insofar as we are all such remnants—only at that level where each of us is no more than just such a worthless, good-for-nothing, ready-for-the-junk-heap remnant—that we can be encouraged in our pure singularity, our "ipseity" as Santner calls it (following Ricouer and others), from Latin *se* for "self" (so that "ipseity" would be "it-self-ness," in effect). Our "identity" is always a matter of social construction and what Santner calls "symbolic investiture." For example, it is only through such symbolic investitures, performed through various ceremonies (such as graduation ceremonies for the awarding of academic degrees, wedding ceremonies, and registering of births) that my own identity as a philosophy professor, father, husband, etc., has been established. In contrast, my ipseity is what I am after one subtracts all my identities, all of what can be symbolically invested with any degree of social power and authority.[2]

It is this ipseity of the individual, either before, during, or after having other identity markers are stripped, which The Band often captures, all while implicitly or explicitly exposing the systems which took those identity markers away.

Though they traveled with Ronnie Hawkins as the Hawks before becoming Bob Dylan's backup band and subsequently cutting their own first record, Robbie Robertson commented, "*Music from Big Pink* represented a sharp diversion from the ex-Hawks' previous work. It was about telling a story and getting across what I was trying to write about in a song."[3] Robertson continues, "These were precise stories and emotional experiences. Discovering the soul of music was what was important, getting a song across with as much emotion as we could—that was the objective, not flailing away, and blasting the walls down."[4] He later clarifies that their pursuit of this emotional connection through "precise stories" typically included characters based on people they knew.

Communicating something universal to the listener included creating a recognizable setting, musically and lyrically, to bridge their own personal experience of those characters. This was achieved in part because the general themes, especially on the first two records, are not disconnected between songs. *The Band* worked a kind of loosely connected narrative through both albums, a somewhat novel idea at the time. Helm went as far as to say, "It's like the first two records were the same project. We had songs that didn't get finished in time to go on the first record and we had ideas—we knew the titles of some of the songs that were going to be on the second one."[5]

Perhaps more striking in terms of their departure from past norms was their placement of the slow opener on *Big Pink*, "Tears of Rage." This placement belied the accepted wisdom to begin a record with a fast tune.[6] Moreover, this particular song expressed betrayal by the very nation, which could decide the fate of *The Band* in terms of popular success (e.g., in its reference of "carrying you in our arms" and Independence Day).

Though Band member Richard Manuel claimed he didn't know what the song was about, other critics took liberties to interpret and at times overinterpret. Regardless, we have a few clear allusions in this stanza worth attending. It is at least a reference to America, and likely American ideals, or those "carried" by narratives of American independence in the country's infancy. And while "you'd throw us all aside and put us away" could be a reference to ideals of the founding fathers being trampled, they and their ideals are not the only ones "thrown away" when the notion of equality between persons is trashed. Emotionally resonant here is the painful image of the daughter rejecting her father, likely an allusion (as a few critics have noted) to Shakespeare's *King Lear*. While "the state" or "political theory" remain at one level abstractions, the pain of the broken father-daughter relation personalizes the failing to reach these ideals, a failure causing very real, personal pain for so many.

The most obvious failure might be racial inequalities and the trampling of the Declaration of Independence which nominally guarantees each "man" "the pursuit of happiness." The cruelty at the time Jefferson penned those words was that African Americans were not included because they were not seen as fully human. Yet The Band, as in many other places, do not get *this* specific, at least not in this song. At the time African Americans were overtly denied personhood, women of all races could not vote.[7] Whatever specific failure is referenced here, the song leaves open exactly who is cast aside, as there are too many options within America's broken application of its own social contract. Such an opener draws in the frustrated sufferer from many corners.[8]

As such, the opener to *Big Pink* allows a wide range of emotional resonance, without being too specific and losing the listener who will not identify. While maintaining the listener's agency to cocreate the connection and meaning, more specifics follow in later songs and paint more particular situations and characters with whom the listener can share specific types of alienation.

The second song on *Big Pink*, "To Kingdom Come," sings of a sad warning of a father to a son. Here too, it is not simply a father, but a "forefather," again, perhaps allegorizing the tragic truth of the son's plight as an individual or as a country. It would be easy to apply a few different scenarios here. The song begins in admonishment: the forefather pointing to kingdom come, telling his son to be careful and not tell a word, because it all comes back to you.

The phrase "Kingdom Come" is part of the Our Father, the most practiced of all Christian prayers. The following lines of the prayer after "Thy Kingdom Come" are "thy will be done, on earth as it is in heaven." After looking to Kingdom Come, or perhaps how things stand heavenward, the Father expresses the sad juxtaposition and reality of how things are "on earth." As a result, you better keep your head down and your mouth shut, perhaps common advice to African American youth when confronted by police. Regardless, the stark reality that requires such advice from the forefather is expressed clearly with the mention of a golden calf pointing back.

The golden calf is, of course, a biblical reference to the creation of a statue for worship by the Israelites. Critically, they refer to their own statue as "the god who took us out of Egypt," meaning Yahweh, and not a new or different god. Without going into detail, it represents a false religiosity, as they determine to use the same name and pretend allegiance to the same god, but now under their own rules and controllable terms. This seems an obvious allusion to a "Christian nation," which, despite lofty language and ideals, has no issue leaving people marginalized and worse, turning the word "Christianity" into another golden calf manipulated by the powerful to justify terrible injustices. In this case the father's advice is essentially, "Do not be yourself," as you cannot risk such a thing. The best you can do is to disappear and go unnoticed.

In somewhat of a mood reversal, the most famous, most covered song from *Big Pink* is "The Weight," even though it only reached number sixty-three in the charts, and the album itself reached a modest thirty. Many are quick to point out that the Nazareth referenced is Nazareth, Pennsylvania, yet one cannot ignore obvious double-entendres here and a few other places. In 1994, Band biographer Peter Viney wrote:

> The Weight has been painting pictures for me for nearly twenty-five years now. It's an intensely visual song, and my pictures aren't of anywhere in Pennsylvania. My Nazareth is a dusty western town sometime in the late nineteenth century—neighboring towns might be Jerusalem or Babylon . . . or Jericho. Carmen and the Devil are strutting their stuff, in red silk dresses fringed with black cat fur, along a wooden sidewalk. Chester is the town character straight out of the CBS-TV series *Gunsmoke*, which was set in Dodge City in the 1880s. Carmen might be Miss Kitty, who owned the Long Branch Saloon—a tart with a heart. Old Luke is another town character whose rockin' chair ain't going' nowhere as he puffs his pipe waiting on judgment Day. The Cannonball streams into the station, a great cow-catcher across the front—pure Americana.[9]

On one hand, Viney's western American image could fit the song, yet on another it is impossible, bordering as it does Jerusalem and Babylon. Perhaps the place exists, but only during the song and in the listener's imagination. Yet the impossibility is made possible emotionally and by way of images. Everyone in the song is asking a favor of one sort or another; whether it is a place to rest, a dog sitter, or company for Anna Lee, suggesting that such favors are part of daily life here. Viney goes on to say that his dry western town does not make sense in certain places, especially with Chester catching the narrator in the fog. Still, that is what the song brings his way.

But whether it is rolling into Nazareth to look for a bed, the reference to "Go Down Miss Moses" (*Go Down, Moses* is the name of a William Faulkner collection of loosely connected short stories), Luke and Judgment Day, Carmen and the devil, the religious references act as familiar signposts in this town's daily life, as they do all across American small towns. This is especially true for southern small-town characters, even if nothing particularly spiritual is taking place beyond requests for little favors that go unfulfilled.[10] Each character's comfort in making those requests goes to their familiarity, providing emotional substance for the listener; again, a familiarity that first includes The Band, as they knew these characters as real people.

Helm spoke of "Crazy Chester":

Crazy Chester was a guy we all knew from Fayetteville (Arkansas) who came into town on Saturdays wearing a full set of cap guns on his hips and kinda walked around town to help keep the peace. He was like Hopalong Cassidy and a friend of The Hawks. Ronnie (Hawkins) would always check with Crazy Chester to make sure there wasn't any trouble around town, and Chester would reassure him that everything was peaceable and not to worry, because he was on the case.[11]

Much like a character in a Faulkner tale, Chester created an unusual self; perhaps crazy, perhaps comical, and probably both at once. What is important is that this recognizable setting (whether western or southern or something else) allows Chester to exist in his radical, if not absurd individuation, and this seems to follow for every other oddball about town. The sort of freedom for a character to create his strange self and be known and accepted provides a cathartic, emotional freedom for the listener, grounded by the familiar religious language that is at the least recognizable, and for some holds a level of hope and acceptance not often found "down here."[12]

Yet in another reversal, The Band's next song from *Big Pink*, "We Can Talk About It," is far more specific in terms of the African American plight, slavery, and by implication the continued systemic racism and battle for equal rights over the last three hundred and fifty years. The content is made clear later in the song, with references to pulling the eternal plough, finding a sharper blade (or making a new one), and direct mention of "no need to slave" and the "whip in the grave."

The song's very title references the psychological difficulty of talking about any traumatic situation, made especially true when the reflection includes some responsibility for the trauma. We find this today when people claim that America is "post-racial" despite the somewhat obvious rise (or continuation?) of white supremacist groups. In fact, the narrator hits on a common American fear of talking about cultural failures in the first stanza. To speak objectively about American failures is often seen as a sort of disrespect, be it to a flag or to an idea a flag represents. Suddenly, for many, you are less American when you wish to discuss failures honestly. In his work *Anti-Semite and Jew*, French thinker Jean-Paul Sartre pointed out the strange silence surrounding the dawning horror that so many French Jews had gone missing and not returned after the war. Non-Jews would not speak of it even while the depth of the tragedy had become obvious. The resistance to speak of collective trauma, especially one where I may be partly the cause, typically leads to a continued deepening of the trauma, sometimes over three hundred and fifty years. Later in the song, the narrator laments about holding to something under our tongues and a preference to being burned in Canada rather than freeze in the South.

The psychology of denial, in this case, is held physically (even if metaphorically). Just one song after "The Weight," in which The Band capture a kind of quaint and, for some, small southern-like setting, resides the dark brutality beneath such romanticization and what can insidiously aid its continuance. As will be increasingly clear, The Band are able to convey a sympathetic character in all settings, even if the setting itself has at times made possible some of the worst injustices that remain the focus of these two albums.

"Lonesome Suzie" tells of a character "always losing," who "sits and cries and shakes." Without giving the listener too much to understand her situation, it seems that this is part of the problem, that the narrator is left helpless, "wondering what to do." It is not simply that Suzie has been traumatized, but the one who cares about her—and it seems that few have, as she is just "hoping for a friend"—seems paralyzed.

We get a glimpse of the empathetic narrator trying to think of something, anything, at one point saying he might have "a friend to lend" and that "anyone who's felt that bad might know what to say." The profound grasp of empathy which arises from suffering, and especially the awareness of the narrator that he has not suffered enough to know what to say, is still potentially helpful to the one who *has* felt that bad. He does not turn away and, more effectively, does not pretend to grasp what he cannot. Knowing his limitations, expressing them while saying he "cannot overlook her" is perhaps the most empathetic thing he can do. All of this is set within the ambience of Garth Hudson's Sunday-morning church organ.

He even understands that Suzie "might just get mad" at the one who *is* able to relate to her situation, a complex emotional response to serious trauma, the potential disappointment that someone else *can* relate when one might simply wish to disappear. And yet, "She might be better off that way"; or she might be better off expressing anger as part of her healing than being stuck in limbo shaking like a leaf. She resembles one in a space without a self, or that her sense of self has been crushed and she is unable to move. At a certain point the narrator becomes worn down by it all, entering her loneliness to declare, "Why don't we get together? What else can we do?"

We gain a clear image of a suffering woman, but the listener is left to fill in the gaps, invariably reflecting upon his or her own suffering and ability to empathize. The subjectivity and imagination of the listener is required, making Suzie's plight potentially very different for different listeners. While this song does not have much of a story or setting beyond these two people, nor does it speak of the "issues" found in a few preceding ones, Suzie is another outcast, perhaps as a result of the failed ideals sung about elsewhere. At one level, we get a more complete picture of the desperate narrator trying to help in a situation beyond his abilities.

This song is another example of The Band's ability—within the same album—to move from universal ideas to particular people. Yet even with the latter, they allow a diversity of interpretation in terms of what happened while conveying relatable, psychological insight to a situation between a friend and one who suffers.

After beginning the album with "Tears of Rage" and "To Kingdom Come," The Band close *Big Pink* with Bob Dylan's "I Shall Be Released," a hopeful, quasireligious bellowing of a sufferer (perhaps prisoner) who can see his day of liberation and himself "somewhere high above this wall." An album that began with the failure to live up to American ideals ends with an individual having seen a sign for legitimate hope. Once again, not much is known beyond the fact that he, like every man, "needs protection" and "must fall."

As with "Lonesome Suzie," this character is both specific and vague at once, allowing a diverse array of listeners to identify and participate in the meaning. Ultimately, even within the need for liberation from social oppression and the cruelty of nominal ideals, resides the possibility of intimacy, whether asking a favor in Nazareth or merely sitting with a friend. This portion of the narrative ends with the day of liberation in sight.

THE BAND: *THE BAND*

On their second LP, The Band continue zeroing in on American settings in order to give emotional resonance to universal themes. According to Robbie Robertson,

> This record could have been called America. It was thematically such a mirror, so many things that we knew from somewhere, some story, or somebody telling us something. Even if we were talking of a certain place, and something very American, it did have a universal quality to it.[13]

Music journalist Greil Marcus had this to say:

> The album felt like a passport back to America for people who had become so estranged from their own country that they felt like

foreigners even when they were in it. It made people think, "Yes, the Civil War is part of me. Yes, a time when people worked on farms and were destroyed by bad weather, when they were vulnerable to things, this is part of me."[14]

By beginning this record with "Across the Great Divide," one gets the sense that American darkness has been shed. It is now time to pick your plot, settle down, raise a family, and have a grand old time. After grabbing your pistol and telling your woman to "understand your man the best you can," the second stanza belts out that imperative "across the great divide," to grab your hat, take a ride, get a bride, and bring the children to the riverside.

Thematically flipping from the start of *Big Pink*, this is American romanticism at its finest. As from "The Weight," one gets the picture of quaint family picnics on the western frontier with nary a care in the world. But as with "The Weight," there is much more to come, hidden beneath the song's rosy picture.

The most famous song from *The Band*, "The Night They Drove Old Dixie Down," might be interpreted as a romanticization of the South and the southerner, the phrase "Old Dixie" conjuring something positive and laudable without its obvious sins. Still, The Band achieve the feat of deep empathy toward the narrator despite the obvious fact that the South fought for (at least in part) white supremacist values.

The focus of the song is one who bewails the loss of a noble agrarian simplicity handed down by his family. Virgil, the storyteller poet, gives an idea of who he is straight away: Virgil Kane served on the Danville Train until Stoneman's calvary came; in the winter of '65, just barely alive; May the tenth, Richmond had fell, it's a time he remembers well.

Virgil farmed like his father, having a crucial part of his identity passed down between the work and the land itself. After seeing his brother killed, he watches the North return to decimate the means to their family sustenance and any semblance of his inherited identity.

We must not lose sight that the vast majority of southern farmers had no slaves and did not farm cotton. Most were sustenance farmers for their own families and small communities. As such, Virgil is one who likely had no interaction with plantation owners and their operations. More than this, the post-Reconstruction South was made in the image of the North, with new technology that would eventually obliterate the lifestyle of small farm living.[15] This sped up commercial farming toward what would eventually become the megafarm phenomena, as former small farmers were forced to become tenant farmers and often into cotton farming for the first time. This particular southerner, while not a slave, did suffer oppression in the sense that two of his identity markers—the work and the land—not to mention his brother, were all destroyed.[16]

Along these lines, author and philosopher Walker Percy once remarked that the South had so many writers because it had experienced a "fall," a reference to this post–Civil War destruction—the burning of Atlanta, tearing up of rails, etc.—until the situation of the Deep South had the quality of aftermath. This theme, art as a response to a "fall" and (despite all the religious talk) the lingering of a largely absent but occasionally ghostlike religious presence through overused religious language, created a vacuum in which cultural outsiders were forced into a self-creation without the luxury of inheriting any portion of their name. Nowhere is this more obvious than the case of slaves themselves. Forbidden from learning to read, slaves were left to create an identity out of nothing and with few tools for doing so. This was made all the more complicated by the spiritual reliance on biblical narratives of escape from slavery while the majority of slave owners were nominally Christian.

Virgil, on the other hand, previously enjoyed this security, knowing who he was, working the land like his father before him, etc. He describes this life as one in which you "take what you need and leave the rest," singing what sounds like a community moral value, as you cannot horde food for the future like stock options. The emotional resonance involves a sincerity amidst his loss of identity, on top of the obvious material suffering all around. It is precisely this identity loss that allows a deep identification for the listener, even some hundred and fifty years later. Many can relate to the material suffering, many cannot. But far more people can connect emotionally to this identity loss, even if the listener's identity loss does not come from a family's living being taken by outside forces. While there is no resolution to Virgil's existential plight, one can only imagine having to create a new identity within this sudden void. Keeping Percy in mind, whoever he becomes moving forward will require an artistic, imaginative response to a fallen identity. The response must occur in the despair and limbo space of loss.

Following the plight of Virgil Kane, The Band pirouette once more with their lusty, upbeat ballad "Up on Cripple Creek," a song about a trucker who gleefully sings of his on-again/off-again woman somewhere in Lake Charles Louisiana, who is "a drunkard's dream." Ralph Gleason writes:

> It is a salty, sexy, earthy (rather than funky) ballad. . . . Levon's chuckle towards the end is surely the nastiest, dirtiest, evilest sexual snort in the history of the phonograph record, and again the rhythmic tension

created between the interplay of the bass and drums and the line of the voice sets up a tremendously moving pulse.[17]

While the song is celebratory in tone, even this is a daydream from one lonely on the road. There is an obvious sexual tension, but the sexual surface is made shamelessly powerful by the narrator's deeper existential need to connect from living off the road. This explosive revelry, even if only within a lonely man's imagination, is surely cathartic for any listener who ever felt lonely or sought for an evening some "shelter from the storm." Robertson comments:

> Up on Cripple Creek is somehow an extension of American mythology. We're not dealing with people at the top of the ladder, but the people in that house out there in that field. What does this person think, with one light on upstairs, and that truck parked out there? That's who I'm curious about—the story of this person, as he drives trucks across the whole country, and the characters that he drops in on in his travels—just following him, with a camera, is really what this song's all about.[18]

In response to the cliché that history is told by the winners, The Band repeatedly return to stories told by those who are not typically allowed their say.

From one type of loneliness to another, "Rockin' Chair" strikes a deeper emotional chord. Completely different in tone from "Cripple Creek," "Rockin' Chair" is a poignant reflection of an old man, his friend, and his beloved home, "old Virginny." Each song is a response to loneliness, but the latter is about going home with a longstanding best friend, knowing that "going home" in a larger sense lay just up the road.

As with "Lonesome Suzie" and "Cripple Creek," "Rockin' Chair" seems to be a departure from any "issues" per se, while still giving voice to the depth of two friends sharing their late stage of life. The simplicity of having a best friend, returning to Virginia as homeland and a rocking chair, puts immediate perspective on what remains important to them and to what their lasting identity markers are. Whatever they've experienced in their long lives, the friendship, a sense of place, and a view from a chair create the space for them to be their truest selves. This song provides a deep breath for the listener, as the narrator here seems satisfied with what he has.

Still, this exhale does not last long. Without tracking the whole record, "The Unfaithful Servant" is thematically important for our purposes. Having little to do with the New Testament parable of the same name, the song is less about an admonition to a servant than a sad goodbye. There has been an offense against the lady of the house, and according to Pat Brennan, there was a Robertson songbook that claims the master is bidding goodbye to a female servant with whom he's had an affair. While there is no direct evidence the setting takes place in the gothic South (much less the Civil War era), such projections are conceivable and likely intentional. Robertson spoke in a few places of his love of Faulkner and Tennessee Williams, among others.

Regardless of where and when, if Brennan is correct about the intended meaning, it could just as easily be called "Unfaithful Master." What strikes home is that the servant is the one who must take the blame, and the sad master must enforce a regrettable punishment by sending her away. Not only does she take the blame, but she also does so for a relationship based on unequal power, a common theme found among America's founders and their slaves. Still, as in other places, it is not clear enough to know if she is a slave, or even that the servant is necessarily female. While there is no structure being criticized that is specific to America, a few are implicitly present depending upon interpretation.

Finally, *The Band* concludes with "King Harvest Has Surely Come," a closing song of either hope or desperation, as the autumn weather must come through for the farmer without any guarantees. Robertson said, "There's a lot of people that the idea of come Autumn, come Fall, that's when life begins. It is not the Springtime where we kinda think it begins. It is the Fall, because the harvests come in."[19] The romantic beginning of the record, "Across the Great Divide," shows itself fraught with tenuous reliance, not only on weather but also on the need for union protections, both of which play important roles in the song. In short, after a terrible season and a barn "up in smoke," the farmer signs on with the union and thinks he will certainly "come out on top."

Of course, while the early days of unions were necessary to safeguard basic rights, Robertson points out that it is not long before things get messy and unions are overrun by gangsters. But the farmer is convinced of his safety net, as he has no issue paying union dues as long as "you don't judge me by my shoes." Expressing an invincible belief that he will prosper, he is, in reality, a poor man being taken for a ride on all sides, even singing lines of respect for his boss who "hands me down my pay." He is painfully confident that his boss, the union, and the weather will all do right by him, with the listener feeling just as sure none of this might happen. At one level a funky tune of hope, it leaves a deep, sad pit in your gut not found in the idealism of the album's outset.

Throughout The Band's first two albums, *Music from Big Pink* and *The Band*, we find loosely connected themes that paint a complex, impressionist picture of American characters and stories. Perhaps marked most clearly by "King Harvest," a continual theme is the sad delusion that we are simply not what we think we are, whether as a country or as a farmer reliant on the union and his boss. And whether the removal of this delusion is yet to come in "King Harvest," or whether it has already occurred as in "The Night They Drove Old Dixie Down," in each case a new self must arise from the ashes of broken beliefs and ideals. This movement between universal American issues to particular characters affected by them marks one of the more unique contributions in music history. By remaining character driven, there is never a preachy tone, allowing the listener to feel a personal plight rather than presented a didactic lesson. Keeping Percy's words in mind, The Band achieve art as a response to a fall, keeping the open-ended nature of the response continually before the listener's mind.

Notes

1. Frankfurt School theorist, Theodor Adorno once said, "The need to let suffering speak is the condition of all truth." *Negative Dialectics*, 1966, trans. E. B. Ashton, New York: Seabury Press, 1973.
2. Frank Seeburger, *The Open Wound: Trauma, Identity and Community*, CreateSpace Independent Publishing Platform, 2012, 259.
3. Harris, Craig. *The Band: Pioneers of Americana*, Rowman and Littlefield: New York, 2014, 91.
4. Ibid.
5. Ibid., 93.
6. This song was written by Dylan and originally recorded with him on *The Basement Tapes*, a version not released for decades, but which was widely bootlegged in the 1970s.
7. One can argue well that full personhood has still not been granted. But at this time it was not even nominally guaranteed.
8. While "America" is never said in this song, Robertson said this album could have been called "America" in terms of their motivation to paint a picture of the country not typically seen (e.g., see https://www.thedailybeast.com/robbie-robertson-on-the-bands-music-from-big-pink-at-50-it-sounds-like-the-band-i-remember).
9. Harris, *The Band*, 87.
10. *Go Down, Moses* is a collection of related, yet independent, short stories—not unlike *Big Pink* and *The Band* as albums.
11. Harris, *The Band*, 87.
12. Flannery O'Connor was asked why she wrote about so many "freaks" in her stories. She responded, at least in the South we acknowledge them for who they are. Flannery O'Connor, "Some Aspects of the Grotesque in Southern Fiction," 1960.
13. Harris, *The Band*, 94.
14. Harris, *The Band*, 94.
15. The positive impact was that this forced the large plantations to divide.

16. In the New Testament, it is significant that Christ befriends Matthew, a tax-collector. Tax-collectors were typically presented as corrupt and hated by most. The outsider is not merely the poor or the prostitute, but even one of pure heart within a corrupt system, and may be only seen as part of that system from the outside.

17. Harris, *The Band*, 100.

18. Harris, *The Band*, 100.

19. *Classic Albums: The Band*. Video. Rhino/Wea: UK 1997.

Chapter 8

ENTANGLEMENT AND SAINTHOOD

Carrying "The Weight" across the Endless Highway

GEORGE PLASKETES

> "The Weight" is as fine an example of rock and roll record making as existed in the year of its birth and it has dated not a whit.
> —DAVE MARSH[1]

With a group membership that was disproportionally four-fifths Royal Canadian, one-part Arkansian raconteur, The Band embodied the essence of North(ern) Americana. Their songs—rustic and ragged, elegiac and enigmatic, ethereal and evocative, cinematic and simple—consistently conveyed a celebratory sense of world weariness with a front porch, backwoods, churchy sound that evoked echoes of places in the past. Perhaps no song sequence from their rich, rootsy, ragtimey rotation better resonates that spirit than the progression that initiates the majestic 4:35 parable of "The Weight": A stately tickling guitar, followed by resolved drum beats that preface the lead lyric—"I pulled into Nazareth / Was feeling 'bout half past dead"—announced by Levon Helm, "the only drummer who can make you cry."[2] As The Band's most recognizable song from a catalog of gems that includes "Up on Cripple Creek," "Life is a Carnival," "The Night They Drove Old Dixie Down," "Chest Fever," "It Makes No Difference," "The Weight" perseveres with prominence and pervasiveness as a standard, a signature and signpost of the era.

The totality of "The Weight"—its dense, uncanny musical meld of folk, rock, country, and gospel; the visuality and vocal structure; lyric abstractions with literary and religious allusions; and a cast of characters—Crazy Chester, old Luke waiting on the judgement day, Carmen and the Devil, Jack the dog, Fannie (Annie?), Miss Moses, Anna Lee—have unfolded into an enduring, expanding, eminent mythology. As prelude, when Capitol Records sent out a blank-label acetate of The Band's debut, *Music from Big Pink* (1968), to press and radio sources, everyone assumed "The Weight" was "the Dylan song" on the album. "The Band fooled everyone except themselves," said Helm.[3] And "The Weight" almost bamboozled The Band. The song was an afterthought for *Big Pink*. Robertson recalled the group's initial thinking was that the song didn't have a complicated chord progression and was "just kind of traditional, so we'll cut it when we get stuck for a song."[4] Once the song was recorded, their mindset changed to, "Gee, it's kind of effective when you hear it back at you like that."[5] "The Weight" went from a throwaway to album single and centerpiece that bridged sides one and two of The Band's arresting, event-like debut. The *Big Pink* long play contained no lyric sheet or group photo with any ID, including on the album cover, which featured a Bob Dylan painting of five musicians, a roadie, a tree, and an elephant to color his musical imprint inside. Ironically, manager Albert Grossman and Ronnie Hawkins felt it was becoming "vital for The Band to distance itself somewhat from Dylan without losing the value of the connection."[6] Dylan had offered to play and sing backing vocals on *Big Pink*, though Robertson politely declined.

"The Weight" continues its lineage across an Endless Highway, carrying its composition, arrangement, and rehearsal from the basement of an art colony hideaway in the Catskills west of the Hudson River in upstate New York to epic, iconic festivals and farewells, from Woodstock to a Winterland waltz; thru vistas, versions, and a variety of venues; in studios, on screens and stages; in recordings, performances, placements; adaptations and advertisements over the past half century. Along the way, the song has attracted considerable conversation, contemplation, and interpretation.

Not only has "The Weight" enticed reflective writing from an esteemed core of music and culture critics and chroniclers—among them, Dave Marsh, Greil Marcus, Chet Flippo, Barney Hoskyns, Jay Cocks—but also Bandphiles and others have obsessively considered the song, expressing their points of view with postings at outposts across internet sites, in forum threads and on blogs. While "The Weight" may not have a book-length treatment devoted solely to the song itself, such as Marsh's *Louie Louie* (1993) or Marcus's *Like a Rolling Stone* (2005), author, aficionado, and self-appointed Band archivist Peter Viney offset any hard or softcover page shortcomings by establishing a compulsively comprehensive curatorial website dedicated exclusively to "The Weight."[7] The resourceful site evolved out of an article on "The Weight" that Viney wrote for the 1990s Band fanzine, *Jawbone*, published in the UK.[8]

"ALL I COULD THINK OF AT THE TIME": THE IMPOSSIBILITY OF SAINTHOOD

> I just wrote it. It's just one of those things. I thought of a couple of words that led to a couple more, and the next thing you know I wrote the song.
> —ROBBIE ROBERTSON ON WRITING "THE WEIGHT"[9]

Despite the anthemic attributes of "The Weight," fifty years of familiarity, and a fervent following that generates a lively lyric forum, there is an enigmatic, elusive nature that continues to mark the song's chronology. The song's composer, Robbie Robertson, has shaded the mystery with an astute and aloof manner that is evenly inadvertent and intentional. By his own admission, Robertson "has a funny attitude to words," which includes sneering at printing song lyrics on album sleeves. "I learned all the words to Little Richard's songs the best I could and what I couldn't figure out didn't matter," states Robertson, sounding downright dismissive, if not defiant.[10] Robertson's principled objection—"Is my diction that bad?"—has contributed to ongoing weighing of the verses. Among the most haunting phrases to fanalysts: "off/of Fannie?" (the "f" in "off" running into the "A" in "Annie" has proved problematic; "fix my rack (or rat or rag?)"; "Carmen (or karma?) and the Devil?" "Caught me in the 'fall' or 'fog?'"

Robertson's discerning indifference and aura-enhancing posturing waver between his providing glimpses of virtuosity and shrugs of nebulous nonchalance when addressing, or not addressing, the song's lyrics, origins, and meanings. At the insightful end of the response spectrum is an interview published in the British music magazine *Vox* (October 1991), as it began its second year of publication, in which Robertson loftily contextualizes his writing "The Weight" as experimenting with and reinventing a North American mythology using his "connection to the universal language."[11] That dialect refers to a hypothetical and historical mystical means of communication intended to be understood by all living beings.

Preceding this perspective by a few years is an excerpt from a Robertson interview with Rob Bowman printed in the liner notes of the thirty-one-song double album *To Kingdom Come: The Definitive Collection* (Capitol, 1989). A portion of that interview was subsequently recycled in The Band anthology of eighteen *Greatest Hits* (Capitol, 2000), a streamlined paradoxical package just in case the declared "definitive" collection from eleven years earlier or the three-disc box set *Across the Great Divide* (Capitol, 1994) were not somehow "ultimate" or comprehensive enough. The cinematic citation is striking in its sophistication and specificity. Robertson's refined rumination frames the song's narrative as a contemplation on "the impossibility of sainthood," a theme inspired by Spanish surrealist filmmaker Luis Buñuel, whose works explore hypocrisies of religion, patriarchy, and middleclass culture. Count Band mate Helm a true believer and Robertson acolyte, offering "amen" affirmation to his "struggles of sainthood" premise, "I've sung that song enough times to agree with him."[12] Robertson reads "The Weight" as analogous with the iconoclast Buñuel's works such as *Nazarin* (1959), centered around a dedicated priest, a knife-wielding prostitute, and her psychotic sister, and *Viridinia* (1961). Robertson was drawn to films such as Buñuel's "that had these religious connotations . . . but it wasn't necessarily a religious meaning."[13] Buñuel's narratives depicted crises of faith, superstition, jealousy, violence, and "people trying to be good . . . trying to do their thing."[14] At one point in *Nazarin*, the suicidal, psychotic Beatriz reaches out to Nazario, the cursed priest who is trying to do good but whose well-intentioned efforts only stir constant trouble. She offers to take Nazario's burdens: "If I can carry your load on my back, I will."[15] Robertson's film-to-songwriting correlation takes a conversational course:

> In "The Weight" it was this very simple thing. Someone says, "Listen, would you do me this favor? When you get there will you say 'hello' to somebody or will you give somebody this or pick up one of these for me? Oh? You're going to Nazareth, that's where the Martin guitar factory is. Do me a favor when you're there." This is what it's all about. So the guy goes and one thing leads to another and it's like "Holy Shit, what's this turned into? I've only come here to say 'hello' for somebody and I've got myself in this incredible predicament." It was very Buñuelish to me at the time.[16]

In prosaic contrast to that particularly poetic passage, and apparently absolved from the benefit of additional decades of reflection, Robertson's memoir, *Testimony* (2016), is songwriting-source scant. Perhaps conscious of not wanting to echo his previous commentaries, The Band's principal songwriter fills in few blanks, and is seemingly content to allow interpretations and inside jokes to continue to run their critical course in free-for-all forums, without providing clarification of the persistent lyric puzzles. Throughout *Testimony*, Robertson's reflections on his song craft are more restrained than they are revealing. Case in point: while setting up in the studio to record "The Weight," producer John Simon's captivation and curiosity with the lyrics compelled him to ask Robertson, "Where did you come up with this?" Robertson's response was conspicuously meager and mundane, a counter to his usual charismatic presence in print and person: "I'm not good at explaining song lyrics, but basically, it was all I could think of at the time."[17] The generic tone lingers, devoid of detail: "As a songwriter, 'The Weight' was something I had been working up to for years. I just heard what I was looking for. The images, the stories, I had been putting away in my imagination's attic, had been brought out into the light."[18]

Robertson's accounts of "The Weight" studio sessions and the song's production elements, particularly its staggered vocal structure, are considerably more illuminating than his discreet detailing of the writing process and lyric denotations. And with good reason, as the vocal and instrumental components are central to its allure. Robertson conveys the song's delicate performance within the unconventional studio recording setup—The Band in a circle arrangement with eye-to-eye contact—utilizing low-quality mics. And chief engineer Phil Ramone's repeated, "That's fucking incredible," with finger-wagging praise at the songwriter upon listening to "The Weight."[19]

The song's conspicuous communal vocals were carefully constructed into an adroit thread that heightens the song's splendor. Following Robertson's lead lick on acoustic guitar, characterized by Bowman as "part Curtis Mayfield and part country," Helm's drum, and Hudson's honky-tonk piano in the key of A advance into Levon at the helm of the lead vocal for the first three verses.[20] The following fourth verse belongs to Rick Danko. Robertson thought it would be interesting to have Danko's "down to earth sound" narrate the "Crazy Chester" stanza. "It might have seemed random at first but when we ran it down it sounded unexpected and refreshing," explained Robertson.[21] Helm and Manual share the final verse ("Catch the cannonball . . . "), with Manuel's splendid falsetto "turnaround melody," at Roberston's request, providing a chorus crescendo.

The mutual method, described by critic Dave Marsh as "harmonies passed around like live grenades," produce elegant eruptions between the vocal trinity, with songwriter Robertson not among the chorus.[22] Ascending "aaaands" cascade seamlessly from Helm to Danko to Manuel, then crown into Helm's lone "you put the load," which arrives at a triumvirate of majestic mingling, "you put the load, you put the load right on me." Marsh was not alone in taking note of The Band's vocal virtuosities highlighted in "The Weight." The salient taking-turn technique struck a chord across the critical continuum. In his eloquent liner notes for The Band's box set *Across the Great Divide* (1994), Chet Flippo writes that the group began to develop a curious, telepathic-like phenomenon as they worked on the songs at Big Pink:

Although they never discussed it, they began to work so closely together that sometimes one would finish another's vocal line or another's instrumental lick, and to answer each other in a call and response. It was as if telepathy were whipping around in a closed circle. The singers began unconsciously developing complex ripple leads, rotating leads, and using novelistic approach of shifting points of view, and having alternating narrators bounce the storyline from character to character. They also quickly learned to achieve balance among themselves volume-wise as well as harmony-wise.[23]

THE LORE OF THE LYRICAL LOAD: "ANYONE'S ENTANGLEMENT"

> So, the story is revealed, and concealed, in flashes, dreams, pieces of unresolved incident, rumbles of doubt exiting through a joke.
> —GREIL MARCUS[24]

> You could ask those guys [The Band] what the song was about and they'd say. "We don't know." I guess they didn't want to go through a long explanation. My brother said, "Mavis, I know what the song is about. This song is about *drugs.*"
> —MAVIS STAPLES[25]

Producer John Simon's initial intrigue with the lyrics before the song was recorded lies at the forefront of the emblematic, enduring fascination with the song's compound meanings. Counter to Robertson's admirable aims to reinvent, experiment and connect mythology and the universal language through the song's narrative, common comprehension of the lyrics is limited. Interpretations abound, in factual fiction and fictional fact; in religious and literary abstractions, analogies and allusions, from the Old and New Testaments to William Faulkner; in setting and circumstance, landscapes and locations that stretch from the Deep South to Appalachia to the Wild West to Dylan's "Desolation Row"; and in critical curiosities and conversations seeking to identify the quirky cast of characters and to elucidate "the load" and "the weight."

The song's evocative parable path is established immediately as the first phrase pulls into a "Nazareth," at once presenting possibilities of place between the holy land setting in the Arab capital of Israel and the Pennsylvania town located eleven miles north of Bethlehem, and home to C. F. Martin & Company, manufacturers of legendary Martin guitars. The company, established in New York in 1833, settled in Nazareth six years later. Critic Jay Cocks's *Time* magazine (January 12, 1970) cover feature on The Band magnified the song's mythos into the mainstream, reading the opening stanza's familiar no-room-at-the-inn narrative as a "mock-serious" meeting between a Bible character and road weary Band member hoping to find a bed. "It was a little off handed," said Robertson of the locality of the lead lyric.[26] "Well I don't know if the Nazareth that Jesus came from is the kind of place you pull into, but I do know that you pull into Nazareth, Pennsylvania. I didn't mean to take sacred precious things and turn them into humor."[27]

Sense of place is central to Robertson's songwriting. He is clearly comfortable playing with time and locale. In 1987, he stated that in his mind, there is "this mythical place in America where *the storyteller* lives, and he tells stories based on this place and the people who have passed though. I've never been there, but we all know it's there."[28] Among his excellent adventures are "Up on Cripple Creek," which leaps from the late 1850s to circa the 1940s or 1950s, relocating a mountain man character from the foot of Pike's Peak during Colorado's gold rush to Lake Charles, Louisiana, watching Spike Jones on the box. "In a typical Robertson lyric, a century or so of chronological time is abruptly made to collapse between us and an event," observes Clive James in his in-depth analysis of Robertson's songwriting and his use of language in a 1972 article in the rock and roll monthly *Creem*.[29] "Suddenly we are involved in it, hearing the contemporary voices, seeing things happen. And a crucial part of the strategy is that the event tends to remain uninterpreted: we might be given a dramatic interchange between two partially specified characters, or an unbroken monologue from some onlooker to an occurrence of which the details are clear but the pattern incomplete, and from this we try to sort out what is going on, unaided by any logical commentary."[30]

The surreal twin Nazareth setting established in opening may be the song's most decipherable riddle. The verses that follow are less resolved, inviting widespread interpretations that have continually captivated, been rumor-rampant, and accumulated varying degrees of adhesion in the analytical sphere. A standard, symbolic, and surface reading of "the weight" suggests, among other things: a universally human dilemma, or something heavy, maybe a temptation, guilt, a burden or bearing a responsibility; life's toll that may leave a person's "bag sinkin' low," or a predicament—in this case, a sleep deprived weary traveler finding a place to lay his head. In (Greil) Marcusian summation, "the weight," in all its complexity and emotion, is "some combination of love, debt, fear and guilt—a perfect image of anyone's entanglement."[31]

Among the more unusually common translations is that the "the load" is code for "the clap," slang for the sexually transmitted disease gonorrhea. The well-known chorus—"Take a load off Fannie / take a load for free . . . and you put the load right on me"—can be decoded disparately as resting or carrying a condition or an affliction, such as contracting and disseminating an STD. In this mildly graphic inference, "fanny" is situated between two usages—the American and Canadian slang slant as "buttocks," and the British euphemism aligning taboo as "female genitalia." In further support of the carnal premise, Viney's comprehensive compilation of correspondence and commentary mentions a Canadian source who implies that the song's subtext may be as much based in bordello, blowjob, and heartbreaker boys in The Band as it is biblical, pointing to "Go down Miss Moses / there's nothin' you can say." The personal possibilities are predictably linked to the endless procession of young groupies and nightly party life on the road, resulting in "Band babies" that were spitting images of group members.

Perhaps the verse's most frequent folklore hovers around The Band's involvement with notorious groupie Cathy Evelyn Smith, who connected with the Hawks-turned-Band in 1963 in Ontario when she was sixteen. Smith got pregnant while traveling with The Band; the baby's paternity was undetermined. By most accounts, Smith was in love with Helm and was certain that he was the father, though she ended up with Richard Manuel, who offered to share the burden of the pregnancy predicament.[32] Smith later achieved infamy for her presence at the Chateau Marmont on Sunset Boulevard in Los Angeles on March 5, 1982, where she administered a fatal heroin and cocaine "speedball" to comedian/actor John Belushi, one of *Saturday Night Live*'s seven original cast members from the mid-1970s. The Smith story may be more alluded to than it is literally linked to explaining "the load" or "The Weight," though it contains certain surreal Buñuel qualities of human dilemma that defies a clear good/bad dichotomy.

Further contextualized, the "go down Moses" line is literary. In addition to being an African American spiritual describing book of Exodus events, *Go Down, Moses* (1942) is the title of a William Faulkner short story, the most concise and concluding story of a work of seven related fiction pieces compiled in a collection considered to be an episodic novel. The central character in the small-town southern short story, Lucas Beauchamp ("old Luke?"), is an African American, whose grandson is on death row awaiting execution. Robertson may not have been deliberately referencing Faulkner, or other literary echoes such as those of Carson McCullers (as Hoskyns suggests), but the southern accent and atmosphere, not to mention characters, are patently present, underscored by the black and white blend of gospel and country in the sound.

In addition to the clap construing chorus, the "load" and/or "weight" have been commonly considered drug related, with the literal-dope view elicited by words and phrases located in or out of context, such as "fix" and "my bag is sinking low" (also construed as scrotal droop). The expanded phrase "fix my rack" (also heard as "rag" and "rat") has attracted interpretations that include references to a pickup-truck gun rack and nickname for a Chevy block engine to bunk beds in barracks or aboard ships, to an obscure slang meaning "knock your teeth out."

The final verse, "Catch the cannonball / now take me down the line," conveys multiple transport translations across various terrains. From the spiritual to a dark vision of a phantom train as a means of escape from "a nightmare-circus place" (Daniel), to a more palpable western Americana, railroad image of the traditional streamliner, cowcatcher plow and all, with a soundtrack to the rickety rhythm of the tracks from the late nineteenth century American folk tune "The Wabash Cannonball," a mythical train rolling along the Great Rock Island Route. Recorded in 1929, and released three years later by the Carter Family, the song became Roy Acuff's signature tune, and is estimated to have sold more than ten million copies following its release in 1936. Johnny Cash, Boxcar Willie, and Bing Crosby are among other artists who caught the Cannonball into the recording studio. The traditional hobo train tune is the oldest song on the Rock and Roll Hall of Fame's "500 Songs That Shaped Rock and Roll" list. A far more esoteric, yet plausible connection links the lyric with the late 1950s British-Canadian (syndicated in the US) episodic thirty-minute television drama *Cannonball*. "The Weight" worthy central storyline of the TV series is driven by two truckers hauling loads of cargo across Canada and the US.

The procession of characters in "The Weight" has also stirred steady and lively identity crises and commentary. On behalf of his Bandmates, Levon Helm asserts in his biography that the song is "full of our favorite characters." According to Helm, Luke was Jimmy Ray Paulman of the Hawks; "Young Anna Lee" and "Crazy Chester" were fellow Arkansasians—Anna Lee Williams (Amsden), the subject of the song "Anna Lee" on Helm's solo record, *Dirt Farmer* (2007), was from Helm hometown Turkey Scratch, and Chester hailed from Fayetteville. A friend of Ronnie Hawkins, Chester was particularly colorful, and lived up to his "crazy" prefix, coming into town on Saturdays wearing a full set of cap guns on his hips and a toupee on his head, walking around to help keep the peace.[33] Helm likened Chester to the fictional cowboy hero Hopalong Cassidy, a character created by Clarence E. Mulford in 1904 and presented in popular short stories, novels, and western movies. Hopalong Cassidy also capably conjures the limping deputy Chester Goode (Dennis Weaver), Dodge City lawman Marshall Matt Dillon's (James Arness) trusty sidekick on the long-running television western series *Gunsmoke* (CBS; 1955–1975), which evolved out of a radio serial. The Cassidy comparison, along with the Spanish name Carmen (meaning "garden"), which invokes a temptress or perhaps prostitute walking side by side with the Devil, again shifts or points "The Weight" Wild Westward.

Firsthand sketches and authentication through The Band members' "personal folklore" have not deterred lyric translators from their passionate pursuit of additional possibilities and preferred positive IDs of "The Weight" troupe. Historical and religious allusions are commonly circulated. Among the common, Miss Moses as Civil War abolitionist Harriet Tubman, Anna Lee as Mary Magdalene, and Chester as Jesus's apostle Paul on the road to Damascus. Other accounts attribute Chester's actuality to a Rick Danko neighbor in Ontario who owned a tobacco farm, and had a dog named Jack and a horse named Fannie that worked the fields, a counter view to Helm's take that Fannie "just seemed to fit the picture." Chester's dog, Jack, is often considered to be an opportune reference to Dylan's dog, Hamlet, a frequent pet presence lying on the floor during the recording sessions in the Big Pink basement.

As the lyrics linger in an endless enigmatic and entangled shroud, critic extraordinaire Greil Marcus naturally rises above the interpretive fray that unfolded. In his seminal work, Marcus downplays, without dismissing, the importance of deciphering and understanding the lyrics throughout the songs that make up *Music from Big Pink*:

> When the music is most exciting—when the guitar is fighting for space in the clatter, while voices yelp and wail as one man finishes another man's line or spins it off in a new direction—the lyrics are blind baggage and they emerge only in snatches. This is the finest rock 'n' roll tradition.[34]

Marcus locates Robertson's songwriting approach within this "older tradition," in which

> the instinct of the American artist to put his story in disguise, to tell his tale from the shadows, probably because that is where he usually finds it. Those who mean to seduce do not announce their intentions

through megaphones. On the other hand, those who are too subtle wind up laying their seductions in the mirror.[35]

VERSIONS AND VISTAS

Not only has "The Weight" become a lyrical lodestone attracting continuous deciphering and discussion, but also a rich discography of musical interpretations of the song, in recordings and live performances, has accumulated, elevating the song into modern-standard status. When "The Weight" was released as the single from the basement of the Big Pink in September 1968, The Band's original version was not alone: the cover course was instantaneous with varied interpretations along a stylistic spectrum of singles and album cuts. The Staple Singers, who, according to Helm, were the original inspiration for The Band's vocal blend, were first in line in 1968, bonding with the song's gospel footings.[36] Jackie De Shannon, notable for a string of early 1960s hits that included a cover of the Searchers "Needles and Pins," "When You Walk in the Room," and the Burt Bacharach/Hal David "What the World Needs Now Is Love," before her highest charting song in 1969, "Put A Little Love in Your Heart," reluctantly recorded "The Weight." Aware of The Band's original, De Shannon steadfastly refused to record their song. She requested that her label get confirmation that The Band were not releasing "The Weight" as a single. Given that impression and with presumed permission, De Shannon became the first of many female vocalists who recorded "The Weight." "The record's going up the chart and all of the sudden here comes The Band's single. Then Aretha Franklin's version comes out," said De Shannon.[37] "So I was at a radio station talking to the program director, and there were two other people promoting the same record outside the door."[38]

The Band's "The Weight" peaked at the modest position #63 on the US charts in 1968; it reached #35 in Canada; and climbed to #21 in Britain, where its popularity may have been somewhat influenced by the *New Musical Express* defying The Band's purported Dylan detachment by reporting that the *Big Pink* album "is said to carry on the current Dylan preoccupation with mystical country and western folks tales."[39]

De Shannon's cover eclipsed The Band's original on the US charts, placing at #55. Franklin's mighty version, accented by background vocal bursts, horns, and graced by Duane Allman's presence playing slide guitar using an empty bottle of decongestant pills, carried considerable weight, reaching #19 in March 1969, and #3 on the soul chart. The Top 20 showing remains the highest placement for any version of "The Weight." While Hoskyns labeled

Franklin's interpretation "improbable," the version recognized, tapped into, and celebrated the song's gospel and choral components that became a (Mavis) staple.[40]

Numerous soul variations followed Franklin's lead. In a collaboration featuring Diana Ross and the Supremes with the Temptations, "The Weight," as the single from their Motown duet LP *Together* (1969), reached a respectable #46. Rotary Connection, a Chicago-based psychedelic soul outfit founded by Marshall Chess, whose lineage lies with the legendary blues and rhythm and blues Chess Records label, includes "The Weight" on *Songs* (1969), a collection of covers of songs by Cream, Stevie Wonder, Otis Redding, and the Jimi Hendrix Experience. The group's experimental approach yielded a kitschy and sometimes spacey sound that may be best known for the operatic soprano of vocalist Minnie Riperton, before her short-lived solo success by way of a number one hit in 1975, "Lovin' You," which showcased the singer's glass-shattering, freaky five-octave range.

The scope of "The Weight" also encompassed instrumental, international, and live renderings clustered between the 1968–69 bracket. A pair of intriguing instrumental interpretations of "The Weight" surfaced alongside other popular songs of the era on cover-concentrated albums. Funk soul saxophonist King Curtis's version is also graced by Allman on slide guitar, alongside interpretations of "Hey Joe," "Hey Jude," "Wichita Lineman," "Games People Play," "Sing a Simple Song," "Little Green Apples," among the twelve songs on the album *Instant Groove*. The seminal surf combo the Ventures included "The Weight" among other period pieces such as "Born to Be Wild," "Sunshine of Your Love," "Down on Me," and "Light My Fire" on the album *Underground Fire*. Another instrumental rendering on *The Live Adventures of Mike Bloomfield and Al Kooper* (1969), a double album recorded at the Fillmore West, set the stage for numerous live concert versions of "The Weight" that followed on recordings by Isaac Guillory (1986), the Grateful Dead (1993), New Riders of the Purple Sage (2003), and Joe Cocker (2005). There were global entries from the Welsh group Amen Corner and the bluesy progressive outfit Spooky Tooth, featuring Gary Wright, with a version that added a touch of harmonica. Also, in the same late-1960s timeframe, and of inspirational rather than interpretive note, the Scottish band Nazareth, which formed in 1968, took its name from the opening verse of "The Weight."

The broad spectrum of cover versions that spanned soul stylings to surf sounds was indicative of the music-genre cross section inherent within "The Weight." The song has attracted an array of interpretations in genres that include folk, rock, Americana, country, jazz, blues, gospel, and New Age. A survey of the soundscape reveals prominent representation among female musicians and vocalists. From the 1970s forward, the cover chorus of women artists who followed the late 1960s first responders Staples, De Shannon, and Franklin in recording versions of "The Weight" ranged from Dionne Warwick (1972) to Shannon Curfman's (1999) blues rock; blues and jazz readings by New Orleans' sultry songstress Marva Wright (2000), followed two years later by Joan Osborne and Cassandra Wilson; Michelle Shocked's interpretation on her gospel album, *ToHeavenURide* (2007), recorded live at the Telluride Bluegrass festival; and Rickie Lee Jones's sparse and sprawling (6:33), prayerfully aching piano recitation with sporadic percussion thumps in 2013.

Country contributions include Sammi Smith's traditional reading in 1971; Deana Carter's deliberate melodic rendition on a twelve-song cover collection, *The Chain* (2007); and Lee Ann Womack's raspy, soulful Nashville version on The Band tribute album *Endless Highway* (2007), with mandolin and pump organ and vocal accompaniment from Buddy and Julie Miller. Other notable country covers feature Marty Stuart joined by the Staple Singers (1994), John Denver (2004), Canadian Aaron Pritchett (2006), and Garth Brooks, who includes "The Weight" on the "Melting Pot" sequence of his cover-abundant eight-disc box set, *Blame It All on My Roots* (2013).

The song's impressive genre breadth also encompasses folk (Hoyt Axton, 1990), Canadian jazz, blues rock (Jeff Healey, 2008), country-rock swing (Giant Sand, 1988), a New Age variation (Japanese harmonicist Koichi Matsuda, 1987), and a rap-rock-country-pop rendition by Uncle Kracker on the *My Name is Earl* (NBC) television soundtrack (2006). The Band original also aired during an episode of the situation comedy but is not included on the soundtrack album. Rock renditions include Ringo Starr and His All-Starr Band (1990); Scott McClatchy (2001), who recruited Willie Nile, the Del Lords' Scott Kempner, and the legendary Dion Di Mucci to share verses of his blue-collar, twangy take; Weezer's lazy strumming version, which appears as a bonus track on their *Red Album* (2008); Little Feat with Bela Fleck on banjo delivering a jazz-funk-country rock fusion (2008); and Thrice (2009). A number of worthy, widely circulated versions such as those by the Black Crowes live, Elle King's bluesy acoustic reading, and Panic! At the Disco's take with a strong vocal by Brendon Urie, have never been released or recorded.[41]

The song's prevalent presence between 1968 and 1969, the year of and after its release, was conspicuous beyond the charting renditions receiving radio airplay, the variety of album cuts, the soul saturation, and as The Band's tenth and closing song of their set before "half a million strong" on the third day of the nearby Woodstock Festival on Max Yasgur's dairy farm in Bethel, New York, on August 17, 1969. One month earlier, "The Weight" colored another counterculture classic, carrying its cinematic sensibility and splendor as a song visually to the silver screen in the film *Easy Rider*.

The counterculture western, directed by Dennis Hopper, features Harley-riding hippies as latter-day cowboys, Wyatt (Peter Fonda) and Billy (Hopper), in leather and fringe, with an American flag motif embossed on a jacket, helmet, and fuel tank that is holding a dope deal stash. The rebel riders are on a cross-country vision quest from Los Angeles destined for New Orleans and Mardi Gras. The travel chronicle, which includes hitchhikers, LSD tripsters, and Jack Nicholson wearing a white suit, whisky, and a leather football helmet as a joyriding passenger, is a meditation on individualism, with frontier images of new possibilities derived from drugs, sexual freedom, vague spirituality, and adventure in uncharted territory.

"The Weight" provides ideal accompaniment—lyrically, musically, visually, geographically—for the classic romantic gospel of the outcast wanderer. Roberston's opening acoustics cue with the bikers at Sacred Mountain gas station somewhere north of Flagstaff. "I pulled into . . ." begins as they pull out on their hogs, continuing into the Great Wide Open, passing the Mittens across Monument Valley, Arizona, through spectacular strata, panoramas and pueblos in pinks and grays and orange tints in the Painted Desert, locations that are film familiar from John Ford's *Stagecoach* and *The Searchers*. The 2:30 scene is lengthy by current soundtrack standards, though the time is swept up into the song and spectacular surroundings.

The desert tableau of "The Weight" is precedent-setting; in form, a polished precursor to music video, still twelve years away from its official arrival on the cable television network MTV on August 1, 1981, with its "Ladies and gentleman, rock and roll" proclamation accompanied by the Buggles "Video Killed the Radio Star." Ironically, the 1981 announcement circled to 1969, with MTV's "new frontier" allusions, accentuated by astronaut Neil Armstrong's "one small step, one giant leap" Apollo moon-mission moment analogous to *Easy Rider*'s counterculture cowboys' cross-country quest. The vivid sequence of "The Weight" in the film is archetypal, its sound and spirit imprinted within virtually every open road scene set to music since *Easy Rider*.

"The Weight" is one of the several standout soundtrack scenes that thread *Easy Rider*. The film advanced a music-visual aesthetic that was emerging in mid-1960s cinema, particularly in films with youth appeal. Influential director Richard Lester, who has been referred to as the "father/godfather/founding father/forefather of music video," set the stage with his conceptualization, conventions, and production style in the Beatles' films *A Hard Day's Night* (1964) and *Help!* (1965). *The Graduate* (1967) further anticipated use of music as an artistic statement that complemented plot and visuals. Director

Mike Nichols integrated Simon and Garfunkel songs—primarily from the duo's Grammy-winning album *Sounds of Silence*—throughout the satire as "interior monologues" within the alienated and adrift recent college graduate Benjamin Braddock played by Dustin Hoffman.

The music in *Easy Rider* is deftly placed throughout as commentary that emphasizes theme and enhances location and sense of place. From the pitch-perfect Steppenwolf songs in the opening scenes—from "The Pusher" "god damning" over an airport drug deal then seguing into the anthemic title theme, "Born to Be Wild"; to the Byrds' folk easy, wind-in-your-hair take on the Carole King-Gerry Goffin nonconformist composition "Wasn't Born to Follow," through the aerial crane shot ascending over the closing scene, a punctuation mark as the credits roll to "The Ballad of Easy Rider." 1960s folk-rock lore has it that Dylan allegedly scribbled the song's lead lyrics—"the river flows, it flows to the sea"—on a napkin that he then gave to Peter Fonda, instructing him to pass it along to Roger (then Jim) McGuinn of the Byrds, saying "He'll know what to do with it."

Ten songs from the film were compiled into the *Easy Rider* soundtrack album on Dunhill Records. The Band's "The Weight" was not included due to a licensing dispute. However, the group Smith recorded a close cover version of "The Weight" as a satisfying soundalike substitute that filled in the blank for the absent original on the album. The soundtrack reached #6 on the *Billboard* charts, earning gold status in 1970.

Easy Rider inaugurated the song's intermittent presence in film and television soundtracks that continues to the present in varying presentations and atmospheres. Among the song's range of placements are in *The Big Chill*'s (1983) Motown heavy Baby Boomer rotation; the bio-based *Patch Adams* (1998), starring Robin Williams as the Gesundheit Institute founder; and in the mental-institution setting of the psychological drama *Girl, Interrupted* (1999).

The tune's tone turns foreboding in the paranormal horror film *1408* (2007), adapted from a Stephen King short story. In the film, "The Weight" is playing in a café as Mike Enslin, a ghostbuster author whose writings document the supernatural, is going through his mail and receives an anonymous and ominous postcard depicting the Dolphin, a New York City hotel. The message warns him not to enter room 1408.

The Scottish rock group Travis's pleasantly melodic and gritty, faithful cover of "The Weight" punctuates the coming-of-age black comedy *Igby Goes Down* (2002). The closing scene of the satire is presented in music video form. There are frequent lyric literal camera shots—"no was all he said" as a person shakes his finger; "picked up my bag, I went looking for place to hide" as Igby exits—and discernable thematic conveyances of the weight and the load of family relationships, from dysfunction to redemption. The three-minute "Weight" narrative accompanies the misanthropic Igby, from a church memorial service for his mother Mimi, to a hospital visit to his schizophrenic father, to his seat on an airplane before the jet soars into the sunset sky, to the parallel ascension of the chorus line "and, and, and you put the load right on me," and a fade to black.

A few of the more recent soundtrack uses of "The Weight" are tinted in similar darker shades. There is an apocalyptic undertone in *Dawn of the Planet of the Apes* (2014), with "The Weight" playing at a gas station after the electricity is turned on following a power outage. In an episode of the Americana mythological fantasy series *American Gods* (Starz), fellatio turns fatal in a closing scene that centers "The Weight" in a sexual, comic, and tragic convergence. Laurie asks Robbie to sing along with "The Weight" chorus playing on the car radio as she performs oral sex on him, a prelude to their deadly car accident.

In lighter contrast, in the film remake of the 1970s television cop series *Starsky and Hutch* (2004), Ben Stiller and Owen Wilson trade in their Ford Gran Torino for Harley Davidsons as they adopt the Billy and Wyatt personas in an abbreviated parody of the song's desert ride scene from *Easy Rider*.

CONSPICUOUS CONTEXTS: COMEDY AND COMMERCIALS

"The Weight" continued to surface sporadically on other stages and settings, from prominent to peculiar. Among the notable venues were off-Broadway (2009) and Broadway (2010). In the Mennonite showbiz memoir *Everyday Rapture*, featuring lead Sherrie Rene Scott, who is backed by two singers called "the Mennonettes," Robertson's composition is part of a jukebox musical mix that includes Judy Garland, Johnny Mercer and Harry Warren standards, songs from the PBS children's series *Mister Rogers' Neighborhood*, and works by David Byrne and Sharon Jones and the Dap-Kings.

While the stage musical was a striking traditional production setting for the song, there were comic and advertising commercial presentations that provided equally, if not more, unexpected backdrops. In a sketch during the twentieth episode of the thirty-second season (May 19, 2007) of Lorne Michaels's supremely iconic late-night comedy variety show *Saturday Night Live* (NBC), guest host Zach Braff selects "The Weight" on the bar's jukebox. The song triggers bawdy reminisces between Braff and three drinking buddies (Will Forte, Jason Sudeikis, Bill Hader) sitting together at a table. The four friends pass around unusual and coarse life-changing memories over the song's verses, in between belting the sing-along "take a load off" chorus. Whether intended or not, the raunchy roundtable recollections in the sketch evoke the song's STD subtext, while also paying boisterous homage to its chorale qualities.

Braff's presence provided a trace of music credibility to the jukebox bar sketch. The "stuck in your head song" premise with "The Weight" marking a moment as a vital cut on a personal soundtrack was a subtle reprise to Braff's directorial debut, *Garden State* (2004). The film features a fabled scene in which Sam (Natalie Portman) hands headphones to a despondent Andrew (Braff) and swears to him that the Shins' "New Slang" would change his life. She was right, on screen and off. Braff, who had been part of the comic ensemble in the television comedy series *Scrubs* (2001–2010), was anointed an indie music arbiter as *Garden State* helped cultivate a new generation of indie-rock fans with its weepy, wistful soundtrack. Though the lightning-in-a-bottle moment was not as big a soundtrack surprise as *O Brother, Where Art Thou?* (2000) and its 7.9 million in soundtrack sales which helped to affirm the arrival of Americana as a music hybrid genre, *Garden State*'s 1.5 million copies was sizeable for a soundtrack for an independent film. The internet's growing sense of community at the time also contributed to the impact as word of the soundtrack, its songs and bands, was circulated online across boards and blogs. The *Garden State* soundtrack was considered pivotal as it represented a cool entry point to new music. Taking a cue from *Garden State*, more Hollywood films attempted to craft similar soundtrack epiphanies through emotional, epic, song-stuck-in-your-head moments buoyed by a stirring indie rock song.

The Braff and beer-drinking-buddies singalong sketch ricochets forward nine years with additional *SNL* association and "take a load off" relevance to painfully lengthy baseball championship droughts. Following the Chicago Cubs series-tying victory over the Cleveland Indians in game six of the 2016 World Series, which put the longstanding loveable loser Cubs on the brink of their first title since 1908—not to mention Cleveland not winning a championship since 1948—long suffering North Side die hards, comedian/actor/singer Bill Murray and Pearl Jam front Eddie Veddder, along with Derek Trucks, led a drunken, celebratory "take a load off" chorus of "The Weight" during a Wrigleyville house party. Documentation of the rendition was widely dispersed, accompanied by low-quality footage and audio.

"The Weight" made other rounds through the late-night television landscape via talk show host/comedians Conan O'Brien and Jimmy Fallon. In both instances, the homage overshadowed the humor. In April 2010, O'Brien embarked on the Legally Prohibited from Being Funny Tour across thirty cities, following a timeslot conflict with *The Tonight Show* (NBC) that resulted in O'Brien resigning from his position as host of the legendary late-night show in January. O'Brien and NBC reached a settlement that restricted him from appearing on television until September 2010. However, the legal agreement did not prevent O'Brien from performing before a live audience in a concert setting. The tour employed a variety-show format, veering from O'Brien's standard television structure that featured a monologue and desk interviews. "The Weight" was the showpiece of the tour's music set list, often as finale or encore. With O'Brien on guitar fronting an enhanced nine-piece house band, the group delivered a live performance of "The Weight" that was patently proficient, highlighted by verse-sharing vocals of two soulfully strong female singers. In June 2010, Conan and the Legally Prohibited Band recorded their version of "The Weight" straight to tape and pressed to vinyl (with four other songs) live at Jack White's Third Man Records in Nashville.

On February 7, 2014, Fallon ended his five-year run as host of *Late Night* (NBC), graduating to take his turn presiding over the longest-running show of its kind on any network, *The Tonight Show*, its esteemed broadcast history of hosts featuring Steve Allen, Jack Paar, Johnny Carson, Jay Leno, and Conan O'Brien. Fallon was keenly and comically aware that such showbiz goodbyes traditionally call for, if not demand, a musical send off, even if remaining in house and going to a nearby studio down the hall to step into your former show's lead-in one hour earlier. True to his precise rock-star impersonation shtick, Fallon inventively marked the momentous occasion by paralleling his *Late Night* parting with The Band's grand Winterland farewell in 1976, recreating their memorable performance of "The Weight" with the Staples Singers as presented in Scorsese's concert documentary *The Last Waltz* (1978). Fallon, who opened his finale doing Dylan, does not announce or reference The Band's concert event or the accompanying documentary film, presumably content that his audience might "get it" and recognize his *Late Night* "last waltz" connection to the rock touchstone, or simply enjoy the song. The staging, lighting, framing and the overall look and feel of the Fallon replication studiously mirrors the Scorsese production. With the Muppets sweetly and colorfully cast in chorus as The Band and the Staples, Fallon assumes the role of the late, great Levon Helm, perched in the background, steadily percussing and taking the first verse. He is then joined by Dr. Teeth and the Electric Mayhem, Animal, Bunsen and Beaker, among others, and Muppet luminaries Miss Piggy and Kermit the Frog in a celebratory singalong.

The song's familiarity enticed major advertisers to employ the song as a soundtrack for pitching products, among them, a diet soft drink, a cell phone, and a smart phone game app. By the 1990s, the soundtrack of the 1960s was commonplace across the cultural landscape, with the sellout stigma somewhat softened, though haunting. In 1994, The Band enlisted in rock's corporate ranks as "The Weight" was adapted for an ad for the American classic Coca-Cola, directed by the late Tony Scott, the prominent filmmaker whose credits include *Top Gun* (1986) starring Tom Cruise. In the opening shot of the thirty-second commercial, the lyric "I pulled into Nazareth" audibly escorts a convertible sharply sidewinding a rural street corner, kicking up dust and abruptly stopping in front of a pool hall. The woman driving gets out from behind the wheel, her hostility evident as she proceeds to throw luggage, clothing, and guy stuff presumed to belong to her now-ex. She is presumably keeping the dog that sits on the car's passenger side. Fittingly, "take a load off me" synchronizes as part of the purge as she finishes emptying the car, drives off, moves on.

Ten years and another convertible later, Cingular/AT&T wireless employed "The Weight" in a cross-country road trip narrative. In the expanded sixty-second spot, the familiar opening sequence of "The Weight" cues as a guy loads his belongings in the car and checks his phone. The camera shot shows the inbox with a text message that reads: From: Annie. GET HERE SOON. Whether sweetheart or sister, "Annie" is a lyrical nod, a nice touch and inside-out joke that playfully prods the song's Fannie/Annie loop. He sets out, from East through the Heartland headed West, with the cascading chorus "and, and, and, you put the load right one me" punctuating the coast-to-coast traveler's arrival in San Francisco and a celebratory stomp up the front steps to embrace an awaiting Annie.

The Cingular/ATT commercial in 2004 foreshadowed the lengthy CD mix montage that concludes Cameron Crowe's film *Elizabethtown* (2005) the following year. With his recently deceased father's ashes in an urn buckled up in in the passenger seat, Drew (Orlando Bloom) sets off on a ceremonial cross-country trek elaborately (and improbably) mapped out, scrap booked, and playlisted into "This Is Your Road Trip" by Claire (Kirsten Dunst). The samples that thread the lengthy sequence are a self-contained soundtrack that occupies the film's closing twenty minutes, and acts as a prelude to *Elizabethtown*'s saturated soundtrack, a rare two-separate-set compilation with volumes containing sixteen and fifteen songs, a precursor to the *Pirate Radio* (2009) double-album film soundtrack.

The omission of "The Weight" from the carefully arranged road trip rotation is mildly surprising. The song's cross-country cachet alone, not to mention its religious underpinnings, appeared a poignant and thematic fit for Drew's journey and the emotional weight of the load he was carrying.

The parallels to Igby's exit scene in *Igby Goes Down* are also palpable. Mere oversight is doubtful, considering the *Almost Famous* teen rock journalist Crowe's reverent, meticulous, curatorial approach to music as a film director. The absence or appropriateness of "The Weight" for the scene never stirred speculation across the prevalent internet sites and forums devoted to The Band, including Peter Viney's clearing house for commentary on "The Weight."

In 2014, "The Weight" received a tech upgrade in an ad for a free download of the popular mobile video game Hay Day. In a sixty-second commercial (expanded from the standard thirty seconds), Cowboy Craig Robinson enters the Hay Day farm on foot, guitar in hand, singing "The Weight." Strumming solo acoustic, he walks slowly down the lane, passing familiar farm iconography—fences, coops, a tractor, hay bales—attracting digitally animated sheep and other affable livestock and farmhands leaving their chores to fall in behind, forming a pied piper parade, rising to a solo gospel-like chorus "take a load off . . . right off me." Using a sly turn of phrase, the voice over cleverly rearranges "take a load for free" into a similar sounding tag "Download Hay Day for free."

WOODSTOCK TO WINTERLAND: A TRIUMPHANT TWO STEP WALTZ

> It was so beautiful to me . . . I've had a lot of great moments in my life and my career. But that is something where I could put my chest out and hold my head up and I can just be super proud.
> —MAVIS STAPLES, ON PERFORMING "THE WEIGHT" FOR *THE LAST WALTZ*[42]

The song's community qualities through its genre-blending, verse-sharing vocal structure and inviting singalong chorus make the song a natural for a live setting. Predictably, live performances of "The Weight" abound since the late 1960s, among them the Grateful Dead, Joe Cocker, Bruce Hornsby, and the Black Crowes. As a significant strand of interpretation, many are documented on You Tube and other internet sites. Among the memorable and frequently referenced performances are those that were presented in posthumous tributes to Levon Helm following his death in 2012, with renowned lineups taking turns on verses in typical Weight fashion. At the eulogistic appreciation of Helm during the 2012 Grammy Awards ceremony, the essential Mavis Staples, Sir Elton John, Mumford and Sons, Brittany

Howard of Alabama Shakes, and the Zac Brown Band shared "The Weight." Similarly, Bonnie Raitt, Richard Thompson, Helm's daughter Amy, Brittany Howard again, Booker T. Jones, Emmylou Harris, Sam Bush, and John Hiatt converged in verse and chorus at the 2012 Americana Awards at the Ryman in Nashville. In a solo homage, Graham Nash paid tribute to Helm via the lovely requiem "Back Home" from his album *This Path Tonight* (2016). Nash and cowriter Shane Fontayne integrate "The Weight" as a refrain—"Take a load off / take a load off / lay your burden down"—occupying the phrase within a soul-departing lexicon of lyrics that includes throughout—"the end of the journey, dust to dust, ashes to ashes, Mother Earth will soon be calling you." "Take a load off" becomes a coda that complements the chorus: "As the curtain is falling / And you sing your last song / May the circle be unbroken / As the Band plays on."

In another strand of homage and an ancillary badge of legacy, "The Weight" was adapted into a band name. The Weight, the band, is comprised of musicians and songwriters with extensive personal and musical heyday connections with The Band that run from the Midnight Rambles at the Barn, Helm's Woodstock studio, to latter-day and post-Band configurations on albums such as *Jericho* (1993) and *Jubilation* (1998), and separate side projects by Helm, Garth Hudson, and Rick Danko. Among The Weight's consistent membership is bandleader Jim Weider, who was with The Band for nearly fifteen years beginning in 1985 following Robertson's departure, Randy Ciarlante, Albert Rogers, Brian Mitchell and Marty Grebb. Though their set lists are predominantly Band songs often packaged and performed in nostalgic *Rock of Ages*–type tours, The Weight's connections and history with the original group make them more than a pure cover or tribute band. At least in their view, as The Weight's members consider themselves an alternate or extension of The Band that is honoring Helm's dying wish in 2012 for carrying on the group's storied music and spirit through continued performance.

Of the various versions of "The Weight" that echoed and interpreted the 1968 original over the past five-plus decades, both live performances and on record, perhaps the most monumental may be The Band's rendition(s) from *The Last Waltz*. The valediction gathering on Thanksgiving Day, 1976, at San Francisco's Winterland Ballroom featured a renowned roster that included Dylan, Joni Mitchell, Neil Young and Diamond, Van Morrison, Ringo Starr, Paul Butterfield, Eric Clapton, Ronnie Hawkins, Muddy Waters, and Emmylou Harris among others. Despite the legendary lineup assembled to celebrate The Band in an epic concert that commenced at 9:00 p.m. and ran through a 2:15 a.m. encore, the group consensus in the aftermath was that "there was still something crucial missing."[43] The Band's frustration ranged from what they considered a poor-quality soundtrack that required rerecording, remixing and overdubbing, to the 160,000 feet of film footage shot with eight cameras to chronicle the end-of-an era event. Scorsese insisted that if The Band were not satisfied with the footage, the film would never be released, which would have resulted in the most expensive home movie ever.

Among The Band's "outspokens," Robertson contended that though the show embraced many different genres and flavors of music, they did not pay adequate tribute to country or gospel; Helm felt that the concert was "too lily white."[44] Acknowledging the concerns, Scorsese reassembled The Band at the historical MGM soundstage on the Culver City studio lot, the sacred site where a significant number of the classic Hollywood musicals were filmed. There they would reshoot songs and some segments of the group telling stories about their days on the road. They recruited Emmylou Harris to bring her exquisite country comfort to Robertson's new composition "Evangeline" and old friends the Staple Singers to gospel up a rendition of "The Weight" with The Band. Helm, who had been prickly about Scorsese's Robertson-centric documentary, acquiesced, motivated by the opportunity to sing Emmylou and Mavis. Helm was also forthright about his dissatisfaction with The Band's Winterland rendition of "The Weight," saying that it "had come too late in the show," and that "my performance was, to say the least, less than magical."[45]

Behind the scenes, the take two at the soundstage further underscored the song's religiosity eight years into the song's presence. In a passage from Mary Pat Kelley's biography, *Martin Scorsese: A Journey* (1991), cited by Peter Viney as the "last word to Robbie" and conclusion to his "Weight" article/website, Robertson relates a disagreement between Scorsese and cinematographer Michael Chapman over the mood and lighting for "The Weight" during the reshooting.[46] According to Robertson's account, Scorsese insisted on a "very Catholic vision, it had to be," while the resolute Chapman countered that "The Weight" is "a very Protestant story; it's Baptist," pointing to the song's gospel music undertones for supporting sound evidence.[47]

Robertson, who was raised Catholic, said he appreciated the artistic and dogmatic debate between Scorsese and Chapman, adding that he was amused at the credit they were attributing to him, since Robertson never really thought of any of those views when writing the song. Robertson mediated the filmmaker divergences, restating his "impossibility of sainthood premise" as "the load":

For me it was a combination of Catholicism and gospel music. The story told in the song is about the guilt of relationships, not being able to give what's being asked of you. Someone is stumbling through life, going from one situation to another, with different characters. In going through theses catacombs of experience, you're trying to do what's right, but it seems with all the places you have to go, it's just not possible. In the song, all this is "the load."[48]

The Last Waltz collaboration on "The Weight" between The Band and the Staple Singers stands as the song's transcendent and triumphant version, a reverent rendition that certifies the song's essence, from gospel to the vocal allocations. The partnership became permanent. From that performance forward, Mavis Staples was jubilantly bound and devoted to "The Weight." In that instant, the song became a Mavis staple, figuratively and literally—an adoption, a surrender, a common inheritance, a soulmate's possession. She visibly treasured that musical moment on the soundstage. Swept up, her response rested somewhere between basking and being overwhelmed, if not lost in the performance. In the documentary, as "The Weight" winds down, the camera settles on the Staples family: "Pops" out of focus in the background and his daughters. Mavis, closest to the camera, tosses her head back, leans in toward the mic and faintly, in a lip-reading-legible whisper, says, "Beautiful." Staples illuminates her wonder:

> It was just a *feeling* that brought that on. The excitement of being with our friends . . . to be singing with them, and knowing that this is going to be on the big screen, the silver screen, it was just a moment in time for me. You could probably, had you been there, you would have heard my heart pounding . . . Anytime I watch it, it's refreshing, It's like the first time. You never get tired of it, you know. And I remember everything about it. I remember every moment that we had doing that.[49]

That "Mavis feeling" and singalong-with-friends sensibility with "The Weight" have been commonly conveyed on slightly smaller scales in other backstage settings, notably a dressing room rehearsal with Mavis, Nick Lowe, and Wilco backstage at Chicago's Civic Opera House in 2011. Mavis has collaborated with Wilco front Jeff Tweedy numerous times, with Tweedy as songwriter, producer, and guitarist on Staples's Grammy winning *You Are Not Alone* (2010), *One True Vine* (2013), and *If All I Was Was Black* (2017). Playing like a casual conversation, Staples takes the first few verses before Lowe and Tweedy take their turns, with everyone in the room, of course, joining in on the chorus. Following the run through, Tweedy asks Lowe, "You okay with that verse?" as Mavis punctuates the impromptu with a positive proclamation,

"Sounds good!" The five-minute performance, available on You Tube,[50] not only reinforces the requisite verse sharing but also the diverse music genre appeal, as Wilco has been cross categorized as alternative, country, folk, rock, and occasionally psych since their formation in 1994.

The group effort and genre bending are similar, though minus Mavis, in the cross-generational electric-guitar documentary *It Might Get Loud* (2008), which calmly concludes with the focal points of the film, Jimmy Page, the Edge, and Jack White, seated in a semi-circle, recreating The Band's Big Pink basement studio arrangements, while delivering an impromptu, organic take of "The Weight." The unplugged rendering triangulates the Yardbirds, Led Zepplein, U2, the White Stripes and Raconteurs; skiffle, blues, garage, punk, and rock; and London, Dublin, and Detroit.

In *Across the Great Divide*, Hoskyns, despite his lingering skepticism of Aretha's "improbable" cover version from 1969, frames the song's lineage in a precis that encapsulates the critical consensus, from Marcus to Marsh and beyond. The central premise is that the post-Winterland version of "The Weight" epitomized the pluralism and community at the heart of The Band's greatest music:

> when the group took the stage with the Staple Singers, they brought together men and women, whites and blacks, young and old, North and South, creating a parable of their career, and an elegy for it. Elegaic or not, it made for magnificent spectacle, with Mavis completely losing herself in the song. It certainly made a lot more sense than Aretha Franklin's version.[51]

"The Weight" of *The Last Waltz* turned out to be two step. In sizeable contrast to the initial version in the Winterland ballroom setting with a 5,400-seat capacity, the MGM soundstage concert revisitation of "The Weight" took place in front of an audience of 250 people. Numbers aside, the more intimate performance of "The Weight" at MGM, rather than the San Francisco spectacle, was the veritable finale, the final step of *The Last Waltz*, a monumental marker of the last time The Band would appear on stage together. The end of an era.

CODA: "BEAUTIFUL"

Among its multitude of meanings and compound contextualization, "The Weight" is essentially a Band bookend, emerging from Big Pink's basement to being bracketed by a stage introduction at Woodstock in 1969 to a waltzing departure at Winterland in 1976. In between and beyond, the song has continued to show up across the Great Divide at destinations along the Endless Highway, further etching its influential and indelible musical mile markers along the way.

In addition to the documentation on Peter Viney's resourceful online archive, and across various versions, vistas, and venues, the "The Weight" has been routinely registered, ranked and recognized, and continually and widely commemorated and catalogued as a "classic." Among the listings, "The Weight" reigns as Number One in *Rolling Stone* magazine's list of "The Band's Greatest Songs." The song is also #41 on *Rolling Stone*'s "500 Greatest Songs of All Time," published in 2004; Pitchfork Media's #13 "Best Song of the Sixties"; and one of the Rock and Roll Hall of Fame's "500 Songs that Shaped Rock and Roll." Not confined to the idiosyncratic inventories of music publications and institutions, reflective essays on "The Weight" have crossed the Culture Desk of the *New Yorker* magazine (2014) and blogs such as the *Huffington Post*'s "Songs That Matter."[52]

In yet another list, this one in Dave Marsh's *The Heart of Rock and Soul: The 1001 Greatest Singles Ever Made* (1989), "The Weight" places at #616, a modest if not disappointing number even when factoring subjectivity and scope. "The Weight" seems uneasily situated between Gregory Abbott's "Shake You Down" (1987) at #615 and the Three Degrees "When Will I See You Again (1974) at #617. In Marsh's capsule that accompanies the entry, the venerated music critic states that The Band's "oblique and masterful" single "is as fine an example of rock and roll record making as existed in the year of its birth and it has dated not a whit."[53] The commentary, published in 1989, was based on the song's formative first twenty years. Three more decades down the Endless Highway, Marsh's conviction persists with profound relevance and resonance. "The Weight" carries on, a prevailing parable aging gracefully in sound and spirit, still "the perfect image of anyone's entanglement." The song's multiplicity of meanings, from the "the impossibility of sainthood" to contracting the clap, its contexts and quirky characters, the music and lyrics, vocals and visuals, accumulating into a totality of timelessness, tradition and triumph.[54] Vintage Americana. Rock of ages. An enduring echo of Mavis Staples's wondrous whisper: "Beautiful."[55]

Notes

1. Dave Marsh, *The Heart of Rock and Soul: The 1001 Greatest Singles Ever Made*, New York: Plumb, 1989, 400.

2. Greil Marcus, *Mystery Train: Images of America in Rock and Roll Music*, New York: E. P. Dutton, 1982, 55.

3. Helm, *This Wheel's on Fire*, 175.

4. Robertson, *Testimony*.

5. Hoskyns, *Across the Great Divide*, 155.

6. Ibid., 163.

7. To be found here: http://theband.hiof.no/articles/the_weight_viney.html.

8. Peter Viney, *Jawbone*, vol. #4, Spring/Summer 1997.

9. Peter Viney, "The Weight," Accessed March 3, 2017: http://theband.hiof.no/articles/the_weight_viney.html.

10. Marcus, *Mystery Train*, 55.

11. Viney, "The Weight."

12. Helm, *This Wheel's on Fire*, 167–68.

13. Bowman, *Liner Notes*.

14. Ibid.

15. Ibid.

16. Ibid.

17. Robertson, *Testimony*, 301.

18. Ibid.

19. Robertson, *Testimony*, 301.

20. Bowman, *Liner Notes*.

21. Robertson, *Testimony*, 300.

22. Marsh, *The Heart of Rock and Soul*.

23. Flippo, *Liner Notes*, 28.

24. Marcus, *Mystery Train*, 55.

25. Elon Green, "Culture Desk: Mavis Staples Remembers Singing 'The Weight,'" *New Yorker*, June 17, 2014.

26. Robertson, *Testimony*.

27. Ibid.

28. Hoskyns, *Across the Great Divide*, 155–56.

29. Clive James, "Robbie Robertson: In the Shadow of The Band," *Creem*, July 1972.

30. Viney, "The Weight."

31. Marcus, *Mystery Train*, 55.

32. Hoskyns, *Across the Great Divide*, 67.

33. Helm, *This Wheel's on Fire*, 167.

34. Marcus, *Mystery Train*, 55.

35. Ibid.

36. Helm, *This Wheel's on Fire*, 270.

37. Bruce Pollock, "They're Playing My Song: 'Put A Little Love in Your Heart,'" December 11, 2012, accessed April 3, 2017: http://www.songfacts.com/blog/playingmysong/jackie_deshannon_-_put_a_little_love_in_your_heart_/.

38. Ibid.

39. Hoskyns, *Across the Great Divide*, 173.

40. Ibid.

41. See the last footnote in this essay for a limited list of covers from 1968–2013.

42. Green, "Culture Desk."

43. Robertson, *Testimony*, 492; and Helm, *This Wheel's on Fire*, 270.

44. Ibid., 492; and Ibid., 270.

45. Helm, *This Wheel's on Fire*, 270.

46. Viney, "The Weight."

47. Ibid.

48. Viney, "The Weight."

49. Green, "Culture Desk."

50. https://www.youtube.com/watch?time_continue=24&v=2WmlUXsjSv8.

51. Hoskyns, *Across the Great Divide*, 354.

52. Anne Margaret Daniel, "Songs That Matter: The Band, 'The Weight,'" accessed February 3, 2017: https://www.huffingtonpost.com/anne-margaret-daniel/songs-that-matter-the-ban_b_3592027.html.

53. Marsh, *The Heart of Rock and Soul*, 400–401.

54. For a recreation of the complete lyrics, see http://www.songfacts.com/detail.php?lyrics=420.

55. A selected discography (1968–2013) of cover versions of The Band's "The Weight" follows. 1968: the Staple Singers, *Soul Folk in Action* (Stax Records); Spooky Tooth, *It's All About Spooky Tooth* (Island). 1969: Jackie De Shannon, *Laurel Canyon* (Imperial); Diana Ross and the Supremes, with the Temptations, *Together* (Motown); Smith, *Easy Rider Film Soundtrack* (Dunhill); Smith, *A Group Called Smith* (Dunhill); Rotary Connection, *Songs* (Cadet); Mike Bloomfield and Al Kooper, *The Live Adventures of Mike Bloomfield and Al Kooper*, (Columbia); Amen Corner, *Farewell to the Real Magnificent Seven* (Immediate); the Ventures, *Underground Fire* (Liberty); King Curtis, *Instant Groove* (Atco). 1970: Aretha Franklin, *This Girl's in Love with You* (Atlantic). 1971: Sammi Smith, *Lonesome* (Mega Records). 1972: Dionne Warwick, *From Within* (Wand). 1973: Kings Road, *Watkins Glen* (Pickwick). 1974: Bob Dylan and The Band, *Before the Flood* (Asylum Records, U.S, Island Records, UK. 1986: Isaac Guillory, *Live* (Personal Records). 1987: Koichi Matsuda, *Les Enfants* (Polydor). 1988: Giant Sand, *Storm* (Demon). 1990: Ringo Starr, *Ringo Starr and His All-Starr Band* (Rykodisc, US; EMI, UK); Hoyt Axton, *Spin of the Wheel* (Compendia). 1993: Grateful Dead, *Another Day in the Sunshine* (KTS). 1994: the Staple Singers and Marty Stuart, *Rhythm, Country and Blues* (MCA Records). 1995: Ronnie Hawkins (with The Band), *Let it Rock* (Quality). 1999: Shannon Curfman, *Loud Guitars, Big Suspicions* (Arista Records). 2000: Marva Wright, *Marva* (Aim). 2002: Cassandra Wilson, *Belly of the Sun* (Blue Note Records); Joan Osborne, *How Sweet It Is* (Compendia); Scott McClatchy (featuring Willie Nile, Scott Kempner, Dion DiMucci), *Redemption* (LIB Recordings); Travis, *Igby Goes Down* film soundtrack (Spun Records). 2003: New Riders of the Purple Sage, *Live* (Columbia). 2004: John Denver, *Definitive All-Time Greatest Hits* (RCA). 2005: Joe Cocker. *Mad Dogs and Englishmen* (reissue of 1970 original) (Universal). 2006: Aaron Pritchett, *Big Wheel* (deluxe version) (OPM Records); Uncle Kracker, *My Name is Earl* television soundtrack (Shout! Factory). 2007: Lee Ann Womack, *Endless Highway: The Music of The Band* (EMI/429 Records); Michelle Shocked, *To Heaven You Ride* (Mighty Sound); Deana Carter, *The Chain* (Vanguard). 2008: Weezer, *The Red Album* (bonus track)

(Geffen); Jeff Healey, *Mess of Blues* (Ruffhouse); Little Feat (featuring Bela Fleck), *Join the Band* (429 Records). 2009: Sherie Rene Scott, *Everyday Rapture* Broadway soundtrack (Sh-K-Boom/Ghostlight Records); Gaslight Anthem (featuring Thrice), *Beggars* (Vagrant Records). 2011: Conan O'Brien & the Legally Prohibited Band, *Conan O'Brien Can't Stop*, motion picture soundtrack (Lakeshore); Conan O'Brien & the Legally Prohibited Band, *Live at the Third Man* (United Records); Levon Helm, *Ramble at the Ryman* (Vanguard). 2012: Rickie Lee Jones, *The Devil May Know* (Fantasy Records). 2013: Garth Brooks, *Blame It All on My Roots*, box set (Pearl).

Chapter 9

LOUD PRAYERS

Communion, Transcendence, and the Blues in Scorsese's *The Last Waltz*

KEVIN C. NEECE

Martin Scorsese was the perfect filmmaker to capture The Band's farewell concert at San Francisco's Winterland Ballroom. Scorsese's films, while well known—as they especially were in the 1970s—for telling stories of violent crime and melancholic urban discontent, have always grasped at something transcendent, hidden inside the guts and sinew of the harshest realities of life. Take for example two of Scorsese's classic films, still fresh at the time—*Taxi Driver*, which had been released the February before The Band's final concert in November of 1976, and *Mean Streets*, Scorsese's 1973 breakout success.

In *Mean Streets*, New Yorker Charlie Cappa (Harvey Keitel) tries to balance his Catholic faith with the world of crime and gang violence in which he finds himself by seeking to bring reconciliation between local rivals and attempting to mentor the wild, self-destructive "Johnny Boy" (Robert De Niro). "You don't make up for your sins in church," the opening narration, spoken by Scorsese, says, "You do it at home. You do it in the streets. The rest is bullshit and you know it."[1] As a hard cut catches Charlie apparently startled to waking, we get the sense that he has dreamed these words, revealing his own inner struggle to balance his commitment to his faith with the criminality by which he is surrounded and to which he is sometimes party. He can't clean the mean streets and therefore struggles to clear his own haunted conscience.

Taxi Driver's Travis Bickle (also De Niro) searches for meaning and purpose within a New York City he describes as "like an open sewer" and "full of trash and filth." Travis also is troubled by the condition of his city but sees himself as somehow connected to an almost Old Testament-style cleansing. Bemoaning the presence of "Whores, skunk pussies, buggers, queens, fairies, dopers, [and] junkies," whom he describes as "sick" and "venal," Travis dreams on a rainy day that "someday a real rain will come and wash this scum off the streets." "Thank God," he says earlier, "for the rain."[2] Travis seeks a sort of divine cleansing—more for the world around him than for himself. Where Charlie Cappa is spurred on by his own guilt, Travis Bickle seems motivated by disgust.

Both stories, however, represent a struggle between what might be called the sacred and the profane, a sense that things are not as they should be and that something better—indeed, something that might be called transcendent or divine—is waiting to break through. Both films embrace religious or near-religious imagery, and both end in bloody, violent climaxes that feel tragic, inevitable, and also strangely redemptive. Travis Bickle especially seems to exorcise something from within himself—at least for a time—as he ascends to a bloody and bizarrely Christlike act of salvation for a young prostitute (Jodie Foster). These characters reflect Scorsese's own struggles, living in the same context of crime-ridden streets while wrestling with his own Catholic faith. They also capture an unrest felt by many in 1970s New York, while providing an unblinking view of that city's darker elements during a period of decline.

The Band share with Scorsese a sense of the sacred mundane, if not the sacred profane, as the exultant wave of their music swells beneath stories of gamblers, washed up Confederate soldiers, and woebegone artistic dreamers. The poetic stew of The Band's lyrics and music—both raw and strangely redemptive—is a perfect musical counterpart for Scorsese's deft melding of the earthly and the ethereal.

Music has long been an important element in Scorsese's films, in their orchestral scores, but perhaps more notably in their adapted scores. Largely curated by Scorsese himself, these collections have frequently drawn from both classical and modern sources. The classical influence had not been seen as much by 1976. Though *Mean Streets* included some traditional *canzone napoletana*, or Neapolitan songs, sung by artists like Renato Carosone and Giuseppe Di Stefano (an apparent nod to generational divisions in the film),[3] Scorsese would not draw from classical Italian opera until *Raging Bull* in 1980. Still, the influence of Italian opera can be felt not only in the more traditional pieces Scorsese chose for *Mean Streets*, but also in his selections for later films of music from Pietro Mascagni and Gaetano Donizetti, as well as by such artists as Dean Martin and Tony Bennett, who, like Scorsese, were themselves influenced by the music brought to America by Italian immigrants like Scorsese's grandparents. As Scorsese explains,

> My grandparents, who came from Sicily between 1910 and 1912, only spoke Sicilian and would sing occasionally as they were working in

the house—that was another way I heard opera when I was young. Besides listening to the old Italian soap operas on the radio, we'd listen to music on the radio and a lot of it was opera.[4]

That operatic sensibility may underlie much of Italian American music and culture, as reflected in Scorsese's films, but from his earliest films to contemporary times, Scorsese is most known for his use of pop music, which is on full display in *Mean Streets*. The film's soundtrack is populated by doo-wop, rhythm and blues, and rock and roll from such artists as the Paragons, the Shirelles, and the Rolling Stones. As rich as Scorsese's operatic roots may be, he is equally inculcated—if not more so—in these popular, distinctly American musical forms, which often provide a through line in his work. For example, also included in the *Mean Streets* soundtrack was a song by the band Cream, whose guitarist Eric Clapton would go on to appear in *The Last Waltz*. Similarly, the Rolling Stones would be the subject of, to date, Scorsese's only other concert film, *Shine a Light* in 2008, forty years after the release of *The Last Waltz*.

The stage at the Winterland Ballroom was decorated for the Last Waltz[5] by production designer Boris Leven, not only with the customary amps, cables, microphones, and speakers one might expect for a rock concert, but also with chandeliers and large, beautifully carved archways, adorned with ornate draperies and candelabra sconces—set pieces borrowed from the San Francisco Opera Festival's production of *La Traviata*. Thus, fittingly for a Scorsese film, an Italian opera provided the backdrop for a rock concert. It was a night that would be as much a send-off for The Band as a celebration and exploration of the elements and amalgamations of American music that informed their musical journey.

Like Scorsese, The Band were intimately entwined with American roots music, which they also intermixed with their own Canadian cultural heritage, in songs such as "Acadian Driftwood," which traces Louisiana Creole culture and language back to French Canadian migration into the southern United States.[6] Also like Scorsese, Robbie Robertson's lyrics frequently recount history through compelling, humanizing, first-person narratives that focus more on story than on plot, and show more than they tell.[7] *The Last Waltz*, then, is not merely a document of a concert, but a conversation, not only between The Band and Martin Scorsese, but also between the various influences—musical and cultural—that shape the two.

Collaboration is a theme at the heart of the film—collaboration between the members of The Band, between The Band and Scorsese, and between The Band and an impressive list of musical friends who "dropped by" for the occasion, including Muddy Waters, Eric Clapton, Bob Dylan, and Joni Mitchell. The film radiates with the intended cooperative spirit of the concert, which was famously preceded by a Thanksgiving banquet. The American myth of the "first Thanksgiving," while broadly inaccurate, is still a fitting symbol for the marrying of cultures that is at the heart of the formation of rock music and exemplified in the Last Waltz concert.

As Band drummer Levon Helm—the Canadian group's sole American member—recounts to Scorsese in the film, "Near Memphis, cotton country, rice country, the most interesting thing is probably the music. . . . So bluegrass or country music, you know, if it comes down to that area and if it mixes there with rhythm and if it dances, then you've got a combination of all those different kinds of music: country, bluegrass, blues music."

"The melting pot," Robertson interjects.
Helm finishes, "Show music."
"And what's it called?" Scorsese asks.
Helm replies, "Rock and roll!"[8]

The core of rock and roll, and indeed the core of the majority of the musical styles on display in *The Last Waltz*, is found in the blues. The legacy of the blues in The Band's music is highlighted in a series of segments beginning with a story told by Robbie Robertson during one of The Band's interviews with Scorsese at their Shangri-La studio in Malibu. Robertson relates a particularly memorable night during a visit the group made to drummer Levon Helm's hometown, when they decided to look up local resident and blues legend John Lee "Sonny Boy" Williamson. "In my opinion," says Richard Manuel, "he's the best harp player—that's, like, harmonica, blues harmonica—that I've ever heard."

Robertson agrees, "He's the big Daddy of 'em,"[9] and continues with the story of the late night conversation and impromptu house concert the group had with Williamson during their visit.

> He would sit there and he was playing for us. And we were getting drunk and trying to figure out where we were. He was spitting in a can. I thought he was dipping snuff. I thought he had something in his lip. And he kept spitting in this can and playing, and we kept getting drunker. Finally, I looked over in the can and I realized it was blood. He was getting pretty tired and pretty drunk by then. And we made big plans for the future and all kinds of things we were gonna do. And it was tremendous. A great night. A couple of months later,

we got a letter from his manager, or whoever it was, saying that he had passed away.[10]

Just after the story of The Band's encounter with Sonny Boy Williamson and the letter carrying the news of his death, Scorsese cuts to a performance in the Last Waltz concert by Paul Butterfield, whose blues harmonica work carried forward the musical conversation begun by greats like Williamson. Butterfield represents a younger generation of blues men, taking the lead on "Mystery Train," a driving blues rock song that carries the musical conversation forward, even as its roots are showing. Butterfield came to notoriety with his Butterfield Blues Band, whose 1966 release *East-West* was a popular blues album, despite the fact that The Band was fronted by and primarily composed of white musicians. It may also seem paradoxical that the album is also considered a psychedelic recording, but the blending of the two points to the "in-between" state of Butterfield's generation of musicians—drawing heavily on the past while moving in new musical directions. Surprisingly, blues legend Muddy Waters himself, at the behest of his producer, blended blues and psychedelia on his 1968 album *Electric Mud*. The album even features a psych/blues version of his classic song, "Mannish Boy," which Waters himself performed in a more traditional form at the Last Waltz. The song immediately follows Butterfield's performance and Helm's description of American roots music. Musically and symbolically, Waters's performance may be the keystone of the entire film. As Scorsese explains,

> It was my love for music, which has never stopped growing, that led me to do *The Last Waltz*. I wanted to make it more than just a document of The Band's last concert. Because it was more than just a musical tribute—it was a tapestry of music history, The Band's music history. And every one of those performers—one legend after another—made up a thread in that tapestry. But when Muddy Waters walked onto that stage and sang "Mannish Boy," he took control of the music, the event, the history, everything. He electrified the audience, took it all up to another level and back to the source at the same time. He gave a phenomenal performance, and I will always consider myself privileged to have been there to witness it, to film it, and to give it back to millions of people with the finished film. It was a defining moment for me.[11]

Perhaps Waters's signature song and now considered a blues standard, "Mannish Boy" (originally "Manish Boy") was both an arrangement of and an answer to Bo Diddley's 1955 song "I'm a Man."[12] Waters's version, as the title suggests, contrasts Diddley's spelling of "M-A-N" in the chorus with that of "B-O-Y." "No, B!" Waters declares, "O, child. Y. That mean mannish boy." Of "M-A-N," he says, "That represent I'm grown." Indeed, Waters was older than Diddley at the time, suggesting that his declaration of manhood speaks to more than Diddley's then-recent coming of age. In Waters's version, this contrast between the words "man" and "boy" brings into stronger relief the song's underlying social and cultural meaning.

More than just a declaration of sexual prowess with lines like, "When I make love to a woman, she can't resist," and "I can make love to you, girl, in five minutes' time,"[13] the song is in direct opposition to southern oppression of black people in daily life in the first half of the twentieth century. In that context, white people would frequently refer to black men as "boy," undercutting both their maturity and their humanity by placing them in a lower, submissive cultural stratum. By rejecting the word "boy" and declaring, "I'm a man!" Waters directly pushes back against the dehumanization of black Americans in the South, prefiguring the "I AM A MAN" signs worn and carried by black protesters in the Memphis sanitation strike of 1968. The slogan became a rallying cry for the civil rights movement and could even be traced back to the eighteenth-century Quaker abolitionist slogan, "Am I not a man and a brother?" used in the fight against slavery in England.

As Waters's official website states, "'Mannish Boy' is not only an assertion of black manhood but also, free from southern laws in his new home of Chicago, the song is nothing less than a black Declaration of Independence."[14] As such, it stands also as a declaration of essential humanity. As a man, and not a "mannish boy," or a man who is called a boy by his white neighbors, Waters seems to say he is a person who is due equality, respect, and human rights. Couching this declaration of humanity in terms of sexual prowess serves as perhaps a more crass version of Shylock's "If you prick us, do we not bleed?"[15] After bragging of his lovemaking skills, Waters asks, "Ain't that a man?"

The message is strong, but perhaps not immediately clear to a white audience. This is not unlike a technique used in early blues songs, which were composed by black workers in the South, it is said, as a way to secretly complain about the white people for whom they worked, substituting "the boss man" with a woman—a lover—who mistreats the narrator of the song. The theme is not as well hidden as that in Waters's lyrics, or even in Diddley's, but it is veiled just enough to continue to fly under the radar of suppression, spreading a humanizing, liberating message to those who have ears to hear.

This sense of humanity and liberation runs right through the Last Waltz concert and film, from the story of a self-described "drunkard" and the woman who offers him shelter and comfort in "Up on Cripple Creek," with which The Band opened the evening, to the rousing cry for freedom from imprisonment in "I Shall Be Released," in which almost the entirety of the evening's performers participated and which closes the concert portion of the film.

Immediately following Waters's performance in the film, cut so closely as to almost suggest the next musician had been waiting on the other end of the stage, Scorsese brings in another of those younger blues men, but from a different branch of the blues family tree: British guitar legend Eric Clapton. He may be a legend now, but Robertson wasn't so taken with him during his days with the Yardbirds in the 1960s. "I heard the records from England," Robertson recalled in a 1982 interview. "I wasn't very impressed, at the time." Clapton had even, according to Robertson, come to the attention of Sonny Boy Williamson, but to perhaps worse acclaim. As Robertson tells it, Williamson said of the Yardbirds, "God, I went to England. Those kids over there, they buy me everything, they treat me like God and they all want to play with me and they're terrible. They can't play worth a shit."

In the same interview, Robertson offers of Clapton, "He got better."[16] Apparently, Clapton did indeed "get better," enough that he was invited to play at the Last Waltz[17] in what became a fiery duel of guitars between himself and Robertson, wherein the two seem well matched in the film, though their differing styles are on display. Clapton's presence, playing "Further on up the Road," a Texas shuffle from 1957, represents a particular connection to earlier blues greats that is not as apparent in the film as it is in the complete concert recording. In Scorsese's film, Muddy Waters's contribution is truncated. Not only is the slightly non-sequitur, gospel-esque opening of "Mannish Boy" not included, but also the film's edit removes an entire verse of that song, as well as the previous song Waters performed, "Caldonia." Another standard, "Caldonia" comes from a decade before "Mannish Boy" in 1945 and is an example of the jump blues genre, an upbeat version of blues that is considered the precursor to rhythm and blues and rock and roll. In fact, a version of "Caldonia" recorded by Erskine Hawkins in 1945 was one of the first recordings to be referred to in print with the words "rock and roll."[18]

The connection between Clapton's rendition of "Further on up the Road" and Waters's performance of "Caldonia" is so close that those familiar with *The Last Waltz*, listening to the instrumental improvisations at the end of "Caldonia" for the first time, may wonder what Paul Butterfield is doing playing harmonica on "Further on up the Road." As Clapton and Robertson recreate and reinterpret the jump blues style, pushing the music back and forth at one another (with the help of a loose guitar strap), American,

Canadian, and British musicians, influences, and methods converge, "further on up the road," indeed, from their predecessors, but carrying on the same conversation.

That conversation, soaked as it is in whiskey and shot through with sex and drugs, is never far from—and is arguably rooted in—spirituality, both hoodoo and Christian. Not far into the lyrics of songs from Muddy Waters and Bo Diddley, one encounters voodoo bones and magical plants, as Sister Rosetta Tharpe and Blind Willie Johnson ponder the gospel and the soul. "I want somebody to tell me," Johnson famously sang, "Answer if you can! I want somebody to tell me: What is the soul of a man?"[19] The song and its singer would provide the centerpiece and the title for Wim Wenders's film *The Soul of a Man* in the documentary film series *The Blues*, produced by Scorsese in 2003 for PBS.

The Last Waltz only occasionally dips directly into the waters of religious or spiritual language and often it is to acknowledge the influence of gospel music more than to make any religious claims. In some instances, it may even come off as rather cheeky or irreverent, such as when Manuel, Danko, and Robertson join together in an impromptu rendition of "Old Time Religion"—"for the folks," as Robertson puts it—while sitting on a couch at Shangri-La. While it all seems good-natured, Robertson's guitar might be a little out of tune, Manuel's harmonica playing is a bit halfhearted, and Danko's fiddling seems intentionally sloppy. "It's not like it used to be," Robertson jokingly quips at the song's end. Indeed, while gospel music and religion are a part of The Band's DNA, like the plastic pork pie hat Danko fidgets with on his head during "Old Time Religion," they don't always seem to fit quite right. Still, The Band would not be The Band without them, and the spiritual quality of music is on display in the film.

"There is a view," Garth Hudson says in an interview segment following an edited version of his lengthy "Chest Fever" intro, "that jazz is evil because it comes from evil people. But, actually, the greatest priests on 52nd Street and on the streets of New York City were the musicians. They were doing the greatest healing work. And they knew how to punch through music which would cure and make people feel good."[20] Scorsese, having considered entering the Catholic priesthood himself before deciding instead to become a filmmaker, likely understands the priestly nature of artistic expression. He had found solace and sanctuary in movie theatres, especially as a young boy in New York, spending his days indoors, as he suffered from asthma. Though he demurred at the idea that he himself is something of a cinematic priest in a 2016 interview, he did offer that his famously quiet sets, "are like sacred spaces; there's no doubt about it."[21]

There is some sense of this sacred quietness, of time and space and unhurried care, in the segments of the "Last Waltz Suite," three songs shot with The Band and some guests, well after the Last Waltz concert at MGM Studios: "Evangeline" with Emmylou Harris, "The Weight" with the Staples Singers, and "Theme from *The Last Waltz*." "Evangeline," representing both the influence of country music and the contemporary generation of country artists with then-new star Emmylou Harris, carries a sense of the ethereal with its blue and purple lighting and misty atmosphere. The song ends to no applause and a pull back to reveal members of the crew appearing through the mist—fog machine smoke, which Levon Helm waves away with his arms. The lyrics touch on familiar ground for The Band, concerning the ill-fated romance between "Bayou Sam from South Louisiana" and "Evangeline from the Maritimes," a reference to a region of Eastern Canada. Sam is a riverboat gambler on the "mighty Mississippi," which of course runs through the Mississippi Delta, home of the blues of Muddy Waters. Again, The Band bring American, Canadian, and Cajun influences together into a gumbo with country music and (by some extension) Delta blues.

Similarly sacred and culturally inclusive is The Band's performance of their classic "The Weight" with the Staples Singers. The Staples Singers appear in the film as representatives of gospel music on a song that, interestingly, has long tried to shake a reputation as a gospel number. This characterization is often put down to, among other things, its opening line, "I pulled in to Nazareth," which Robertson has long said refers to Nazareth, Pennsylvania, the city of manufacture stamped on the inside of the Martin guitar on which he composed the song. As he wrote, he says, he recalled "going from Canada down to the Mississippi delta when I was sixteen years old. Characters and circumstances—all of it started to come back to me." He continues, "And I could hear these voices, 'and you put the load right on me.'"[22] In Robertson's telling, it's as if the voices of those who had gone before were speaking to and through him—certainly a spiritual event, not unlike the biblical "great cloud of witnesses."[23]

In another sense, the song speaks of sharing a burden, laying it on another person's shoulders, recalling the traditional American spiritual "When I Lay My Burden Down,"[24] sung by both gospel artists and such original bluesmen as Mississippi Fred McDowell and Othar Turner: "Glory, glory, hallelujah! When I lay my burden down. I'm going home to be with Jesus, when I lay my burden down." There is also the Christlike image of self-sacrifice inherent in those lyrics. The Staples Singers, by their very presence as a gospel group, help reinforce the oddly spiritual, almost biblical nature of the song. Again, the studio song ends quietly, with Mavis Staples smiling broadly and whispering, "Beautiful!" as the final notes resonate into sacred silence.

The Last Waltz concert, of course, was anything but quiet. As Scorsese recalled in 1978, "I had an intercom, which was hard to use because you're right on the stage, you know, and it's blasting and all you hear is somebody yelling, 'You're off the line!'"[25] It also may have hardly seemed sacred, littered as it was with references to sex and drugs, in the songs as well as backstage. As Levon Helm recalls, promoter Bill Graham had painted a dressing room white and adorned it with "noses out of Groucho Marx masks," surrounding a "sleek, glass table with razor blades artfully strewn about" as a "tape played sniffing noises." Unsurprisingly, the room was used for snorting cocaine, which was, according to Helm, "a big, big deal at the time."[26] In fact, it was at the Last Waltz that Scorsese first tried cocaine, which led to a years-long addiction, the physical effects of which seem clear in interview footage from the time.[27]

Drugs also played a role in the blues. Muddy Waters's "Mannish Boy" refers to "little Johnny Conqueroo," a nickname for John the Conqueror root, which is a plant used in hoodoo practices. While carried rather than ingested, the root is believed to have mystical powers.[28] In a similar way, people have long sought spiritual enlightenment through plant-derived drugs and other substances. While it's certainly a stretch to suggest that any form of spiritual enlightenment was being sought in the "Cocteau Room," as Graham dubbed his mini coke den, it does perhaps indicate that even the most destructive elements of rock-and-roll culture have some connection to a quest for a sort of higher state, through artistic expression and through drugs taken to fuel the making thereof.

Again, that mismatch with and yet familiar connection to religion appears in *The Last Waltz* when once more the sound dies down. In the original concert there was a late intermission during which several poets read their works. Two of them, Michael McClure and revered beat poet Lawrence Ferlinghetti, are featured in the film. Scorsese shifts McClure earlier in the lineup and moves Ferlinghetti even closer to the end of the evening by removing or shifting a few performances that immediately followed his poem.

Ferlinghetti, looking oddly priestlike in his blue, buttoned-down jacket, black bowler hat, and white beard, steps unassumingly to the microphone and says, "Let us pray." He then reads, from his own handwritten notes, a poem whose title was apt for the evening, "Loud Prayer." Addressed to "Our Father, whose art's in heaven," the poem strikes a satirical tone from the beginning that serves as a pointed critique of the loss of the sacred in modern culture.

"Hollow be thy name," Ferlinghetti says, "unless things change." Bemoaning the idea that "thy will, will be undone on earth, as it isn't heaven," he prays for "daily dread—at least three times a day," possibly referring to daily news broadcasts, and entreats the divine to "forgive us our trespasses on love's territory" before ending, rather than with an "amen," with, "Oh, man!"[29]

After what has, in the film, become Ferlinghetti's fractured benediction on the evening's proceedings, Scorsese moves on to a more sincere blessing, sung by the night's biggest guest star, Bob Dylan. "May God bless and keep you always," he sings, "May your wishes all come true. May you always do for others and let others do for you." It's a sincere, even sentimental rendition of "Forever Young," a song that wishes on its listener the blessing of a youthful soul—a newness of life, if you will, and a restoration of hope. The song then blends into one more raucous moment as Dylan leads The Band in an impromptu reprise of "Baby, Let Me Follow You Down," the first of the song the film audience hears, but a recapitulation of the tune with which Dylan had opened his set. With the gathering onstage of the majority of the night's musicians for The Band's "I Shall Be Released," the film version of the concert ends with celebrations, blessings, and benediction, though on November 25, 1976, the evening was far from over. It was only after more encores and two long jam sessions that The Band actually finished their set at 2:15 on the morning of the 26th with the rendition of "Don't Do It" that opens the film and Robertson's final, "Goodnight. And goodbye." The end is the beginning. One can't help but wonder if the liturgical sensibility that tends toward cyclical narratives ingrained in Scorsese's Catholic mind haven't informed the structure of the film and given something of a prayerful feeling to a rock concert that sought no such thing.

And maybe that's what we see in *The Last Waltz*: loud prayers. They are prayers of hurt and heartache, of hope and healing, of love lost, humanity regained, and souls in search of something missing—something they're uncertain if they've ever found. More longing than knowing, more reaching than grasping, there are a thousand prayers that echoed through Winterland's walls that night, few of them reverent, but all of them reverberant. Perhaps that's why *The Last Waltz*'s opening title card shouts, "THIS FILM SHOULD BE PLAYED LOUD!"—so those loud prayers can be heard as they were intended.

Whatever spiritual processes are taking place in *The Last Waltz*, they are doing so largely outside of established religion—not "in church," but "in the streets."[30] The film may be unintentionally spiritual. It may be fueled by adrenaline, a huge crowd, a late night, and a lot of cocaine, but it is often a picture of human beings reaching outside of themselves from somewhere deep within. Maybe it just so happens that when we share a meal together, it can't help but be a kind of communion. Maybe when we sing songs together, it can't help but be a kind of prayer. And maybe when we give everything we've got in the basement—tapes and otherwise—to our human expressions, something sacred just has to show up. Such seems to be the case in *The Last Waltz*.

To watch Robbie Robertson play guitar in this film is to watch a man sweating off the weight of his life on the road and exorcising demons through his fingertips. As he wrestles with the considerable heft of his guitar—which he'd had bronzed for the occasion, perhaps naively not calculating how unwieldy that process would render the instrument—he is finding release from another weight: the potential impending doom that awaits musicians who stay too long on the touring circuit. "Or maybe it's just superstitious," he says of the motivation to end The Band's journey. "You can press your luck. The road has taken a lot of the great ones. Hank Williams. Buddy Holly. Otis Redding. Janis. Jimi Hendrix. Elvis. It's a goddamn impossible way of life."[31]

Eerily, the names he lists read like a history of American music not unlike the one embodied by the guest stars featured at the Last Waltz. They represent the roots and the branches of The Band's musical family tree: country, rockabilly, blues, soul, and rock and roll. The list of those lost runs the gamut of musical progress—from the unbroken circle to the uncharted psychedelia. It's a chilling trend of tragedy that makes one wonder, especially after the early deaths of Rick Danko and Richard Manuel (the latter by suicide on tour with a reformed version of The Band), if Robertson hasn't got a pretty good point.

It's not hard to be convinced of just about anything The Band's leading figure suggests. There's a kind of spiritual mysticism about Robertson that echoes through his work, his interviews, and his memoir. He seems to be a philosopher, a sage, and a prophet, in touch with something somewhere beyond merely the music. So, perhaps it was wisdom that led to the Last Waltz. Perhaps it was, as Robertson says, "superstition." Perhaps it was dumb luck. Whatever the case, the waltz was danced—between the members of The Band and their guests, The Band and the audience, The Band and Scorsese, and with the heritage of music that brought The Band into being. It is perhaps this unique feeling of culmination that leads many to think of the concert and the film as "the end of an era."

Perhaps it was and perhaps it wasn't. But it was certainly the end of The Band, at least as it had been. The film is the coming together of musicians, traditions, cultures, and ideas at the moment of The Band's irreparable fracturing. "Something got broken," Robertson says, "and it was like glass.

It was hard to put back together again."³² Indeed, the members other than Robertson did reunite and even made records as The Band, but something was missing. Eventually, beginning with Manuel and then Danko, too many of the group's members were lost and now, with the death of Levon Helm in recent years, only Robertson and Hudson remain. The glass is indeed shattered and can never be repaired.

But the spiritual impulse, the religious instinct, is a way of hoping for what was and what will be again. It sings along with and through the blues of sorrow and pain, and scratches out a gospel song on a fiddle slung low. Maybe The Band and Scorsese keep bumping up against the sacred in the mundane and the profane because that's the only place we ever truly find it—where we live, at home, in the streets. We've got a lot of blues to play in this life. Things are not as they should be. We still get our daily dread, at least three times a day. Earth isn't heaven. But when we make our loud prayers together—"Oh, man!"—it can sure come close.

Notes

1. Martin Scorsese, *Mean Streets*, Warner Bros., 1973.

2. Martin Scorsese, *Taxi Driver*, Columbia Pictures, 1976.

3. Salazar, David, "Opera Meets Film: How Giuseppe Di Stefano's Inclusion in 'Mean Streets' Explores Generational Conflict through Music," *OperaWire*, November 28, 2019.

4. McCarthy, James. "My Music: Martin Scorsese," *Gramophone*, April 2, 2013. https://www.gramophone.co.uk/features/article/my-music-martin-scorsese

5. Throughout this piece, I will be using the non-italicized "Last Waltz" to refer to the Last Waltz concert and the italicized *The Last Waltz* to refer to the film that documents the concert.

6. The Band, *Northern Lights—Southern Cross*.

7. This is particularly true of Scorsese's 2002 film, *Gangs of New York*, for which Robbie Robertson served as musical supervisor.

8. Scorsese, *The Last Waltz*, 1978.

9. Williamson has similarly been called "the peerless innovator who did for the harmonica what Louis Armstrong did for the trumpet" (Devi, Debra, *The Language of the Blues: From Alcorub to Zuzu*, True Nature Books, 2012).

10. Scorsese, *The Last Waltz*.

11. Martin Scorsese, *Feel Like Going Home*, director interview, PBS Official Website, https://www.pbs.org/theblues/aboutfilms/scorseseinterview.html, accessed February 25, 2020.

12. Muddy Waters, Official Website, https://muddywatersofficial.com/pages/mannish-boy, accessed February 17, 2020.

13. This lyric differs from Diddley, who brags that he can accomplish the task "in an hour's time." This seems to be Waters bragging of even greater sexual prowess, though this

thinking is probably backward. Most would more likely consider the better lover to be the man who can last longer, not the one who finishes first. This focus on speed, though, demonstrates the male-centric viewpoint of the song, which is rather out of place today, but which stands as a symbol of a sense of masculine power that has frequently been an anchor of male identity.

14. Muddy Waters, Official Website, https://muddywatersofficial.com.

15. It was the character of Shylock in Shakespeare's *The Merchant of Venice* who argued for the humanity of Jewish people by asking, "Hath not a Jew hands, organs, dimensions, senses, affections, passions?" and famously, "If you prick us, do we not bleed?"

16. Joshua Baer, "The Band: The Robbie Robertson Interview," *Musician—Guitar Special*, no. 43, May 1982.

17. Clapton would also later induct The Band into the Rock and Roll Hall of Fame in 1994, in a ceremony at which Martin Scorsese was present and thanked from the stage by Robbie Robertson. Scorsese's connection with Clapton and the blues would continue two years later when he served as an executive producer for *Nothing but the Blues*, a documentary film about Clapton's love of blues music, starring and narrated by the musician.

18. Larry Birnbaum, *Before Elvis: The Prehistory of Rock and Roll*, Scarecrow Press, 2013.

19. Blind Willie Johnson, "The Soul of a Man," Lyrics, Columbia, 1930.

20. Scorsese, *The Last Waltz*.

21. Krishnan Guru-Murthy, *Interview with Martin Scorsese*, BBC Channel 4 News, Aired December 6, 2016, youtube.com/watch?v=87VRx9IQYqw, accessed February 26, 2020.

22. Daniel Roher, *Once Were Brothers: Robbie Robertson and The Band*, Imagine Documentaries, 2019.

23. Hebrews 12:1.

24. Also known as "Glory, Glory (Lay My Burden Down)."

25. Paul Soles, *90 Minutes Live*, "Robbie Robertson, Martin Scorsese, and The Last Waltz," CBC, Aired April 14, 1978, https://www.cbc.ca/archives/entry/robbie-robertson-martin-scorsese-and-the-last-waltz, accessed February 26, 2020.

26. Helm, *This Wheel's on Fire*.

27. Soles, *90 Minutes Live*.

28. Tony Kail, *A Secret History of Memphis Hoodoo: Rootworkers, Conjurers, and Spirituals*, History Press, 2017.

29. Scorsese, *The Last Waltz*.

30. Scorsese, *Mean Streets*.

31. Scorsese, *The Last Waltz*.

32. Roher, *Once Were Brothers*.

BIBLIOGRAPHY

Aaron, Peter. *The Band FAQ: All That's Left to Know about the Fathers of Americana.* Milwaukee, WI: Backbeat Books, 2016.

Adorno, Theodor. *Negative Dialectics.* Trans., E. B. Ashto. New York: Seabury Press, 1973.

Adorno, Theodor, and Max Horkheimer. *Dialectic of Enlightenment.* Stanford University Press, 2002.

Aronowitz, Alfred G. "Friends and Neighbors Just Call Us the Band." *Rolling Stone*, August 24, 1968. https://www.rollingstone.com/music/music-news/friends-and-neighbors-just-call-us-the-band-45805/.

Baer, Joshua. "The Band: The Robbie Robertson Interview." *Musician—Guitar Special*, no. 43, May 1982, archived at http://theband.hiof.no/articles/1982_interview_band_rr_musician.html. Accessed February 17, 2020.

Baldwin, James. "Sonny's Blues." *Going to Meet the Man.* New York: Dial Press, 1965.

The Beatles. *The Beatles Anthology.* Chronicle Books, 2000.

Birnbaum, Larry. *Before Elvis: The Prehistory of Rock 'n' Roll.* Scarecrow Press, 2013.

Bivins, Jason C. *Spirits Rejoice! Jazz and American Religion.* New York: Oxford University Press, 2015.

Bomar, Scott B. *Southbound: An Illustrated History of Southern Rock.* Milwaukee, WI: Backbeat, 2014.

Bowman, Rob. *The History of The Band*, "Playing with Bob Dylan," from the article, "Life Is a Carnival." *Goldmine*, July 26, 1991, Vol. 17, No. 15, Issue 287.

Bowman, Rob. Liner Notes. *The Band Greatest Hits.* CD. Capitol Records, 2000.

Bowman, Rob. Liner Notes. *Music from Big Pink.* CD. Capitol Records, 2000.

Bowman, Rob. Liner Notes. *Moondog Matinee.* CD. Capitol Records, 2001.

Buber, Martin. *I and Thou.* Charles Scribner's Sons, 1970. Ed. Walter Kaufman, 1970.

Burks, John. "The Band: Stage Fright." *Rolling Stone.* September 17, 1970. http://www.rollingstone.com/music/albumreviews/stage-fright-19700917.

Clapton, Eric. "Interview." By Tom Pinnock. *Uncut.* November 30th, 2012. http://www.uncut.co.uk/features/eric-clapton-on-cream-i-was-in-a-confrontational-situation-24-hours-a-day-27997.

Clay, Alexa. "Utopia Inc." *Aeon* magazine. https://aeon.co/essays/like-start-ups-most-intentional-communities-fail-why.

Cocks, Jay. "Down to Old Dixie and Back." *Time.* January 12, 1970.

Collier, Rob. "How to Danko: A Lesson in the Style of Rick Danko." *Bass Musician* magazine. https://bassmusicianmagazine.com/2012/04/how-to-danko-a-lesson-in-the-style-of-rick-danko-by-rob-collier/.

Cott, Jonathan, ed. *Dylan on Dylan: The Essential Interviews*. London: Hodder, 2007.

Cuddon, J. A. *A Dictionary of Literary Terms: Revised Edition*. New York: Penguin Books, 1982.

Daily Trivia. "Daily Trivia: James Baldwin." https://ijustliketoread.wordpress.com/tag/james-baldwin/

Daniel, Anne Margaret. "Songs That Matter: The Band, 'The Weight.'" https://www.huffingtonpost.com/anne-margaret-daniel/songs-that-matter-the-ban_b_3592027.html.

Devi, Debra. *The Language of the Blues: From Alcorub to Zuzu*. True Nature Books, 2012.

Didion, Joan. "Slouching Towards Bethlehem." *Slouching Towards Bethlehem*. Farrar, Straus and Giroux, 1968.

Doyle, Patrick. "Levon Helm's Last Years Captured in 'Ain't in It for My Health.'" *Rolling Stone*, April 15, 2013. http://www.rollingstone.com/music/news/levon-helms-last-years-captured-in-aint-in-it-for-my-health-20130415.

Durkheim, Emile. *The Elementary Forms of Religious Life*. Trans. Karen E. Fields. New York: The Free Press, 1995.

Dylan, Bob. *Chronicles: Volume One*. New York: Simon and Schuster, 2004.

Dylan, Bob. "Bob Dylan—Nobel Lecture." Nobelprize.org. June 5, 2017. https://www.nobelprize.org/nobel_prizes/literature/laureates/2016/dylan-lecture.html.

Eagleton, Terry. *The English Novel: An Introduction*. Hoboken, NJ: Wiley-Blackwell, 2004.

Electro-voice. "Electro-Voice RE15 Manual." https://www.electrovoice.com/binary/RE15%20Engineering%20Data%20Sheet.pdf.

Flippo, Chet. *Liner Notes. The Band: Across the Great Divide*. Box Set, Capitol Records, 1994.

Forte, Dan. "Robbie Robertson: The Many Sides of." *Vintage Guitar Magazine*. http://www.vintageguitar.com/11786/rockin-robbie-robertson/.

Gilmore, Mikal. "Bob Dylan Unleashed: A Wild Ride on His New LP and Striking Back at Critics." *Rolling Stone*. September 27, 2013. http://www.rollingstone.com/music/news/bob-dylan-unleashed-a-wild-ride-on-his-new-lp-and-striking-back-at-critics-20120927.

Gleason, Ralph. "Bob Dylan: The Children's Crusade." *Ramparts Magazine*. March 1966, 27–35. http://unz.org/Pub/Ramparts-1966mar-00027.

Gleason, Ralph. "Dylan Has Returned with 'John Wesley Harding': So John Wesley Harding Has Been on the Turntable for a Few Days Now and This Is a Preliminary Report." *Rolling Stone*. February 10, 1968. http://www.rollingstone.com/music/news/dylan-has-returned-with-john-wesley-harding-19680210.

Green, Elon. "Culture Desk: Mavis Staples Remembers Singing 'The Weight.'" *New Yorker*. June 17, 2014. https://www.newyorker.com/culture/culture-desk/mavis-staples-remembers-singing-the-weight.

Greene, Andy. "Readers' Poll: The Band's 10 Greatest Hits." *Rolling Stone*. December 4, 2013. http://www.rollingstone.com/music/pictures/readers-poll-the-bands-10-greatest-songs-20131204.

Griffin, Sid. *Million Dollar Bash: Bob Dylan, The Band, and the Basement Tapes*. London: Jawbone Press, 2014.

Gritz, Jennie Rothenberg. "The Death of the Hippies: The Photographer Joe Samberg Remembers How Drugs Destroyed the Telegraph Avenue Scene." *The Atlantic*. July 8, 2015.

Guru-Murthy, Krishnan. Interview with Martin Scorsese. BBC Channel 4 News, Aired December 6, 2016, youtube.com/watch?v=87VRx9IQYqw, accessed February 26, 2020.

Harris, Craig. *The Band: Pioneers of Americana*. Rowman and Littlefield: New York, 2014.

Helm, Levon. *This Wheel's on Fire*. Chicago Review Press, 1993.

Helm, Levon. *This Wheel's on Fire: Levon Helm and the Story of The Band*. Chicago: A Capella Press, 1993.

Hoskyns, Barney. *Across the Great Divide: The Band and America*. Milwaukee, WI: Hal Leonard, 1993.

Hoskyns, Barney. *Across the Great Divide: The Band and America*. New York: Hal Leonard, 2006.

Hunt, Lynn. "The Sacred and the French Revolution." *Durkheimian Sociology, Cultural Studies*. Jeffrey Alexander, Ed. Cambridge: Cambridge University Press, 1988.

Ignacio, Don. "*Stage Fright* (1970)." http://donignacio.com/music/bandpage.html.

Jacobi, Martin. "Bob Dylan and Collaboration." In *The Cambridge Companion to Bob Dylan*, edited by Kevin J. H. Dettmar, 69–79. Cambridge: Cambridge University Press, 2009.

James, Clive. "Robbie Robertson: In the Shadow of the Band." *Creem*, July 1972.

Jones, Christine Hand. "Bob Dylan and the End of the (Modern) World." PhD dissertation, University of Texas at Dallas, 2013.

Joyce, James. *A Portrait of the Artist as a Young Man*. London: B. W. Huebsch, 1916.

Kail, Tony. *A Secret History of Memphis Hoodoo: Rootworkers, Conjurers, and Spirituals*. History Press, 2017.

Kelly, Mary Pat. *Martin Scorsese: A Journey New York*. Thundermouth, 1991.

Kerrin. "Garth's Gear—The Classic Years." http://theband.hiof.no/articles/ghs_keyboards_knz.html.

Laderman, Gary. *Sacred Matters: Celebrity Worship, Sexual Ecstasies, the Living Dead, and Other Signs of Religious Life in the United States*. New York: New Press, 2009.

LeDrew, Chris. "*Music from Big Pink*: Myth Debunked, Genius Retained." *OnStage* magazine. May 9, 2013. http://www.onstagemagazine.com/music-from-big-pink-myth-debunked-genius-retained/.

Lepidus, Harold. "Roger Waters Talks about Influence of Bob Dylan and the Band in New Interview." *Bob Dylan Examiner*. http://www.examiner.com/article/roger-waters-talks-about-influence-of-bob-dylan-and-the-band-new-interview.

Lytle, Mark Hamilton. *America's Uncivil Wars: The Sixties Era: From Elvis to the Fall of Richard Nixon*. New York: Oxford University Press, 2006.

Mailer, Norman. *Advertisements for Myself*. Cambridge: Harvard University Press, 1992.

Marcus, Greil. "Rock-a-Hula Clarified." *Creem*. June 1971.

Marcus, Greil. *Mystery Train: Images of America in Rock 'n' Roll Music*. New York: E.P. Dutton, 1982.

Marcus, Greil. *The Old, Weird America: The World of Bob Dylan's Basement Tapes*. New York: Picador, 1997.

Marsh, Dave. *The Heart of Rock and Soul: The 1001 Greatest Singles Ever Made*. New York: Plumb, 1989.

Marqusee, Mike. *Chimes of Freedom: The Politics of Bob Dylan's Art*. New York: New Press, 2003.

Miller, Timothy. *The 60s Communes: Hippies and Beyond*. Syracuse, NY: Syracuse University Press, 1999.

Minturn, Neil. *The Last Waltz of The Band*. Hilldale, NY: Pendragon Press, 2005.

Nash, Graham, and Shane Fontayne. "Back Home." *This Path Tonight*. Blue Castle Records, 2016.

O'Connor, Flannery. "Some Aspects of the Grotesque in Southern Fiction." 1960. http://www.en.utexas.edu/Classes/Bremen/e316k/316kprivate/scans/grotesque.html.

Pareles, Jon. "A Wiser Voice Blowin' in the Autumn Wind." *New York Times*, September 28, 1997. http://www.nytimes.com/1997/09/28/arts/pop-jazz-a-wiser-voice-blowin-in-the-autumn-wind.html?mcubz=3.

Payne, Bill. "Richard Manuel's Piano." *Bill Payne Creative* (website). https://billpaynecreative.com/writing/richard-manuel.

Percy, Walker. *Signposts in a Strange Land*. Farrar, Straus and Giroux: New York, 1991.

Petrusich, Amanda. *It Still Moves: Lost Highways and the Search for the Next American Music*. New York: Faber and Faber, 2008.

Pinnock, Tom. "The Band, Bob Dylan and *Music from Big Pink*—the Full Story." *Uncut*, July 31, 2015. http://www.uncut.co.uk/features/the-band-bob-dylan-and-music-from-big-pink-the-full-story-69989#mvtU7okxgBDU8iu6.99.

Pollock, Bruce. "They're Playing My Song: 'Put A Little Love in Your Heart.'" December 11, 2012. http://www.songfacts.com/blog/playingmysong/jackie_deshannon_-_put_a_little_love_in_your_heart_/.

Preminger, Alex, and T. V. F. Brogan. *The New Princeton Encyclopedia of Poetry and Poetics*. Princeton, NJ: Princeton University Press, 1993.

Robertson, Robbie. "Song Review." *All Music*. Review of "Up on Cripple Creek," by Bill Janovitz. https://www.allmusic.com/song/up-on-cripple-creek-mt0011252707.

Robertson, Robbie. *Testimony*. New York: Crown Archetype, 2016.

Rogovoy, Seth. "How Robbie Robertson Learned He Was Jewish and the Son of a Gangster," https://forward.com/culture/444583/how-robbie-robertson-learned-he-was-jewish-and-the-son-of-a-gangster/.

Roher, Daniel. *Once Were Brothers: Robbie Robertson and the Band*. Imagine Documentaries, 2019.

Romano, John. "James Baldwin Writing and Talking." Interview with James Baldwin. *New York Times*. September 23, 1979. http://www.nytimes.com/1979/09/23/archives/james-baldwin-writing-and-talking-baldwin-baldwin-authors-query.html

Rosenweig, Franz. *The Star of Redemption*. University of Wisconsin Press: Madison, 1971.

Schäfer, Stephanie. *"Cashville"—Dilution of Original Country Music Identity Through Increasing Commercialization*. Hamburg: Diplomica Verlag, 2012. http://ebookcentral.proquest.com/lib/dalbapt-ebooks/detail.action?docID=1035426.

Scorsese, Martin. *Feel Like Going Home*. Director interview. https://www.pbs.org/theblues/aboutfilms/scorseseinterview.html. Accessed February 25, 2020.

Seeburger, Frank. *The Open Wound: Trauma, Identity, and Community*. CreateSpace Independent Publishing Platform, 2012.

Shelton, Robert. *No Direction Home: The Life and Music of Bob Dylan*. New York: Da Capo Press, 1997.

Shepherd, Reginald. "A Few Thoughts on the Dramatic Monologue." http://reginaldshepherd.blogspot.com/2007/07/few-thoughts-on-dramatic-monologue.html.

Simon, John. *Truth, Lies and Hearsay: A Memoir of a Musical Life in and Out of Rock and Roll*. Independently published, 2018.

Slate, Jeff. "Robbie Robertson on the Band's 'Music from Big Pink' at 50: 'It Sounds Like the Band I Remember.'" *Daily Beast*. September 1, 2018. https://www.thedailybeast.com/robbie-robertson-on-the-bands-music-from-big-pink-at-50-it-sounds-like-the-band-i-remember

Soles, Paul. *90 Minutes Live*. "Robbie Robertson, Martin Scorsese, and The Last Waltz." April 14, 1978. https://www.cbc.ca/archives/entry/robbie-robertson-martin-scorsese-and-the-last-waltz. Accessed February 26, 2020.

Song Facts. "'The Weight' by The Band." http://www.songfacts.com/detail.php?id=420.

Stanley, Bob. *Yeah! Yeah! Yeah!: the Story of Pop Music from Bill Haley to Beyoncé*. New York: Norton, 2015.

Sylvan, Robin. *Traces of the Spirit: The Religious Dimensions of Popular Music*. New York: NYU Press, 2002.

Thomson, Elizabeth, and David Gutman, eds. *The Dylan Companion*. Boston: Da Capo Press, 2001.

Thompson, Toby. *Positively Main Street: Bob Dylan's Minnesota*. Minneapolis: University of Minnesota Press, 2008.

Viney, Peter. *Jawbone*. Vol. 4, Spring/Summer 1997.

Viney, Peter. "The Weight." http://theband.hiof.no/articles/the_weight_viney.html.

Wald, Elijah. *Dylan Goes Electric!: Newport, Seeger, Dylan, and the Night That Split the Sixties*. NY: Dey St., 2015.

Waters, Muddy. Official Website. https://muddywatersofficial.com/pages/mannish-boy. Accessed February 17, 2020.

DISCOGRAPHY/FILMOGRAPHY

The Band. "King Harvest (Has Surely Come)." On *The Band*. Capitol Records, 1969.
The Band. "The Night They Drove Old Dixie Down." On *The Band*. Capitol Records, 1969.
The Band. "Up on Cripple Creek." On *The Band*. Capitol Records, 1969.
Classic Albums: The Band. Rhino/Wea: UK 1997.
Dylan, Bob. "When the Ship Comes In." Recorded October 23, 1963. In *The Times They Are A-Changin'*. Vinyl recording. Columbia, 1964.
Dylan, Bob. *Highway 61 Revisited*. Vinyl recording. Columbia, 1965.
Dylan, Bob. "It's Alright Ma (I'm Only Bleeding)." Lyrics. *Bringing It All Back Home*. Dwarf Music, 1965.
Dylan, Bob. "Mr. Tambourine Man." Recorded April 12, 1965. In *Mr. Tambourine Man*. The Byrds. Vinyl recording. Columbia, 1965.
Dylan, Bob. "Sad Eyed Lady of the Lowlands." In *Blonde on Blonde*. Vinyl recording. Columbia, 1966.
Dylan, Bob. *John Wesley Harding*. Vinyl recording. Columbia, 1967.
Dylan, Bob. "I Shall Be Released," in *Music from Big Pink*. Vinyl recording. Capitol, 1968.
Dylan, Bob. "Quinn the Eskimo." In *Self Portrait*. Vinyl recording. Columbia, 1970.
Dylan, Bob. *The Basement Tapes*. Vinyl recording. Columbia, 1975.
Hall, Gregory. *The Band*. DVD. Nashville: TH Entertainment, 1995.
Harrison, George. "Interview." *Classic Albums, The Band*. DVD. Eagle Rock Entertainment, 2005.
Hatley, Jacob. *Ain't in It for My Health: A Film about Levon Helm*. Film. Amazon Video, 2013.
Helm, Levon. *Classic Albums, The Band*. "Interview." DVD. Eagle Rock Entertainment, 2005.
Johnson, Blind Willie, "The Soul of a Man." Lyrics. Columbia, 1930.
Jones, George, and Tammy Wynette. "God's Gonna Get'cha for That." Lyrics. *George Jones and Tammy Wynette's 16 Greatest Hits*. Sony BMG, 1999.
McLean, Don. "American Pie." Recorded May 26, 1971. In *American Pie*. Vinyl Recording. United Artists, 1971.
Robertson, Robbie. "Daniel and the Sacred Harp." Lyrics. *Stagefright*. Capitol Records, 2000.
Robertson, Robbie. "To Kingdom Come." Lyrics. *Music from Big Pink*. CD. Capitol Records, 2000.

Robertson, Robbie. "The Shape I'm In." Lyrics. *Stagefright*. CD. Capitol Records, 2000.
Robertson, Robbie. "The Weight," in *Music from Big Pink*. CD. Capitol Records, 2000.
Robertson, Robbie. "Interview." *Classic Albums, The Band*. DVD. Eagle Rock Entertainment, 2005.
Scorsese, Martin. *Mean Streets*. Warner Bros., 1973.
Scorsese, Martin. *Taxi Driver*. Columbia Pictures, 1976.
Scorsese, Martin. *The Last Waltz*. Columbia Pictures, 1978.
Simon, John. "Interview." *Classic Albums, The Band*. DVD. Eagle Rock Entertainment, 2005.
Traffic. "Memories of a Rock N' Rolla." *When the Eagle Flies*. 7E520, Island Records, 1974.
The Traveling Wilburys. *The True History of the Traveling Wilburys*. Concord Records. Concord Music Group, Inc. T. Wilbury Limited, 2007.

CONTRIBUTORS

Joshua Coleman is from Birmingham, Alabama. He teaches theology at Regis Jesuit in Aurora, CO. He holds a PhD from an interdisciplinary program between the University of Denver and the Iliff School of Theology in philosophy, theology, and cultural theory.

Christine Hand Jones, PhD, is a singer-songwriter and assistant professor of English at Dallas Baptist University, where she teaches courses in English and songwriting. Her academic work explores the connections between music and literature with a focus on the apocalyptic writings of Bob Dylan. Her artistic work fuses folk rock with soul and draws inspiration from literature, the Bible, and, of course, Bob Dylan.

Kevin C. Neece is author of *The Gospel According to Star Trek: The Original Crew* (Cascade Books, 2016) and producer and host of *The Gospel According to Star Trek Podcast*, as well as a writer and speaker on media, the arts, and pop culture from a Christian-worldview perspective. He served as a contributing editor for *Imaginatio et Ratio: A Journal of Theology and the Arts*, and his work has appeared in Jeff Sellars's book *Light Shining in a Dark Place: Discovering Theology through Film*, *New Identity Magazine*, Reel Spirituality, and Patheos, among others. He has also coedited several multiauthor books, including *The Good, the True, the Beautiful: A Multidisciplinary Tribute to Dr. David K. Naugle* (Pickwick Publications, 2021). A former professor, Kevin holds a BAS in communication and philosophy and an MLA in fine arts. He lives with his wife and son in North Texas.

Charlotte Pence is editor of *The Poetics of American Song Lyrics* and directs the creative writing program at the University of South Alabama. She is also the author of two award-winning poetry chapbooks and the full-length collection *Many Small Fires*, which received an INDIEFAB Book of the Year Award from *Foreword Reviews*. Her poetry, fiction, and creative nonfiction have recently been published in *Harvard Review*, *Sewanee Review*, *Southern Review*, and *Brevity*.

George Plasketes is professor of media studies in the Auburn University's School of Communication and Journalism. A native of Chicago, he studied in Oxford (Mississippi, that is), receiving two degrees (BA, journalism, 1978; MA, mass communication, 1980) and unanimous All-SEC honors as a defensive end (1977). He earned a doctorate at Bowling Green State in Ohio (1985). He is the author/editor of six books, with subjects that include B-sides, cover songs and debut albums, Elvis Presley images and fanaticism in American culture, and the first critical chronicle on one of popular music's most original songwriting antiheroes in *Warren Zevon: Desperado of Los Angeles* (2016). He is currently completing a book on the mid-1960s Chicagoland music scene. He has also published essays, articles, and chapters on a variety of music, media, and popular culture subjects, including *Saturday Night Live* creator Lorne Michaels, baseball pitcher Bill "Spaceman" Lee, the failed television musical drama *Cop Rock*, TaB diet cola, and the music of the television series *Northern Exposure*. Among the courses he teaches at Auburn are Soundtracks; Popular Culture; Fame and Celebrity; Re-producing Popular Culture; and Technology and Culture, an interdisciplinary seminar in the Honors College.

Jeffrey Scholes, PhD, is assistant professor and director of the Center for Religious Diversity and Public Life in the Department of Philosophy at the University of Colorado. His areas of interest include Christianity and political economy, material religion and culture, and religion and sports.

Jeff Sellars, PhD, teaches in Northern California and along the Oregon coast. His main area of academic interest centers on media, culture, and technology.

Toby Thompson is author of five books of nonfiction: *Positively Main Street—An Unorthodox View of Bob Dylan*, *Saloon*, *The '60s Report*, *Riding the Rough String*, and *Metroliner—Passages, Washington to New York*. He has written for magazines as varied as *Esquire*, *Vanity Fair*, *Outside*, *GQ*, *Playboy*, *Rolling Stone*, *Sports Afield*, *Gray's Sporting Journal*, *Big Sky Journal*, *Western Art & Architecture*, the *New York Times*, the *Washington Post*, and many others. He teaches nonfiction writing in the creative writing program at Penn State.

Jude Warne was born and raised in Manhattan, amidst two parents who were (and still are) rock and rollers, so she believes very strongly in the power and importance of rock and roll and high-quality music and art criticism, especially that of Lester Bangs and Greil Marcus. She has written numerous reviews for the *Vinyl District*, *The Observer*, *Film International*, *No Depression*, *Journal of Popular Music and Society*, and *Senses of Cinema*, and was also the music columnist at *Red Paint Hill Journal* from 2015 until 2017. Jude earned her BA (cinema studies, 2011) and MA (humanities and social thought, 2015) from New York University. Her master's thesis, "Let the Broken Hearts Stand," explored and examined the disappointed American characters in Sherwood Anderson's *Winesburg, Ohio* and Bruce Springsteen's *Darkness on the Edge of Town*. Jude's six-volume teen fiction series *Crushing* was released in 2017 through Epic Press. She published the biography, *America, the Band*, in 2020 through Rowman & Littlefield.

INDEX

Aaron, Peter, 40, 43, 47n69
Abbott, Gregory, 142
"Across the Great Divide," 112
Across the Great Divide, 17, 45n22, 120, 141
Adorno, Theodor, 116
Allen, Steve, 135
Allman Brothers Band, 43
Almost Famous, 137
"Amen Corner," 129
American Gods, 133
Anthology of American Folk Music, 9, 35
Anti-Semite and Jew, 109
Ashbery, John, 57
"Atlantic City," 49
Aurora Leigh, 57
Austen, Jane, 57

Baer, Joshua, 159
Band, The: and Scorsese, 148, 157–58; and the audience, 157; and their guests, 157
Barrett, Elizabeth, 57
Basement Tapes, The, 17, 34–36, 41–42, 62–63
Beatles (band), 10n2, 12, 32, 74, 76n32, 131
Beggars Banquet, 74
Bender, William, 28
Big Pink (restaurant), 7, 63, 103n13
Birnbaum, Larry, 159
Bivins, Jason C., 94
Blame It All on My Roots, 130
Blonde on Blonde, 17, 37, 65
blues, the, 151–59

Bowman, Rob, 120
Brooks, Garth, 130
Brown, James, 11
Bruno, Bruce, 6
Burks, John, 92
Bush, Sam, 138
Butterfield, Paul, 138, 150, 152
Byrds (band), 20, 40, 43, 132
Byrne, David, 133

Cahoots, 7
Cannonball, 108, 122, 126
canzone, 147
Cappa, Charlie, 146–47
"Carmen and the Devil," 108, 118
Carroll, Hattie, 37
Carson, Johnny, 135
Cash, Johnny, 33, 126
Catholicism, 139
Chain, The, 130
"Chest Fever," 7, 65–66, 68, 73, 118, 153
Chester, Crazy, 41, 69–70, 108–9, 126
"Chimes of Freedom, The," 35
Christian nation, 107
Chronicles: Volume One, 16, 18–19, 45n31
Ciarlante, Randy, 138
civil rights movement, 45n36, 98, 151
Civil War, 19–20, 49, 112–13, 115, 127
Clapton, Eric, 62, 96, 138, 148–49
Cocker, Joe, 129, 137
Cocks, Jay, 119, 124
Cocteau Room, 155
Coleman, Joshua, 8

"Communion," 8, 105, 146–47, 149, 151, 159
Costello, Elvis, 63
Curfman, Shannon, 130

"Daffy Duck in Hollywood," 57
Danko, Rick, 3–7, 11–12, 17, 20–21, 29, 68, 153, 157–58
"Darkness, The," 20, 29, 98–99
Dawn of the Planet of the Apes, 133
De Shannon, Jackie, 128
Dean, James, 26, 29, 44
"Death Tour," the, 11, 22
Delta Supper Club, 13
Denver, John, 130
Dickens, Charles, 57
Dictionary of Literary Terms, A, 51
Diddley, Bo, 13, 151, 153
Donizetti, Gaetano, 147
Dream Songs, 57
"Drifter's Escape," 38
Duffy, Carol Ann, 57
Durkheim, Emile, 93
Dylan, Bob, 4, 6–8, 26–48, 62–64, 76n47, 78, 96

Easy Rider, 39, 131–33
Electric Mud, 150
Eliot, George, 57
Elizabethtown, 136
Endless Highway, 8, 10n3, 118–19, 129–31, 133, 141–45

Faulkner, William, 108, 123, 125
Flippo, Chet, 119, 122
Flying Burrito Brothers (band), 20
folk music, 6, 27–29, 33–35, 40, 43
Franklin, Aretha, 43, 128, 141

"Games People Play," 129
Garden State, 134
Garland, Judy, 133
ghetto streets, 9
Gleason, Ralph, 34, 36, 46n45, 113
Go Tell It on the Mountain, 52

Goode, Chester, 127
gospel extasis, 12
gospel music, 139, 153–54
Graduate, The, 131
Graham, Bill, 155
Great Depression, the, 29
Great Rock Island Route, 126
Great Speckled Bird (band), 20
Grebb, Marty, 138
Griffin, Sid, 32, 45n31
Grossman, Albert, 22, 39, 100, 119
Guru-Murthy, Krishnan, 159

"Hard Rain's A-Gonna Fall, A," 35
Harding, John Wesley, 37
Hardy, Thomas, 57
Harris, Emmylou, 20, 138–39, 154
Harrison, George, 10n2, 62
"Harry Smith Anthology." See *Anthology of American Folk Music*
harsh fundamentalism, 34
Hawkins, Erskine, 152
Hawkins, Ronnie, 4–5, 11, 54, 78, 93, 126, 138
Hawks (band), 4–6, 17–18, 30–31, 81, 95–96, 125–26
Healey, Jeff, 130
Heart of Rock and Soul, The, 142–44
Helm, Levon, 4–5, 11–12, 37, 103n13, 104, 118, 126, 135, 154–55, 158
Helmstrom, Echo, 18
Hendrix, Jimi, 22, 129, 157
"Hey Joe," 129
"Hey Jude," 10n2, 74, 129
Hiatt, John, 138
High on the Hog, 23
"Highway 61 Revisited," 35
Highway 61 Revisited, 37
Hoffman, Dustin, 132
Holly, Buddy, 22, 29–30, 157
"Honky-Tonk Hawkin'," 8
Hooker, John Lee, 104, 149
Hopper, Dennis, 131
Hornsby, Bruce, 137
Hoskyns, Barney, 17, 28, 44–45n22

Hudson, Garth, 5–7, 11, 16, 34, 49, 76n45, 77n48, 122, 138, 153, 158
Huffington Post, 142

If All I Was Was Black, 140
Ignacio, Don, 99
"impossibility of sainthood," 19, 41, 120–21, 139, 142
"In a Station," 19, 68
Instant Groove (Atco), 129
It Might Get Loud, 141

Jacobi, Martin, 31
"Jawbone," 101
Jawbone, 119
"Jericho," 23, 108, 138
John, Elton, 43, 63, 137
John Wesley Harding, 17, 28, 36, 38
"Johnny Boy," 146
Johnson, Blind Willie, 153, 159
Jones, Booker T., 138
Jones, Christine Hand, 8
Jones, Rickie Lee, 130
Jones, Sharon, 133
Joyce, James, 51
Jubilation, 23, 138

Kail, Tony, 159
Kane, Virgil, 50, 55, 112–13
King, B. B., 104
King Curtis (Curtis Ousley), 129
"King Harvest," 5, 17, 51, 57, 59, 115–16

La Traviata, 148
Laderman, Gary, 94
"Lady Lazarus," 57
"Last Waltz, The," 154, 158n5
Last Waltz, The, 3, 8, 11–12, 16, 22–25, 49, 103, 138, 140–41, 146–59
Led Zeppelin (band), 63
Lee, Anna, 41, 67, 108, 118, 126
Lee, Frankie, 37
Leno, Jay, 135
Levy, Morris, 14
Lewis, Jerry Lee, 13, 27

"Liner Notes," 38, 122
"Little Feat," 130
"Little Green Apples," 129
Live Adventures of Mike Bloomfield and Al Kooper, The, 129
"Lo and Behold," 36, 41
"Lonesome Suzie," 68, 110–11, 114
Louie Louie, 119

Mailer, Norman, 14
Manuel, Richard, 5–7, 17, 42, 56, 59, 71, 76n46, 77n48, 149, 157
Marcus, Greil, 32, 35, 78, 111, 143
Marsh, Dave, 119, 122, 142
Martin Scorsese: A Journey, 139
Mascagni, Pietro, 147
"Mavis feeling," 140
McCarthy, James, 158
McClatchy, Scott, 130
McClure, Michael, 155
McLean, Don, 26, 44
Mean Streets, 146–48, 158–59
Mercer, Johnny, 133
"Million Dollar Bash," 36, 41
Miss Fannie, 41–42
Miss Moses, 41, 108, 118, 125, 127
Mississippi Delta, 14, 154
Mister Rogers' Neighborhood, 133
Mitchell, Brian, 138
Mitchell, Joni, 138
Moondog Matinee, 7, 21, 25
Mulford, Clarence E., 127
Music from Big Pink, 7–8, 61–69, 73–78, 92–99, 104–7
"Mystery Train," 21, 143, 150

Nazarin, 121
Neece, Kevin C., 8
Nichols, Mike, 132
"Night They Drove Old Dixie Down, The," 51

O Brother, Where Art Thou?, 134
O'Brien, Conan, 134–35
O'Connor, Flannery, 116

INDEX

"Ohio Prison Fire," 19
One True Vine, 140
Osborne, Joan, 130

Paar, Jack, 135
"paring his fingernails," 52
Pence, Charlotte, 8
Penfound, Jerry, 6
pentatonicism, 33
Perkins, Carl, 13
persona, 51, 58
Petrusich, Amanda, 27
Pirate Radio, 136
Plasketes, George, 8
playing music, 63, 84
Presley, Elvis, 27, 29–30
Priest, Judas, 37–38
Prima, Louis, 13
Pritchett, Aaron, 130

"Quinn the Eskimo," 41

Raging Bull, 147
Rebel Club, 11, 13
Rebel without a Cause, 29–30
Red Album, 130
Redding, Otis, 22, 129
religious album, 92–93
rhythm piano, 6
Robertson, Robbie, 5, 9–11, 23, 29–33, 63–71, 73, 77n55, 79, 81, 96
Rock of Ages, 7, 138, 142
"Rockin' Chair," 114
Rodgers, Jimmy, 18
Rogers, Albert, 138
Rogovoy, Seth, 73
Roher, Daniel, 159
Rolling Stone, 39, 48, 142
Rosenweig, Franz, 105
Ruby, Jack, 15

Salazar, David, 158
San Francisco, 7, 22, 65, 136, 138, 141, 146
Scholes, Jeffrey, 8
Scorsese, Martin, 8, 22, 139, 148, 158–59

Seeburger, Frank, 105
Sellars, Jeff, 8
Sgt. Pepper's Lonely Hearts Club Band, 32, 74
"Shake You Down," 142
"Shape I'm In, The," 21, 25, 85
Shine a Light, 148
Shocked, Michelle, 130
Simon, John, 72–73, 99, 121, 123
Sinatra, Frank, 12
"Sing a Simple Song," 129
Smith, Cathy Evelyn, 125
Smith, Harry, 29, 33, 35
Smith, Sammi, 130
Soles, Paul, 159
"Sonny's Blues," 48–50, 52, 55, 58
Soul of a Man, The, 153, 159
Stage Fright, 7–8, 21, 78–79, 85–93, 99–101
Staples, Mavis, 137, 140, 143, 155
Starr, Ringo, 69, 130, 138
storyteller, the, 38, 88, 112, 124
"struggles of sainthood," 121
Sweetheart of the Rodeo, 43
Sylvan, Robin, 93

Taxi Driver, 146, 158
"Tears of Rage," 7, 17, 65–68, 76n46, 106, 111
Testimony, 13, 15, 17, 20, 39, 121, 143–44
Tharpe, Rosetta, 153
This Path Tonight, 138
"This Wheel's on Fire," 23, 75n21
Thompson, Toby, 8
"Time to Kill," 81–83
Times They Are A-Changin', The, 19
"To Kingdom Come," 68, 101–3, 107, 111
ToHeavenURide, 130
Tonight Show, The, 135
Top Gun, 136
traumatic situations, 109
Tumbleweed Connection, 43

Underground Fire, 129
"Unfaithful Master," 115
"Up on Cripple Creek," 51, 113–14, 152

Vietnam War, 32, 66, 86
Viridinia, 121

"Wabash Cannonball, The," 126
Warne, Jude, 8
Warren, Harry, 133
Waters, Muddy, 104, 138, 149–50, 152–55, 158–59
"We Can Talk," 68, 101
"Weight, The," 3, 5, 7–8, 17, 39–42, 69–70, 72, 74n3, 118–44, 154
"White Negro, The," 14
"Wichita Lineman," 129

Williams, Hank, 22, 33, 157
Williams, Tennessee, 115
Wilson, Cassandra, 130
Womack, Lee Ann, 130
Woody-Guthrie style, 31
Wright, Marva, 130

You Are Not Alone, 140
Young, Neil, 138

Zimmerman, Beattie, 16
Zimmerman, David, 16

www.ingramcontent.com/pod-product-compliance
Lightning Source LLC
Chambersburg PA
CBHW030625230426
43661CB00053B/2144